THE ILLUSTRATED HISTORY OF THE

VIETNAM WAR

THE ILLUSTRATED HISTORY OF THE

VIETNAM WAR

ANDREW WIEST AND CHRIS McNAB

METRO BOOKS
New York

METRO BOOKS
New York

An Imprint of Sterling Publishing
1166 Avenue of the Americas
New York, NY 10036

First published in 2000.
This edition published in 2015.

Editorial and design by
Amber Books Ltd
74–77 White Lion Street
London N1 9PF
www.amberbooks.co.uk

Editor: Christopher Westhorp
Designer: Zoë Mellors

ISBN: 978-1-4351-6110-8

For information about custom editions, special sales, and premium and corporate purchases, please contact Sterling Special Sales at 800-805-5489 or specialsales@sterlingpublishing.com.

Manufactured in China

2 4 6 8 10 9 7 5 3 1

www.sterlingpublishing.com

Contents

CHAPTER 1

In the Footsteps of the French

FRENCH ARMOURED TROOPS ACCOMPANIED BY A COLUMN OF VIETNAMESE ALLIES. THE FIRST INDOCHINA WAR WAS A BLOODY START TO MORE THAN THREE DECADES OF CONFLICT IN SOUTHEAST ASIA, AND IT PROVED THAT EVEN A HEAVILY ARMED AND WELL-STRUCTURED WESTERN ARMY COULD BE DEFEATED BY MOTIVATED AND DISCIPLINED GUERRILLA TROOPS.

The First Indochina War lasted nine years and ended more than six decades of French colonial rule in the region. Facing an enemy who was very efficient in battle, the French suffered crushing military defeats and waning support at home.

Vietnam's history is dominated by wars of resistance against foreign powers. China occupied Vietnam for more than 1000 years from 111BC to AD938 and again from 1407 to 1428. In the medieval period the kingdoms of Champa and Cambodia made frequent incursions into Vietnamese territory, and in the thirteenth century Mongolian invaders were repelled by the forces of Tran Hung Dao, a Vietnamese leader who triumphed through a style of guerrilla warfare that was to appear prophetic.

Vietnam later attracted those European powers with colonial aspirations: Portugal in 1535, the Netherlands in 1636 and France in 1680. All three countries tried to establish Vietnamese trading posts, eager to secure monopolies over silks, spices, porcelain, rubber and timber, and to make a lasting impression through religion (the first Roman Catholic mission was established in Vietnam in 1615 around modern-day Danang).

It was the French influence, however, that prevailed. By 25 August 1883 France had achieved military control of all three of the regions which composed Vietnam: Cochin China (south), Annam (central) and Tonkin (north). By 1893 France had added Cambodia and Laos to its conquests and in so doing it created the extensive territory known as the Indochinese Union.

French rule was harsh and preferential, generally working for the exclusive profit of the mercantile classes, and by the 1920s hostile nationalist organizations proliferated in reaction to this. Perhaps the most significant of these was the Revolutionary Youth League of Vietnam, founded by Nguyen Ai Quoc who would later be better known by the *nom de guerre* Ho Chi Minh (see box below). Few observers in the 1920s would have guessed the incredible effect this man would have on the history of Southeast Asia.

THE GREAT STRATEGIST HO CHI MINH

HO CHI MINH

Born Nguyen Sinh Cung in the northern Annam province of Nghe An, Ho Chi Minh (1890–1969) was a well-educated youth who at the age of 17 took a job as a cook on a merchant vessel bound for Europe. There he lived in London and then Paris, soaking up French socialism while remaining deeply involved with the French capital's Vietnamese community. Ho later renamed himself Nguyen Ai Quoc (Nguyen 'the Patriot') and spent much of the 1920s and 1930s in the Soviet Union and China advising on colonial affairs.

Ho's overriding passion was for Indochinese independence, and in 1930 in Hong Kong he assisted the formation of the influential Indochinese Communist Party (ICP). By 1941, when he returned to Indochina, Nguyen Ai Quoc had renamed himself Ho Chi Minh ('He Who Enlightens'). After leading guerrilla forces against the wartime Japanese occupiers, Ho went on to become the dominant figure of North Vietnamese politics until his death in 1969. He oversaw both the defeat of the French between 1946 and 1954 and much of the subsequent war against South Vietnam, the United States and its allies, which, though he never got to see it, ultimately fulfilled his dream of Vietnamese reunification.

LEFT: CROWDS GREET ALLIED TROOPS IN SAIGON IN AUTUMN 1945 FOLLOWING THE LIBERATION OF INDOCHINA FROM THE OCCUPYING JAPANESE.

THE FIRST INDOCHINA WAR

A cultured and cosmopolitan man, Ho Chi Minh was a committed nationalist who brought together Vietnam's three main communist parties to form the powerful Indochinese Communist Party (ICP). In May 1941, the ICP in turn gave rise to the Viet Nam Doc Lap Dong Minh Hoi ('League for the Independence of Vietnam'), an organization which fought for Vietnamese self-rule against both Japanese wartime occupation and, subsequently, re-established French authority. The name was eventually shortened to Vietminh.

Although occupied by Japan, the French territories in the Indochina region remained nominally under French colonial rule, overseen by the Japanese. This lasted until 11 March 1945 when, in response to a French attempt to seize power, the Japanese declared Indochina's independence and gave power to the young Vietnamese emperor Bao Dai. But the defeat of Japan in 1945 led Ho Chi Minh and the Vietminh to attempt to seize power (they took Hanoi in August but Saigon was more difficult) and he replaced Bao Dai, proclaiming the existence of the Democratic Republic of Vietnam (DRV) on 2 September. This situation, however, was not to last. Disarmament of the Japanese fell to pro-colonial British forces in the south of Vietnam

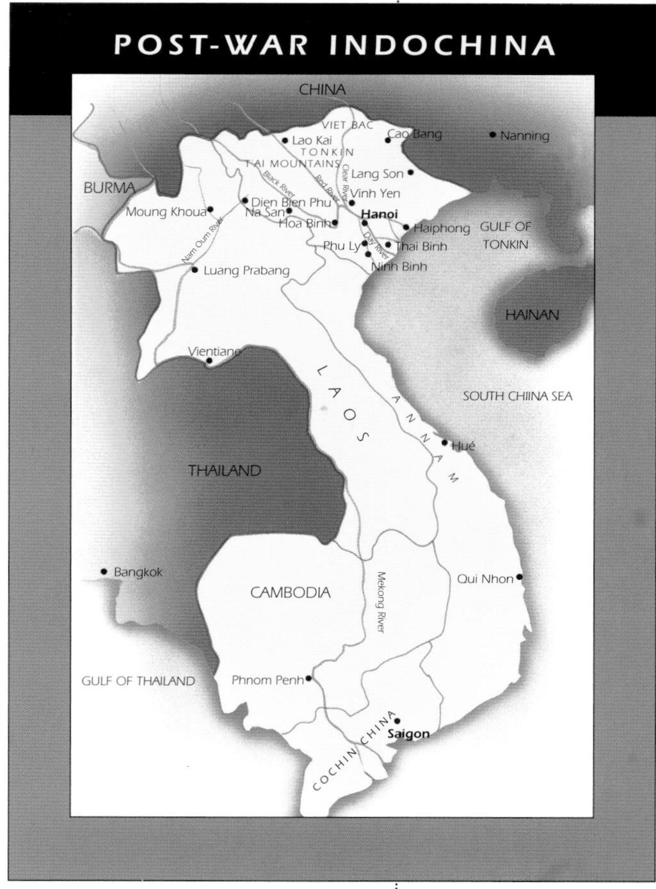

RIGHT: BRITISH AND FRENCH TROOPS GATHER PRIOR TO ACTIONS AGAINST VIETMINH INSURGENTS OPERATING AROUND SAIGON. DISARMAMENT OF JAPANESE FORCES IN SOUTH VIETNAM FELL TO THE BRITISH, THOUGH MANY JAPANESE SOLDIERS WERE UTILISED BY THE BRITISH AS COMBAT TROOPS IN THE EARLY SUPPRESSION OF THE VIETMINH.

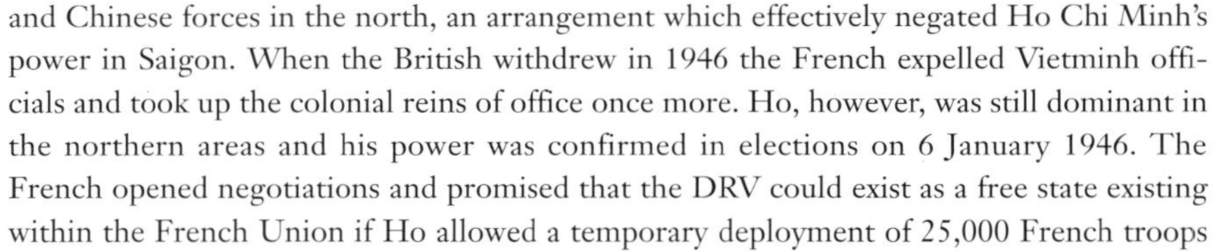

and Chinese forces in the north, an arrangement which effectively negated Ho Chi Minh's power in Saigon. When the British withdrew in 1946 the French expelled Vietminh officials and took up the colonial reins of office once more. Ho, however, was still dominant in the northern areas and his power was confirmed in elections on 6 January 1946. The French opened negotiations and promised that the DRV could exist as a free state existing within the French Union if Ho allowed a temporary deployment of 25,000 French troops in the north, to be withdrawn from Indochina by 1951. Ho accepted, but the French subsequently backed out of the agreement, fearing that the loss of Vietnam would precipitate the loss of other French colonies. The much-aggrieved Ho ominously declared the beginning of '100 years war'.

BELOW: GENERAL DOUGLAS D. GRACEY MEETS JAPANESE LEADERS IN SAIGON. GRACEY WAS TASKED WITH JAPANESE DISARMAMENT BELOW VIETNAM'S 16TH PARALLEL.

Attempting to pinpoint the beginning of the First Indochina War is problematic, yet a key moment must be the battle of Haiphong in 1946. Haiphong was Tonkin's principal harbour; communist controlled, it was a flashpoint which had been blockaded by the French since 20 November 1946. On 23 November Colonel Pierre Louis Debès, the commander of the French forces in the city, received orders to take Haiphong by any means necessary. The French began a massive bombardment using the 3in (76mm) and 8in (203mm) guns of the cruiser *Suffren* and all available artillery and air power. There is no clear indication how many Vietnamese died in Haiphong (estimates vary between 200 and 20,000), but by 28 November, when fighting stopped, the First Indochina War was underway.

THE TIGER AND THE ELEPHANT

The First Indochina War lasted from 1946 to 1954. In nine years of conflict the combined death toll of soldiers would exceed 200,000 as France pitted its conventional firepower and organization against the thoroughly unconventional divisions of Vietminh guerrillas. The French war's significance to the later Vietnam War is paramount. Not only were the foundations of Vietcong and North Vietnamese Army (NVA) tactics laid (the latter's immediate precursor was the People's Army of Vietnam or PAVN, led by Vo Nguyen Giap), but the French forces also made some seminal mistakes which the US would repeat a decade later.

These mistakes are now familiar to any student of Southeast Asian history. The French deployed around 150,000 soldiers in Indochina, yet Vietnam's densely jungled and mountainous terrain could easily absorb such numbers and the French never had sufficient manpower to pacify Vietminh-held territory. Local military commanders had to justify their actions to political leaders based in Paris and Hanoi, who were often members of unstable coalition governments.

One clear advantage the French had, however, was firepower. A typical combat unit could field 9mm submachine-guns and carbines, 0.50in machine-guns, 60mm and 80mm mortars, US-built M4 Sherman and M24 Chaffee tanks, and 75mm, 105mm and 155mm artillery. Air power included Martin B-26 Marauder bombers, and Grumman F-8 Bearcat and Vought F-4U Corsair fighters. Yet such a military machine required huge and reliable logistics and the Vietminh's domination of jungle roads and trails in Tonkin, northern

The French fought the First Indochina War on the basis of a 'domino theory' similar to that which influenced the later US involvement, fearing a deterioration of their authority in French colonies such as Algeria and Morocco should Indochina be 'lost'.

BELOW: A MARTIN B-26 MARAUDER BOMBER IS ARMED AND FUELLED READY FOR STRIKES AGAINST THE VIETMINH.

Below: French troops equipped by the British disembark at Vinh Long in October 1948. France became increasingly reliant on foreign military and economic aid as the war progressed.

Annam and coastal areas of Cochin China meant that this was a near impossibility too. Huge numbers of French troops were to die on ambush-prone roads and rivers, and consequently air supply became vital, with the French relying on their AAC-1 transport aircraft – and, from 1952 on, US-supplied Douglas C-47 Skytrains and Fairchild C-119 Flying Boxcars. Yet once the Vietminh and People's Army of Vietnam had acquired more sophisticated anti-aircraft weaponry, even this source of resupply became increasingly hazardous and undependable.

France had no shortage of excellent commanders, but few were experienced in counter-insurgency warfare. A French tactical cornerstone was the *tache d'huile* ('oil slick') method in which 'hostile territory' was divided up into a grid, each square being systematically 'raked' by offensive forces. The French also constructed defensive fortifications across the north, the most impressive example of these being the hundreds of ferro-concrete emplacements that were built to form the De Lattre Line in 1951 (see page 15 below).

The problems with these tactics soon became clear. 'Oil-slick' methods were too inflexible – the Vietminh were not chained to any square of land and could retreat and attack as they desired. Likewise, defensive fortifications simply tied down large numbers of French soldiers in one isolated and vulnerable spot. Yet in fairness, the French did have some strong tactical units to compensate for this. The *divisions navales d'assaut*, a riverine assault division made up of army and navy troops, and the *groupement des commando mixtes aéro-portés*, an airborne commando group, used rapid deployment tactics with fair levels of success. Likewise, the estimable *legionnaires* and paratroopers were continually used as elite forces wherever the fighting was hardest (11,620 *legionnaires* alone died in Indochina).

Right: Former SS soldiers serving with the French Foreign Legion survey their handiwork. The SS veterans had experience of fighting against partisans on the Eastern Front and were effective combatants in French Indochina, though they proved politically unacceptable.

In remarking upon France's failures, the startling capabilities of the forces at Ho's command should not be downplayed. The Vietminh was a highly motivated revolutionary

THE VIETMINH

The Viet Nam Doc Lap Dong Minh Hoi ('League for the Independence of Vietnam', or Vietminh) was a capable revolutionary army which integrated ruthless military force into effective programmes of support building. They were divided into three structural layers. First was the village militia, a generally unarmed grassroots support used in a whole range of logistical or intelligence duties. The militia was formed in 1949 from a countrywide mobilization of men and women aged between 18 and 45, reaching numbers in excess of 340,000 by 1954. Next were the regional troops, who mingled with the civilian populace but were active in guerrilla operations against the French. These worked in small independent groups or in cooperation with the final layer of the Vietminh, the Chuc Luc ('regular force'). This was a formally organized body of soldiers which by 1954 had some 125,000 troops in seven divisions, well equipped with infantry and support weapons from French, Chinese and Japanese sources. Control of all Vietminh troops cascaded downwards from the revolutionary leadership to regional committees of political officers who oversaw local tactics. From 1946 to 1947 the whole of Indochina was divided into 14 operational regions, reduced to six in 1948 when only the territory of Vietnam itself became the military focus.

Peasants carrying Vietminh supplies.

army. Commanding them, the PAVN/NVA and the later Vietcong, for over 30 years was General Vo Nguyen Giap, a self-taught military leader who mixed pragmatism with a passionate commitment to Mao Zedong's strategies of revolutionary war (see box, page 18). The PAVN, later more popularly known as the North Vietnamese Army (NVA) during the war with the US, was built up as a conventional army in association and cooperation with the Vietminh (the more political wing of Ho's military forces). The PAVN's expansion was rapid, and by 1951 it was to consist of 154 battalions. Giap's army was a totally different animal to that of the French – it had a clear objective, was well motivated, had an intimate knowledge of the terrain and people, and it could generate popular support (which the French, fatally, failed to do). Giap's army could survive and fight on limited resources, though the thousands of volunteers meant that supplies could be reliably carried through by hand to the combatants; and, importantly, it could absorb huge levels of casualties without the weakening of political will or strategic boldness.

In 1946, Ho Chi Minh likened the coming conflict to that of a clash between a tiger and elephant. The elephant could crush the tiger in a straight fight, yet if the tiger did not fight on these terms, repeatedly sneaking out of the jungle to tear pieces from the elephant's hide, the elephant would slowly bleed to death. Spoken at the outset of the war, Ho's words would prove to be accurate.

Below: French troops in operations against the Vietminh in 1948. Until 1950 French leaders consistently underestimated the capabilities of their local opponents.

A cornerstone of Vietminh tactics was evasion. By the act of maintaining a fight only when they were confident they could win, the communists preserved numbers while steadily pushing up French casualties.

RIGHT: MOROCCAN *TIRAILLEURS* ADVANCE THROUGH A BURNING VILLAGE NEAR TONKIN IN 1951 DURING CLEARANCE OPERATIONS.

BELOW: FRENCH TROOPS RIDE ON A US-SUPPLIED M24 CHAFFEE TANK. ARMOUR WAS OF LIMITED USEFULNESS, FOR ON TIGHT JUNGLE ROADS IT WAS PRONE TO AMBUSH.

THE EARLY WAR 1946–50

The first four years of the First Indochina War were a time of low-intensity guerrilla actions, with the Vietminh pursuing tactics of ambushes, murders and bombings while the French replied with fighting-reconnaissance patrols. The action was mainly concentrated in the contested northern territories, particularly the Tonkin region, and after half-hearted peace negotiations failed in May 1947 the French launched their first major offensives: Operation Léa on 7 October and Operation *Ceinture* ('Belt') on 20 November. These had big goals: the capture of Ho Chi Minh and the defeat of his units in the northeastern Viet Bac region and the territories north of Hanoi. French forces took the major outpost of Thai Nguyen and around 7200 Vietminh were killed and 1000 taken prisoner. Yet the DRV leadership evaded capture and, operating with only 12,000 men in 80,000 square miles (207,200sq km) of jungle, the French could not consolidate their advances and withdrew – a pattern that was to be repeated throughout the conflict.

Greater success was achieved by Major General Marcel Alessandri (in overall field control of French forces at this time), who employed 20 battalions to pacify the highly contested Red River Delta area – the territory extending from the junction of the Day and Red rivers just north of Hanoi across to the coast at Haiphong. Alessandri took the region through 'clearing' and 'mopping up' operations by using more flexible land-based and riverine units, and he also made attempts to cut off the Vietminh's rice supplies. Yet the French failed to reinforce the area or make themselves welcome, and the Red River Delta would remain troublesome for the rest of the war.

In 1949 an event outside Vietnam dramatically changed the face of the conflict in Indochina. The civil war in China ended with a victory for Mao's communists, and subsequently China became an invaluable source of supply, training and refuge for the Vietminh. On 18 January 1950, China formally recognized the DRV as a political entity and started to supply arms in increasing amounts, which by 1953 would equal around 4000 tons (4,000,000kg) per month. Of particular value was the supply of heavy weaponry, such as 75mm howitzers and 75mm heavy mortars. These would enable the Vietminh to attempt the final stages of revolutionary war.

Below: PAVN soldiers gather after liberating a village which had been set on fire by French forces. The French were especially vulnerable to enemy attack at the many isolated border and jungle outposts they maintained.

THE PRESSURE IS RAISED

In 1950 the Vietminh went on the offensive. It launched attacks throughout the Red River Delta and northeastern Tonkin, before turning its attention to the isolated French outposts on the Chinese border. Giap was showing a distinct change in tactics. At the French positions at Dong Khe, for example, the Vietminh put up a 75mm artillery bombardment for two days before throwing five PAVN battalions in human waves against the defences. After huge slaughter among the attacking soldiers, Dong Khe fell to the 308th Division on 27 May. It was recaptured by a battalion-strength air-drop of paratroopers, but then shelled into submission by the Vietminh and decisively taken once again using further human wave assaults.

The loss of Dong Khe isolated another French outpost, Cao Bang in the far northeast, and there followed one of the great tragedies of the war. A decision was taken to evacuate Cao Bang's troops along 45 miles (72km) of RC4 (*Route Coloniale 4*) instead of the safer but longer RC3. RC4 ran close to the dangerous Chinese border and consequently the retreat became a hideous slog under continual Vietminh ambushes, the efficiency of which resulted in 4800 French soldiers being killed and a huge amount of French weaponry (including 112 mortars and over 8000 rifles) was added to the Vietminh stockpile.

Other outposts fell and the Vietminh now controlled most of northeastern Vietnam. The French sought a change in military leadership and General Jean de Lattre de Tassigny assumed full military and civilian authority in Indochina. Sensing another Vietminh campaign in the Red River Delta, De Lattre set about constructing 900 forts and 2200 pillboxes which reached from Haiphong out to Vinh Yen and then back to below Phat Diem in the south. Yet in another classic French miscalculation, the 'De Lattre Line' actually made

Right: A machine-gun team armed with the 7.5mm Chatellerault M1924/29 keep a close look out for enemy activity during Operation Lorraine.

Below: Elite airborne soldiers parachute into action at Hoa Binh. The French managed to retain Hoa Binh but Vietminh tactics soon meant that it had little or no strategic value.

the French more vulnerable, tying down 20 battalions of troops more usefully employed otherwise.

In January 1951, 81 Vietminh battalions totalling some 20,000 men attacked 7000 French troops at Vinh Yen, around 30 miles (48km) northwest of Hanoi. But what looked to be a massive impending defeat for the French turned into a major victory. Grumman F-8F Bearcats and Douglas B-26 Invaders used a new munition, napalm, to blast the attacking formations, while French troops and artillery smashed a large-scale PAVN attack on 16 January.

Repeated PAVN attacks in other sectors even threatened Hanoi itself, but for once Giap had overreached and French firepower was brought to bear to inflict a massive defeat. Such was the scale of losses (more than 14,000 dead) that the Vietminh even suffered significant levels of desertion, and Giap backtracked from his premature entry into conventional warfare. And yet the French did not make good on their victory; they did not have the manpower or the tactical foresight to secure the territories they had gained, and overall Vietminh strategy was unhindered as a result.

In 1953 alone, Chinese supplies to the Vietminh included 24 105mm howitzers, 1000 submachine-guns, millions of rounds of small arms ammunition, 40,000 mines and more than 200 tons of explosives.

NEARING THE END

By 1951 French public opinion was swinging against the war. The frightful casualty lists and lack of progress started to make the war politically questionable. A resolution of the conflict was needed and by the end of 1951 the French themselves were going on the

Left: With shellfire raining down, French Foreign Legion soldiers provide covering fire using a Chatellerault M1924/29. The French achieved some significant victories in 1950–51, though not a sustainable momentum.

offensive, with extra military motivation being provided by increased US aid (see Chapter 2) and the pressure of an impending review of the Indochina budget back in Paris. De Lattre's objective was Hoa Binh, a Vietminh-dominated city south of the Red River Delta. On 14 November, three parachute battalions made a daring drop into the city and secured it. The Vietminh, showing their usual strategic vision, retreated. They then gathered five divisions, two of which were directed against the French supply routes to Hoa Binh along RC6 and the Day River. Hoa Binh developed into a punishing slog of ambush, assault and artillery duel for both sides and the Vietminh started to bypass the town to make attacks deep into the Red River Delta. Hoa Binh eventually cost the French 894 killed and missing, and although the Vietminh lost many more (about 9000) the French were eventually forced to withdraw under the sheer scale of enemy attacks.

Giap responded to the Hoa Binh situation with major offensives of his own. Using the 308th, 312th and 316th divisions he attacked French garrisons on the Nglia Ridge in the highlands of northwest Vietnam. Most of the outposts fell, isolated as they were from reinforcements, but of particular note was the performance of the French 6th Colonial Parachute Regiment which, after parachuting into the Tu Le Pass on 16 October, had to execute a 50-mile (80km) withdrawal fighting against the entire 312th Division. They made it to safety with the loss of 91 men killed.

Above: A PAVN soldier mans a Japanese 7.7mm Type 92 machine-gun for anti-aircraft use. Such air defences restricted French air power at Dien Bien Phu.

Giap at his command post near Dien Bien Phu.

GIAP AND 'REVOLUTIONARY WAR'

As commander-in-chief and minister of the interior in Ho's revolutionary government, Vo Nguyen Giap was one of the key strategists behind North Vietnam's success in three decades of conflict. Giap was a brilliant, self-taught military strategist who combined excellent planning with a considered pursuit of Mao Zedong's techniques of 'revolutionary war'. For Giap, this warfare encompassed two types of *dau tranh* ('struggle') – military and political. Military *dau tranh* broke down into three successive phases: phase I, small-scale guerrilla actions; phase II, a mixture of guerrilla and conventional actions; and phase III, outright conventional war. Political *dau tranh* was a broad spectrum of economic, social, psychological and ideological measures to expand support for the revolutionary cause while simultaneously breaking the morale and political will of the enemy.

'Revolutionary war' was the ideal methodology for defeating both the French and the combined South Vietnamese-US initiatives in Southeast Asia. An unpredictable and protracted form of warfare, as practised by Giap it destabilized the enemy at every level of operations. The only criticism of Giap's strategic awareness is that he occasionally pushed to the Phase III of operations too quickly in some sectors, the result being high casualties against superior enemy firepower.

By this point in the war, General Raoul Salan was in control, De Lattre having returned home stricken with cancer. Salan's attempt to reverse the tide of the war was Operation Lorraine, a commitment of some 30,000 troops in various airborne, motorized, commando or tank-destroyer formations which attacked out from the Red River Delta and hoped to suck the Vietminh into the set-piece battles which the French favoured. Launched on 29 October 1952, the objectives were the Yen Bay supply depots about 100 miles (160km) inside Vietminh territory. Yet Giap made no real effort to meet the French in battle, instead using his 304th and 320th divisions to make powerful guerrilla attacks. Overextended and gradually weakened, the French troops withdrew on 14 November but their tribulations were not at an end – an ambush by two Vietminh regiments on 17 November along RC2 resulted in the slaughter of an entire convoy, with 1200 French deaths.

Right: US adviser General John Wilson O'Daniel (right) with French General Christian de Castries, on 2 February 1954.

April 1953 marked another major development in the war when the Vietminh invaded northern Laos. The Vietminh had already taken the Laotian border regions and Laos had

At Dien Bien Phu the French were actually outgunned by the Viet-minh/PAVN forces. Although the French had redirected much of their artillery to the outpost, communist troops dug into the surrounding hills had gathered nearly 200 artillery pieces.

LEFT: PARACHUTING WAS ALMOST THE ONLY METHOD OF INFANTRY REINFORCEMENT ONCE DIEN BIEN PHU WAS CUT OFF.

DIEN BIEN PHU

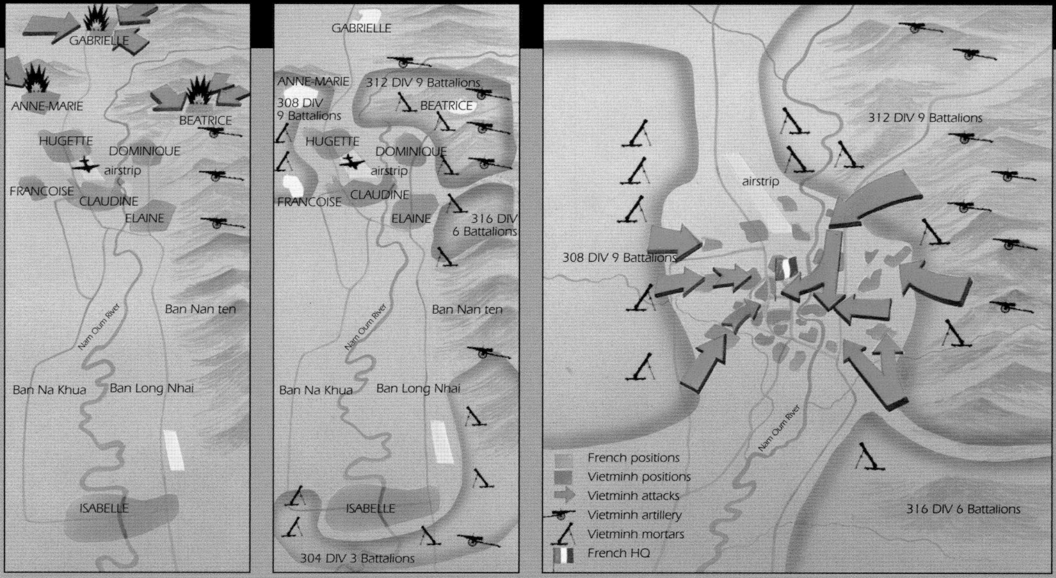

First wave of Vietminh attacks March 1954

Situation 15 April 1954

The French Surrender May 1954

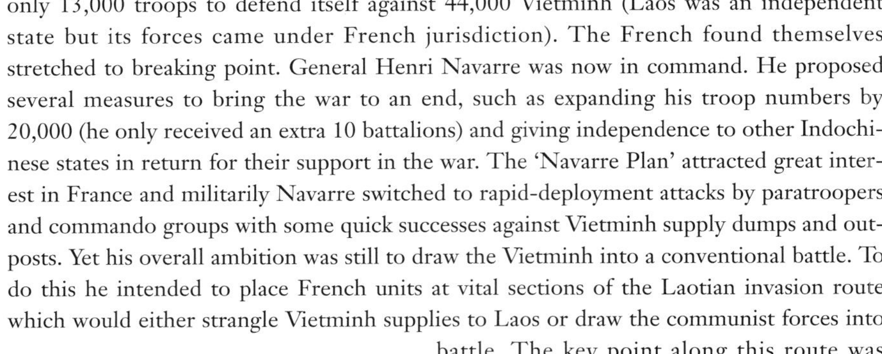

only 13,000 troops to defend itself against 44,000 Vietminh (Laos was an independent state but its forces came under French jurisdiction). The French found themselves stretched to breaking point. General Henri Navarre was now in command. He proposed several measures to bring the war to an end, such as expanding his troop numbers by 20,000 (he only received an extra 10 battalions) and giving independence to other Indochinese states in return for their support in the war. The 'Navarre Plan' attracted great interest in France and militarily Navarre switched to rapid-deployment attacks by paratroopers and commando groups with some quick successes against Vietminh supply dumps and outposts. Yet his overall ambition was still to draw the Vietminh into a conventional battle. To do this he intended to place French units at vital sections of the Laotian invasion route which would either strangle Vietminh supplies to Laos or draw the communist forces into battle. The key point along this route was Dien Bien Phu, a flat valley in the T'ai Mountains some 12 miles (19km) long and eight miles (13km) wide with two small airstrips. The airstrips were important because Dien Bien Phu was only 10 miles (16km) from Laos but 170 miles (275km) from Hanoi, and air supply would be the only viable method of keeping French troops sustained there. Despite the grave concern of other French commanders, Operation Castor – the capture and holding of Dien Bien Phu – was put into action.

BELOW: VIETMINH SOLDIERS PARADE THROUGH HANOI AFTER FRANCE'S DEFEAT IN INDOCHINA. SOME 5000 TROOPS TOOK PART IN THE MARCH WHICH SIGNALLED THE FORMAL OCCUPATION OF HANOI AS THE NORTH VIETNAMESE CAPITAL CITY.

DIEN BIEN PHU

Dien Bien Phu began as a parachute operation when two airborne battle groups were dropped into the valley on 20 November 1953. The elite paratroopers quickly eliminated surprised Vietminh contingents and set about turning Dien Bien Phu into a jungle fortress. They created a series of strongpoints throughout the valley, each one being named after a past mistress of the commander, General Christian de Castries. After a series of large airlifts, the French force at Dien Bien Phu consisted of 10,800 men (later reaching 16,000), their armaments including 75mm and 105mm artillery pieces, four 155mm howitzers and 10 M24 Chaffee tanks.

The French yet again underestimated Giap. Believing that the surrounding jungle-covered mountains would prohibit the deployment of artillery, the French were stunned when heavy shellfire started to rain down on them from the heights. The Vietminh had managed to drag 75mm and 105mm howitzers and numerous mortars through the highlands while avoiding the threat of air strikes by remaining hidden under cover from the dense foliage. French air power was further limited by Vietminh anti-aircraft fire, which now included 64 37mm anti-aircraft (AA) guns in the hands of a Chinese regiment. Throughout the battle of Dien Bien Phu, 62 French aircraft would be shot down.

While the French sent out fighting patrols, five Vietminh divisions had surrounded Dien Bien Phu and started ferocious assaults backed by their formidable artillery fire. The outposts fell steadily, though the casualties inflicted upon the besiegers led Giap to pause operations while he built his army up to a strength of 50,000. Despite further air-dropped reinforcements, the French position soon became hopeless. On 7 May 1954, after yet another mass attack six days earlier, the French were forced to surrender having lost 7184 men killed and wounded compared to Vietnamese losses of around 20,000 (though 11,000 French soldiers were taken prisoner, few would return). Giap's losses may have been excessive, but he still gained the victory he intended. Ho Chi Minh and the DRV had won the war both militarily and politically. The French finally accepted that their rule of Indochina was at an end.

THE GENEVA ACCORDS

The Vietnam War involving the United States can only be understood in the light of the Geneva Conference which followed the French defeat at Dien Bien Phu. During June and July 1954, Vietnamese, Soviet, European, Chinese and American politicians gathered to discuss a settlement for Indochina and the resultant Geneva Accords were finally signed on 20 July. Vietnam was temporarily divided at the 17th parallel into a communist-controlled north and a US-supported south in charge of its own affairs, and France gave up all its claims to Vietnamese jurisdiction (Laos and Cambodia fell under separate agreements). A condition of the Geneva Accords was that national and general elections were to be held by July 1956, elections which were intended to reunify Vietnam under a democratically agreed government. The 17th parallel also bisected a demilitarized zone (DMZ) some 6 miles (10km) wide which would act as a buffer zone between the two nations to prevent any infringement of the accords.

The Geneva Conference drew the First Indochina War to a close, a conflict which had cost the French and their Indochinese allies more than 94,000 dead or missing while the Vietnamese had suffered around 150,000 fatalities. It had resulted in French colonial power being ejected from the region by a ruthless and intelligent enemy that fought a different kind of war than that favoured by Western armies. However, the agreement which concluded the struggle was not to bring peace. By 1954 the United States was already deeply involved in the affairs of Southeast Asia and this exposure would drag the country into a military engagement which mirrored the French catastrophe, though on an even greater scale.

BELOW: THOUSANDS OF FRENCH SOLDIERS TAKEN PRISONER AT DIEN BIEN PHU ARE LED AWAY TO CAPTIVITY. MOST WOULD FACE YEARS OF HARDSHIP, TORTURE AND DEPRIVATION.

CHAPTER 2

Taking a Stand Against Communism

A US military adviser moves across a rice paddy in the company of a South Vietnamese machine-gun team. During the 1960s the distinction between an adviser and a combatant became steadily blurred for the US, and it was inexorably drawn into all-out war.

For the US during the 1960s, Southeast Asia was seen as a linchpin of world stability. With China and North Vietnam already in communist hands, US officials felt themselves morally obliged to act when South Vietnam was threatened.

The relationship between the United States (US) and the forces of Ho Chi Minh was not always a hostile one. From 1941 to 1945 Ho Chi Minh's opposition to and actions against the Japanese occupation of Indochina gained US approval, and President F.D.R. Roosevelt's administration provided the Vietminh with arms and supplies in return for surveillance and sabotage. But Ho Chi Minh and Roosevelt were united in more than just their military pragmatism. Roosevelt's ideals meant that he favoured Vietnamese independence over French colonialism, and US affiliation with Ho Chi Minh grew so warm that the latter even quoted the American Declaration of Independence when he proclaimed the Democratic Republic of Vietnam (DRV) on 2 September 1945.

In April 1945, however, Roosevelt died and was replaced by Harry S. Truman. There began a dramatic cooling of US relations with Ho Chi Minh. In the atmosphere of the new politics of the Cold War, Truman was advised to retain allegiances with the French, especially because of the Vietnamese liberation movement's communist outlook and ambitions. The US cut off communications with Ho Chi Minh and aided the restoration of French rule. This set in train the events that would take the US into the Second Indochina War, better known as the Vietnam War.

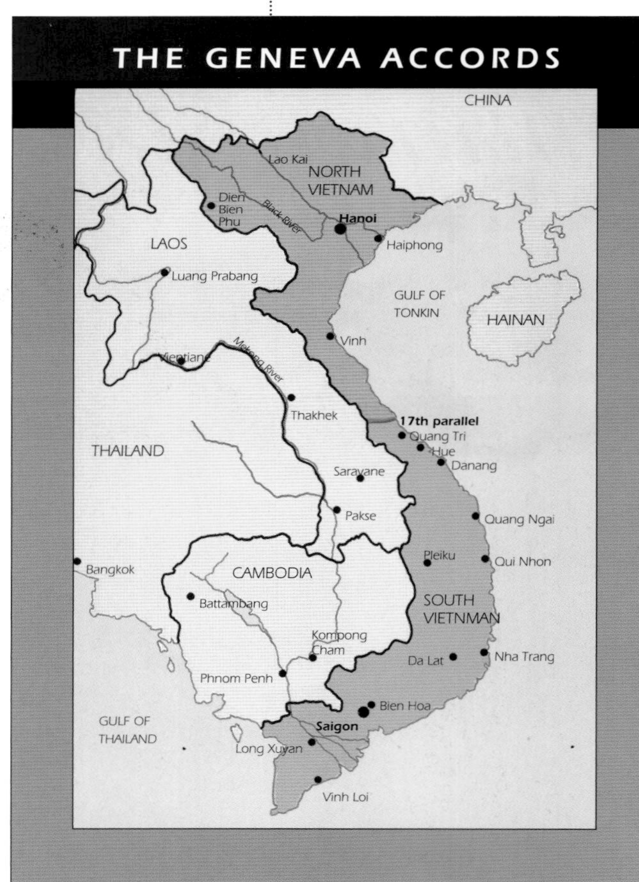

Between 1946 and 1954, and particularly after 1949 when Mao's communists came to power in China, the US started to channel increasing amounts of money, materiel and weaponry to the French. The figures speak for themselves: in 1950 the newly established US Military Assistance Advisory Group (MAAG) gave \$100 million to the French forces; by 1954 that figure had risen to \$1 billion – some 80 per cent of the French costs overall for the war that year. In total, the US contributed \$3 billion over the course of France's nine-year conflict, a massive 60 per cent of France's total war expenditure.

The US drew the line, however, at itself actually becoming involved militarily (apart from the supply of weapons systems). The impending defeat of the French at Dien Bien Phu, however, did provoke alarm in Washington, D.C., especially as \$385 million had just been given to promote France's control of the situation. From 1953 President Eisenhower's government debated the use of air strikes and even nuclear weapons against the Vietminh and PAVN, but caution over dragging the US into a complex conflict ruled the day. Yet what they could not do was ignore the situation. Not only was Indochina a vital trade region for goods such as rice, rubber and iron ore, but it was also seen as a key area in the global struggle between capitalism and communism.

THE VIETCONG

The National Front for the Liberation of South Vietnam was established by Hanoi on 20 December 1960 as the main guerrilla organization committed to establishing communism in South Vietnam. Subsequently known as the Vietcong (meaning 'Vietnamese communists'), it was initially made up of southern-born Vietminh soldiers who stayed on in South Vietnam after the Geneva Accords, and it expanded under an influx of new recruits and later North Vietnamese Army (NVA) support. In 1960, the VC numbered around 5000 and was often organized into battalion-strength units of 300–600 men and women. These would subdivide into an infantry company and a heavy weapons company plus support units such as reconnaissance, signals and communications, and engineers. With many thousands of supporters throughout South Vietnam, by the time of the Tet Offensive in 1968 its numbers were in excess of 50,000.

The Vietcong's early war with the United States and ARVN was mainly in South Vietnam's rural districts, and its elusive style of guerrilla warfare and dexterity with booby traps inflicted thousands of casualties on its opponents. The turning point for it was the Tet Offensive, during which more than 30,000 of its number were killed. Following Tet, the Vietcong would never again operate with the force that it had previously applied, and the NVA took over as the primary communist force.

A Vietcong guerrilla lays a mine.

By the late 1940s, the dominant US attitude to communism was one of containment; unless it was it would spread like a virus through other nations and regions one by one, each falling like the next domino in a chain. This was seen to be confirmed in the USSR's satellite states in eastern Europe, its intrusions into the Middle East, the events of the Korean War, and China and the Soviet Union's recognition of the DRV. On 27 June 1950, President Truman restated Eisenhower's 'domino' theory of communist expansion – the belief that every country that fell to communism would lead to the acquisition of another as part of an inexorable worldwide attempt at domination. Truman had been embarrassed over the 'loss' of China, and by the time of the French defeat in 1954 President Eisenhower did not want to make the same mistake.

Left: Vietminh troops stack up captured US-supplied radio equipment and ammunition at Dien Bien Phu in 1954. The US had debated direct military intervention during the French War, but restricted itself to material and economic aid instead.

Right: Units from the People's Army of Vietnam make a river crossing while on their way to the front in 1953. Vietminh logistics were improvised, incredibly flexible and almost always delivered.

Below: US military advisers became a common sight among South Vietnam's military units during the early 1960s, and they started actively, though discreetly, to lead combat operations.

SUPPORTING DIEM

The Geneva Accords had split Vietnam in two at the 17th parallel. Ho Chi Minh's regime governed North Vietnam, while Bo Dai's US-backed government controlled South Vietnam. Free elections were to be held in 1956 to reunify the country, yet US officials were aware that if this were to take place, Ho's popular nationalism would probably attract about 80 per cent of the vote. Ironically, both Ho and Bo Dai's prime minister, Ngo Dinh Diem, later rejected the accords in favour of unification, though exclusively under their own regimes. So instead of electoral unification, the regimes governing north and south became entrenched and antagonistic political entities. While North Vietnam received Soviet and Chinese support, South Vietnam relied heavily upon US investment to build up its political and military 'independence'.

Yet the US also recognized South Vietnam's need for external protection. Consequently, Secretary of State John Foster Dulles oversaw the creation of SEATO, the South-East Asia Treaty Organization. This alliance of the US, Britain, France, Australia, New Zealand and Pakistan agreed to protect the territorial and political integrity of South Vietnam, Cambodia and Laos from outside interventions. And despite the national diversity of SEATO it became an effective body which enabled some of its members to contribute to the coming war.

The years immediately after the French war saw Ho Chi Minh more concerned with internal disputes than cross-border conquests. Some 900,000 civilians, mostly Roman Catholics from the Red River Delta area, fled from the north to the south following the agreements in Geneva, and North Vietnam was left with economic turbulence and food shortages. North Vietnam produced only 40 per cent of Vietnam's rice but had a larger population than South Vietnam, and in an unwise act of political repression the government had some 50,000 'landlords' (people deemed be in ownership of excessive amounts of Vietnamese land, but many of whom were actually little more than modest farmers) executed between 1954 and 1956. In late 1956 Ho Chi Minh would apologize for this action, but by November he had to quell a serious rebellion and his forces took the lives of some 6000 dissidents.

South Vietnam was by this time under Diem's leadership after he gratuitously rigged national elections in his own favour (Diem received 200,000 more votes in Saigon than there were registered voters). As its premier Diem would lead the Republic of Vietnam (RVN) until 1964, yet it was his arrogant and erratic leadership which made the defeat of communist insurgency that much harder. He consistently alienated the population with either persecution or partisan 'reforms' and thereby enhanced support for Ho Chi Minh among sections of the South Vietnamese people. Despite this, the US felt it had little alternative but to offer military, political and economic support. So between 1955 and 1961 alone, $7 billion would be sunk into Diem's regime and infrastructure. But, more significantly, increasing numbers of US military personnel would find themselves directly involved in combat against the Vietcong.

The South Vietnamese had a substantial army with which to combat the Vietcong. Yet inept and socially divisive government control led to a corruption and inefficiency in the military which the US policy makers and ambassadors found hard to rectify.

IN THE FIELD

By the late 1950s Diem's forces were the beneficiaries of about 750 US military advisers, with officials from MAAG attempting to establish an effective army among the South Vietnamese. In particular, MAAG leaders such as Lieutenant General Samuel T. Williams sought to organize the Army of the Republic of Vietnam (ARVN) as a conventional force capable of resisting a North Vietnamese Army (NVA) invasion across the DMZ. This was far from easy. The ARVN was riven with corruption and equipment shortages. Furthermore, South Vietnam's forces were effectively divided in four between the ARVN and three large private armies with either religious or criminal allegiances. Diem frequently antagonized these private forces, creating a spiral of infighting in 1955 that produced even more recruits for the Vietcong.

LEFT: MEMBERS OF THE VIETMINH GENERAL HEADQUARTERS DURING A PLANNING SESSION. PART OF THE STRENGTH OF THE VIETMINH-VIETCONG WAS THAT ITS LEADERSHIP UNDERSTOOD WESTERN CULTURE AND POLITICS AND SO COULD FIGHT THE WAR ON THE SOCIAL AND MEDIA FRONTS AS WELL AS ON THE BATTLEFIELD.

The Vietcong's volunteers were not the poorly fed fanatics of popular myth. It was a well-supplied and organised body of soldiers with good logistics, intensive training programmes and intelligent tactics. Yet it was also utterly ruthless to those who did not support it.

In 1956 the ARVN's strength stood at around 135,000 men, armed with US weaponry such as 105mm howitzers, 75mm M30 mortars and various small arms. In opposition to them was the National Front for the Liberation of South Vietnam, or Vietcong ('Vietnamese communists'). These insurgents were specifically southern-based as opposed to the conventional NVA north of the DMZ. The Vietcong was initially small in number (about 1000 Vietminh had stayed on in South Vietnam following the Geneva Accords) and conducted only limited operations, mainly because North Vietnam was still committed to a political method of unification.

Initial Vietcong actions consisted of murders, kidnappings and ambushes, but also occasional larger operations against industrial sites and arms dumps. Yet escalation was continual. In 1957–58, for example, 700 South Vietnamese officials were killed by the Vietcong; while in 1960–61 over 6000 were killed. Escalation had been boosted in January 1959 when North Vietnam officially agreed to the partial support of Vietcong activities. The following year, at the third party congress, Ho went the final step and approved the liberation of South Vietnam by military means. Supply routes to the Vietcong were established down through Laos and the Vietcong was expanded by 2000 NVA soldiers who were infiltrated from North Vietnam.

Despite the growing seriousness of the situation, President Eisenhower still kept his soldiers in an advisory role, though on more or more occasions the 'advisers' became engaged in unauthorized participation in ARVN operations, manning machine-guns or giving fire-control. Of real concern was the fact that the Vietcong, now numbering around 12,000 men and operating in units of 50–100, was starting to inflict some significant

NGO DINH DIEM

A significant cause behind the escalation of the Vietnam conflict between 1954 and 1963 was the leadership of the South Vietnamese president, Ngo Dinh Diem (1901–63). A committed Roman Catholic, nationalist and anti-communist from a wealthy mandarin background, following the end of Japanese occupation in 1945 Diem had spent a short time as a Vietminh hostage, during which time he met Ho Chi Minh, who asked Diem to join the communist revolutionary government. Finding out that his older brother, Ngo Dinh Khoi, had been killed by the Vietminh he refused Ho's offer, and after his release he spent two years in the US, attending Roman Catholic seminaries, and two years in Europe.

AFTERMATH OF A VIETCONG TERROR BOMB IN SAIGON.

After the French defeat in Indochina in 1954, Diem returned to Vietnam and at the request of Emperor Bao Dai became prime minister. Diem quickly displaced Bao Dai, achieving the presidency of South Vietnam in 1954 and holding the position until 1963. Diem was undoubtedly a nationalist, but his manipulative attitude, over-influential family and class arrogance led him to alienate many communities and forces in South Vietnam. US-support of Diem was eventually eroded over years of governmental ineptitude, and by the 1960s the South Vietnamese military was demoralized, Buddhist riots were sweeping the country and control of communist aggression was slipping from Diem's grasp. On 1 November 1963 he was forced from government by a faction of army generals and murdered the next day.

LEFT: PART OF THE PAVN'S MOSTLY JAPANESE ARTILLERY ARSENAL IN DECEMBER 1959.

defeats on the ARVN. On 26 September 1959, for example, the Vietcong's 2nd Liberation Battalion killed 12 men from two companies of the ARVN 23rd Division and seized most of their weapons. On 26 January 1960, 200 Vietcong overran an ARVN HQ at Trang Sup. Furthermore, district and provincial capitals were starting to fall to the Vietcong. By the time John F. Kennedy became US president in 1961, the ARVN was losing soldiers in their thousands each year and annual troop infiltration from the north was about 7000 men. The situation in Vietnam was getting out of control.

THE KENNEDY YEARS

As a fervent subscriber to containment theory, Kennedy was determined not to let South Vietnam fall into communist hands. As early as 1956, the then senator Kennedy had referred to South Vietnam as 'the cornerstone of the free world in Southeast Asia', and from the beginning of his presidential office Kennedy increased financial aid and the number of military personnel going to South Vietnam. Despite many cautionary opinions concerning the US's involvement, Kennedy assented to other, stronger voices. Secretary of Defense Robert McNamara and Secretary of State Dean Rusk were powerful advocates of escalation, and their advice would play a central role in American policy on Vietnam. By December 1961 there were around 3000 US military advisers in Vietnam; these included the Special Forces, or Green Berets, instructing the ARVN in counter-

BELOW: TWO VICTIMS OF A VIETCONG EXECUTION SQUAD IN HON HIEP ON 13 OCTOBER 1960.

RIGHT: VIETNAMESE TROOPS WAIT TO BOARD US HELICOPTERS FOR AN AIRLIFT OPERATION AGAINST A POINT OF COMMUNIST CONCENTRATION AROUND THE VILLAGE OF HUNG MY, SOUTH VIETNAM. UNTIL THE US COMMITTED ITSELF TO ACTUAL COMBAT, THE VIETCONG HELD TACTICAL ADVANTAGE IN MUCH OF THE FIGHTING.

BELOW: CAPTAIN RICHARD A. JONES OF THE US RANGERS AND ARVN TROOPS ADVANCE ON A VIETCONG HIDEOUT DURING AN OPERATION IN THE PLAIN OF REEDS AREA IN NOVEMBER 1962.

insurgency warfare and CIA officials organizing the Montagnard mountain peoples into insurgent units known as Civilian Irregular Defense Groups (CIDG). By 1963 the number of advisers would rise to around 16,000.

In 1961 the Vietcong expanded operations. In September, it captured Phouc Vinh, a provincial capital only 55 miles (89km) north of Saigon. Although it was recaptured the next day by the ARVN at heavy cost, the feeling prevailed that South Vietnam was losing the struggle to contain communist elements. In October, military adviser General Maxwell D. Taylor and Special Assistant for National Security Affairs Walt W. Rostow visited Vietnam and returned with the 'Taylor-Rostow plan'. This plan recommended a dramatic increase in US advisory, economic and military support to South Vietnam, including the commitment of 8000 US troops in actual combat roles. Kennedy shied away from this last suggestion, but he acceded to the need for escalating investment. In December

1961 two companies of Boeing-Vertol H-21C Shawnee helicopters, 33 machines in total, landed in Vietnam complete with pilots and around 400 technicians to maintain them. US aircraft carriers also started to 'slip' into Vietnamese waters.

Though no one would admit it, US soldiers were now going into combat against the Vietcong. American helicopter pilots were firing rockets and machine-guns against Vietcong positions during troop deployment and 'fire-support' missions; US Special Forces soldiers were accompanying ARVN troops on covert reconnaissance and ambush operations; and, significantly, Americans were starting to die – some 200 would be killed by the end of 1964.

Most initial media reporting of the situation in South Vietnam was favourable to US policy makers. Only when US casualties started to mount and television journalism portrayed more of war's realities did public opinion start to shift.

Yet for all this activity, Kennedy felt little need for overt US troop commitments. Critical reports on the future of South Vietnam, by Under-Secretary of State George Ball and other influential figures, were disregarded in favour of McNamara's statistical optimism, which saw the war progressing according to plan. Indeed, it was argued that US military investments were starting to bear fruit in the shape of ARVN forces which managed some solid victories against Vietcong strongholds around Saigon and in the Mekong Delta. By May, Australia was also involved in Vietnam, having formed and deployed the Australian Army Training Team – Vietnam (AATTV) to instruct the South Vietnamese in jungle warfare and defence. Under the 'strategic hamlets' programme, designed by Diem and his brother Ngo Dinh Nhu, some 2000 fortified villages (of a planned 14,000) were established so that communities could exist in militarily secure environments. However, the accompanying relocations and forced labour led to much ill feeling among the supposed beneficiaries and the Vietcong propagandists presented these defensive villages as little more than prisons, thereby gaining themselves more new recruits in the process.

ABOVE: A US M-113 ARMOURED PERSONNEL CARRIER CROSSES A RIVER DURING A TRAINING EXERCISE IN MARCH 1963. AMPHIBIOUS CAPABILITY WAS ESSENTIAL IN MANY REGIONS OF VIETNAM.

Kennedy's fortunes in South Vietnam saw a downturn in 1963, mainly because of the erratic behaviour of Diem. Fearful of being supplanted in a military coup, Diem's suspicious relationship with the military started to demotivate the ARVN in its prosecution of the war. For example, in January 1963 evidence was received of a Vietcong unit operating a radio station in the village of Ap Bac near the border with Cambodia. A huge ARVN force was massed against it, which included tanks, US helicopters and 51 US advisers. Yet the ARVN had been poorly served by its intelligence, and on reaching the area of Ap Bac it found it faced the Vietcong's entire 514th Battalion. On previous operations, Diem had rebuked some of his officers for suffering even mild casualties, so the extreme caution and apathy of the ARVN officers at Ap Bac created operational chaos. Five US helicopters

were destroyed and 65 ARVN and three US personnel were killed as ARVN troops ignored or misapplied directions from the US advisers.

Ap Bac created a lot of bad press coverage – something which Kennedy abhorred. Moreover, Diem's elitist rule led to rioting from South Vietnam's large Buddhist community, and Western photographers produced haunting images of Buddhist priests burning themselves to death on the streets of Saigon in protest at infringements of their civil rights. Furthermore, the stony first lady of state, Madame Nhu, flippantly dismissed these suicides and instigated bizarre laws against human practices such as dancing and fortune-telling. By the end of 1963 the US had had enough. So when a group of South Vietnamese generals approached the US government and broached the idea of a coup, the enigmatic response was that it would not endorse any overthrow of Diem, but it would still support a new government. The generals had their green light. On 1 November 1963, Diem was forcibly ousted from government and, after about 24 hours on the run, he was murdered by persons unknown.

On 22 November 1963 John F. Kennedy was himself assassinated in Dallas, Texas. In his lifetime, Kennedy had been passionately committed to stopping the spread of communism in South Vietnam. Haunted by the failure of the disastrous Bay of Pigs invasion of Cuba, Kennedy had famously said of Vietnam, 'Now we have a problem in making our power credible, and Vietnam is the place'. Ironically, it is now known that Kennedy was

BELOW: A US SPECIAL FORCES ADVISER AND ARVN SOLDIERS ON A RIVER PATROL NEAR THE BORDER WITH CAMBODIA WATCH THE BANK INTENTLY FOR ANY SIGNS OF A VIETCONG AMBUSH.

Left: US engineers in Quang Tri province in 1969. Infrastructure was needed to support US logistical needs.

Below: General William Westmoreland, later head of the Military Assistance Command, Vietnam, tours Vam Lang on 1 May 1964 to familiarise himself with the people and terrain.

drawing up plans for a US withdrawal from Vietnam to be steadily delivered after the 1964 presidential elections. Whether the Vietnam War would have proceeded as it did had he not been assassinated can only be speculated upon.

JOHNSON TAKES OVER

Power in Washington, D.C., was now in the hands of President Lyndon B. Johnson who continued to escalate US involvement in Vietnam and took the final step of effectively committing the US to war. The situation he inherited was tremendously serious. Even McNamara and Rusk were reporting the imminent collapse of South Vietnam, a state now led by Major General Nguyen Khanh after a string of unpredictable governments. During December 1963 North Vietnamese infiltration increased dramatically, and by March 1964 around 40 per cent of South Vietnam was under Vietcong control. US aircraft overflying South Vietnam encountered lethal anti-aircraft fire from new Vietcong weapons acquired from China and the Soviet Union. In Saigon terrorist bombs were exploding regularly. All this despite an ARVN force of around 300,000 soldiers.

Since February 1963 US military policy in Vietnam had been controlled by the new Military Assistance Command, Vietnam (MACV) under the leadership of General Paul Harkins. Harkins and other advisers urged Johnson towards stronger military involvement, though Johnson continually showed a reticence to do so – apart from increasing supplies of military technology. Yet on 2 August 1964 an incident occurred in the Gulf of Tonkin which would change events.

Ho Chi Minh timed many of the VC/NVAs greatest offensives to take place during the US presidential election process, when political direction in the US tended to be at its weakest and most hostile to the propagation of war.

THE AUSTRALIANS IN VIETNAM

The deployment of the Australian Army Training Team – Vietnam (AATTV) in 1962 was effectively the beginning of Australia's commitment to the Vietnam War. All AATTV members were elite Australian or New Zealand Army soldiers, drawn initially mainly from the officer or warrant officer class, and their primary role was instructing South Vietnamese troops and communities in jungle warfare, village defence and counter-insurgency. Their training role did not preclude them from engaging in combat duties, however, and from 1965 onwards they were often to be found working in groups of up to 10, setting ambushes on VC trails or attacking isolated VC bases from the Mekong Delta to the DMZ. Their 10-year record of action in Vietnam led to over 100 decorations for bravery, including four Victoria Crosses and two Distinguished Service Orders (DSOs), and out of 1000 AATTV members who served between 1962 and 1972, 33 were killed and 122 wounded.

All Australian troops were withdrawn from Vietnam by December 1972, the last to go being 140 AATTV members who stayed on as training advisers to ARVN, territorial and Cambodian units, though they were by now renamed as the Australian Army Assistance Group (AAAG). As well as individual decorations, the AATTV received the US Meritorious Unit Citation and the Unit Citation of the Vietnamese Cross of Gallantry.

AUSTRALIAN TROOPS IN A FIREFIGHT.

During 1964 the US implemented or supported two covert operations against North Vietnam. The first, 'Op-Plan 34A', consisted of attacks by Republic of Vietnam Navy patrol boats, with US logistical backing, on the North Vietnamese coastline. The second, called 'Desoto', was a US Navy operation which used naval destroyers inside North Vietnam's territorial waters to gather intelligence on electronic coastal defences, particularly shore radar. On 2 August the US 'Desoto' destroyer USS *Maddox* came under torpedo

RIGHT: ONE OF THE NORTH VIETNAMESE PATROL BOATS WHICH ATTACKED THE USS *MADDOX* ON 2 AUGUST 1964. THE INCIDENTS IN THE TONKIN GULF REMAIN ONE OF THE MOST CONTENTIOUS ISSUES OF THE VIETNAM WAR, WITH SOME CLAIMING THAT LATER ATTACKS WERE OUTRIGHT FABRICATIONS USED TO JUSTIFY THE ESCALATION OF FIGHTING.

assault, though the ship was outside North Vietnamese waters. Although the USS *Maddox* did not sustain any damage or casualties, it crippled two of its attackers with its 5in (127mm) guns when defending itself. Responding to this aggression, Johnson now expanded the show of force in the area by deploying the destroyer USS *C.Turner Joy*. Yet shortly afterwards both the USS *Maddox* and USS *C.Turner Joy* reported further attacks and the retaliatory sinking of two North Vietnamese boats. This second alleged attack incident almost certainly did not occur; there was no visual contact with the enemy boats and even some US intelligence officers involved at the time said that the radar indicated only interference from the wake of the USS *Maddox*.

THE TONKIN INCIDENT

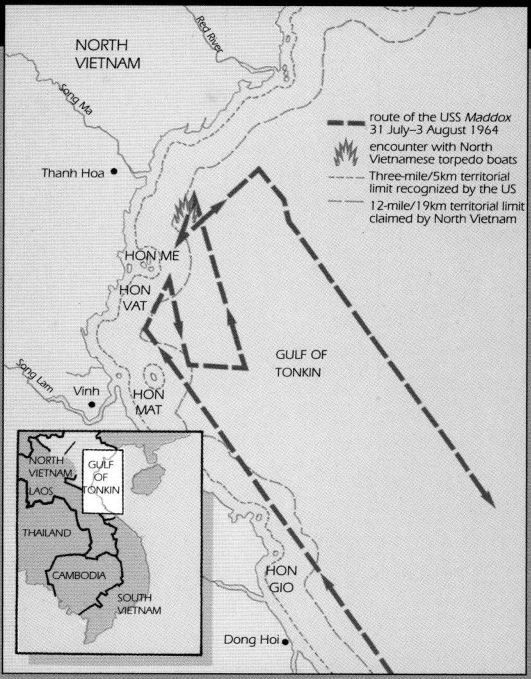

route of the USS *Maddox* 31 July–3 August 1964
encounter with North Vietnamese torpedo boats
Three-mile/5km territorial limit recognized by the US
12-mile/19km territorial limit claimed by North Vietnam

Yet the provocation was enough. In early 1964 Johnson had ordered the US Joint Chiefs of Staff (JCS) to plan contingency bombing raids on North Vietnam in case of attacks on US personnel. On 5 August he put them into action with Operation Pierce Arrow. Fighter-bombers from the US aircraft carriers USS *Ticonderoga* and USS *Constellation* struck four North Vietnamese naval bases and an oil storage depot at Vinh, causing extensive damage at a cost of the loss of two aircraft to anti-aircraft fire. One day before this attack, Johnson had asked the US Congress to pass the 'Gulf of Tonkin Resolution', which effectively would give the president and the US military the power to take whatever steps they felt necessary to successfully prosecute action against the Vietcong and the North Vietnamese. The resolution's wording was deliberately open-ended, allowing the president 'to take all necessary steps, including the use of armed force, to assist any member or protocol state of the South-East Asia Collective Defence Treaty requesting assistance in defence of its freedom'. On 7 August the US Congress approved it and Johnson now had a free hand to take the war to the next level.

MOVING TO WAR

After the Gulf of Tonkin incident, events moved rapidly in Vietnam. US military bases were already coming under Vietcong attack and the US casualty list was steadily rising. There was also increased recognition that only unilateral US action could stem the communist activity. National Security Affairs aide Walt Rostow and the JCS recommended air power as the key, particularly if directed against North Vietnam's fledgling industrial base. Johnson did not immediately implement these solutions, instead advocating retaliatory actions only. There were now around 23,000 US personnel in South Vietnam.

In 1964 there was increased involvement by regular North Vietnamese forces operating with the Vietcong in South Vietnam. This signalled a move towards larger scale engagements which would build up to the proportions of conventional war.

On 18 September, again in the Gulf of Tonkin, two US Navy destroyers (USS *Morton* and USS *Parsons*) engaged North Vietnamese torpedo boats at radar distance and claimed to have sunk two, though the dubious nature of this incident prevented Johnson pursuing counter-attacks. Yet there followed an unequivocal Vietcong action against a US airbase at Bien Hoa which left five US servicemen killed and 76 wounded, along with five Martin B-57 Canberra bombers destroyed. Surprisingly, again there was no counter-attack, primarily because Johnson was conducting a presidential election at the time and could not afford to be seen escalating the conflict in Southeast Asia.

BELOW: US SPECIAL FORCES-TRAINED MONTAGNARD COMMANDOS ABOUT TO SET OUT ON A PATROL FROM THE TRAINING CENTRE AT PLEIYIT.

Johnson went on to win the election, and from then on applied more forceful decision-making to the situation in Vietnam. In late 1964, with US officials becoming increasingly tired of the military performance of South Vietnam's ARVN, escalation became a recommended policy rather than an option. US aircraft pursued bombing raids against North Vietnamese supply routes in Laos while the US Navy started operating against the North Vietnamese coastline in support of covert ARVN operations. These attacks were still very limited in nature – only about two air strikes a week – but it was hoped that they would encourage further reforms in both the government of General Nguyen Khanh and the ARVN.

Meanwhile, the Vietcong grew bolder. On 24 December a bomb in Saigon's Brink Hotel, where officers were being billeted, killed two US servicemen and wounded 51 others. The same month the Vietcong captured the 6000-occupant village of Bihn Gia on the coast near Saigon and held it for four days against several ARVN battalions which suffered appalling casualties. Like the Vietminh before them, the Vietcong appeared to be gaining complete mastery of the military situation through its use of unpredictable and flexible tactics.

RIGHT: US F-100 SUPER SABRE JETS TAKE OFF FROM BIEN HOA AIRBASE FOR A MISSION AGAINST TARGETS IN THE MEKONG DELTA.

Perhaps the Vietnam War truly began in 1965. On 7 February the Vietcong attacked a US military base at Pleiku in the Central Highlands region, killing nine US servicemen and wounding 126. This time Johnson agreed to bomb North Vietnam and launched Operation Flaming Dart 1. On 7 February 49 US Navy Douglas A-4 Skyhawks and Vought F-8 Crusaders attacked the North Vietnamese barracks at Dong Hoi, while the next day the Vietnamese National Air Force (VNAF) attacked communication installations at Vinh. Only a few days later, the Vietcong bombed a hotel at Qui Nhon and killed 23 US servicemen. Flaming Dart 2 was put into action immediately; another combined USN and VNAF attack, with over 150 carrier- and land-based aircraft, this raid was directed at the Chanh Hoa barracks 160 miles (257km) north of the DMZ and military installations around Vit Thu Lu and Chap Le. Two days later, however, on 24 February 1965 the air campaign was transformed when Johnson authorized the infamous Operation Rolling Thunder. This massive and prolonged air war against North Vietnam was effectively a move to all-out war, and on 8 March a large contingent of US Marines was deployed on the beaches of Danang. They would be some of the first US troops to fight in the Vietnam War.

ABOVE: OFFICERS AT THE DUC MY RANGER TRAINING CENTER GET INSTRUCTION ON TACTICAL COMBAT. AWAY FROM THE FRONT, VIETNAM PROVIDED OPPORTUNITIES FOR MILITARY STRATEGISTS AND TECHNICIANS TO EXPERIMENT WITH THE MEANS AND TOOLS OF WAR AS NEVER BEFORE.

LEFT: A SPECIAL FORCES SOLDIER, ACCOMPANIED BY HIS TRANSLATOR, INSTRUCTS MONTAGNARD TRIBESMEN IN HOW TO USE A 60MM MORTAR. SPECIAL FORCES TOOK A MAJOR PART OF THE RESPONSIBILITY FOR THE MILITARY TRAINING GIVEN TO VIETNAM'S CIVILIAN AND ETHNIC GROUPS.

TH
490
SH
372
NEW JERSEY
776

CHAPTER 3

Rolling Thunder

A FLIGHT OF REPUBLIC F-105 THUNDERCHIEFS HEADS FOR ITS TARGETS IN NORTH VIETNAM. AS PART OF THE THREE-YEAR OPERATION ROLLING THUNDER, THE 'THUDS' WOULD CONTRIBUTE TO ONE OF THE MOST SUSTAINED AND FEROCIOUS BOMBING CAMPAIGNS OF THE TWENTIETH CENTURY.

RIGHT: A DOUGLAS A-4 SKYHAWK REFUELS A NORTH AMERICAN RA-5C VIGILANTE RECONNAISSANCE AIRCRAFT. THE VIGILANTE WAS ONE OF THE MOST SOPHISTICATED ELECTRONIC INTELLIGENCE (ELINT) AIRCRAFT PRESENT IN THE VIETNAM THEATRE AND PROVIDED AN INVALUABLE PLATFORM FOR OBSERVING TROOP MOVEMENTS AMONG THE VC AND NVA.

In 1954, the US Air Force lent personnel to the French in Indochina to maintain US-supplied transport aircraft. By 1961 it was actually training South Vietnamese pilots and by 1964 it was in combat.

On 13 February 1965 President Johnson authorized Operation Rolling Thunder, one of the biggest sustained bombing campaigns in history. By late October 1968 more than one million tons (1,100,000,000kg) of US bombs had been dropped inside North Vietnam, an average of around 800 tons (800,000kg) of bombs for every single day of this three-year, 304,000-sortie operation.

The punishment which the aircraft of the US Air Force, US Navy and US Marines inflicted upon the North Vietnamese is undoubted; yet equally so is the fact that Rolling Thunder was conspicuously limited in influencing the outcome of the war. If anything the campaign illustrated the perennial wartime problem of the US, namely that its technology could inflict great losses upon the enemy, but could never quite get to the heart of either its morale or logistics.

THE THUNDER BEGINS

Prior to this series of massive bombardments, there had already been limited US retaliatory bombing actions against North Vietnam. Rolling Thunder, however, was a deliberate decision by the United States government to deliver a sustained and escalating war of attrition through aerial means. The thinking behind this policy was that the bombing of North Vietnam would support an escalation in the US ground presence in South Vietnam (around 535,000 soldiers by 1968) by reducing NVA infiltration into the South and degrading Hanoi's power to govern, as well as helping to keep politically troublesome US casualty figures to a minimum. In addition, McNamara also felt that the bombing would deter China from expanding its involvement with North Vietnam.

In hindsight, the operation's protagonists were overly optimistic, an attitude born from an underestimation of the North's resilience, Johnson's acceptance of the arguments put by JCS military analysts and an overconfidence in the capacities of technology. Some experts from the US State Department assured Johnson that the compliance of the North could be achieved in only a six-month campaign. Yet North Vietnam's protracted strategy of revolutionary war and its massive supportive infrastructure at community level meant that it absorbed such punishment with little overall effect on its practical conduct of the war.

The targets of Rolling Thunder generally fell into three categories. Firstly there were logistical ones such as bridges, roads, railway lines, supply depots and, later, key industrial plants such as the Thai Nguyen steel works, the oil storage depots at Haiphong, cement works and power generators. Second there were military bases, particularly airfields, weapons dumps, troop headquarters, surface-to-air missile sites and related command-and-control centres. Finally there were the actual Vietcong and NVA supply convoys heading from the North down along supply routes through Laos.

ABOVE: A FULLY ARMED AND FUELLED NORTH AMERICAN F-100 SUPER SABRE LIFTS OFF FROM BIEN HOA AIRBASE DURING ROLLING THUNDER IN FEBRUARY 1966.

The US had the greatest resources of airborne firepower in the world. The bulk of Rolling Thunder's sorties were flown in McDonnell-Douglas F-4 Phantoms and Republic F-105 Thunderchiefs, the latter actually flying around 75 per cent of the total. With excellent air-to-air and ground-attack capabilities, the F-4 Phantom found itself operating in both the fighter-escort role and bombing operations, carrying up to 16,000lb (7250kg) of armaments. The F-105 was the campaign's strike-fighter workhorse; with its 20mm M61A1 Vulcan rotary-barrel cannon and up to 12,000lb (5450kg) of external ordnance (including AIM-9 Sidewinder air-to-air missiles and AGM-12 Bullpup air-to-surface missiles), it delivered impressive firepower, though its prominent involvement meant it also suffered a higher percentage of losses.

RESISTING ROLLING THUNDER

The failure of Operation Rolling Thunder was in a large measure due to the extraordinary cooperation among the North Vietnamese in respect of both air raid precautions and damage repair. During the bombing, up to 600,000 of Hanoi's 800,000 people would periodically evacuate the city (the remainder survived in huge underground bunker networks), taking with them military and civilian supplies in small quantities which were distributed safely throughout the countryside. After hits on petroleum facilities, for example, drums of oil of varying sizes were sited throughout remote areas in rice paddies or dense undergrowth. Factories, schools and offices were also dismantled and reconstructed away from the bombing. While these measures preserved NVA supplies in the North, along the 'Ho Chi Minh Trail' other techniques of survival and preservation were used. The NVA was a master of remaining hidden. Trucks and people were covered in foliage and camouflage, cooks used smoke-absorbing ovens, submerged bridges were built, US infrared equipment was foiled by wrapping banana leaves or bamboo around hot surfaces. In addition, the thousands of mostly female members of the Youth Shock Brigades energetically repaired bomb damage as soon as it was inflicted. North Vietnam was totally mobilized in the war against the United States, and this goes a long way to explaining the failure of the air raid operations, for they only cemented the North Vietnamese in a common bond. Thus morale stayed high while the use of the recesses of the Vietnamese countryside meant that enough resources survived to fuel the war effort.

HUMAN INDUSTRY IN NORTH VIETNAM.

As North Vietnamese surface-to-air missile systems improved, the US found itself in a technological race to discover decisive counter-measures. Winning the electronic war thus became vital to the success of Rolling Thunder, though it was never perfectly achieved.

RIGHT: THE MOST BASIC LEVELS OF NORTH VIETNAMESE ANTI-AIRCRAFT DEFENCES STILL MANAGED TO BRING DOWN MANY US AIRCRAFT. HERE TWO NVA SOLDIERS MAN A HEAVY MACHINE-GUN.

Yet these planes were only two of a powerful fleet of attack, reconnaissance and Electronic Counter Measures (ECM) aircraft. Others included the North American F-100 Super Sabre, the USA's first production supersonic fighter; the swing-wing General Dynamics F-111 bomber, with a weapons payload of up to 31,500lb (14,300kg); the Douglas A-4 Skyhawk, which would fly more bombing missions than any other US Navy aircraft in Vietnam; the turboprop-powered Douglas A-1 Skyraider; and the Grumman A-6 Intruder, flown by the US Marines and the US Navy as an all-weather-capable attack aircraft. Slung beneath such aircraft was a rapidly developing body of destructive ordnance, for as well as high-explosive conventional bombs, the Americans would apply napalm, cluster bombs, white phosphorous bombs, defoliants, and, later in the campaign from 1967, the 1000lb (450kg) electro-optically guided munitions known as 'smart bombs'.

The capability of this airborne armada notwithstanding, it could not fly over North Vietnam and unleash its loads without meeting resistance; and as the air war progressed, the sophistication of that stubborn defence would reach quite unexpected levels.

BELOW: THE REPUBLIC F-105 THUNDERCHIEF PUT IN OVER 25 YEARS OF SERVICE WITH THE US AIR FORCE BETWEEN 1958 AND 1984, THOUGH VIETNAM WAS ITS DEFINING MOMENT.

NORTHERN AIR DEFENCES

The steady escalation of US bombing was matched by equally steady advances in NVA air defence technology. In 1965 North Vietnam's anti-aircraft defences were limited – surface-to-air missiles (SAMs) were non-existent and the only weapons for shooting down aircraft were optical-sight anti-aircraft guns, such as the Soviet-made M38/39 37mm

cannon, and infantry-deployed small arms and heavy machine-guns. Despite the basic nature of this armoury, the danger it posed to US aircraft was very real. The early US tactics of fast, low-level attacks often came unstuck in a hailstorm of bullets and cannon shells which took a heavy toll on aircraft and pilots – over 80 per cent of the 3000 US aircraft lost in the war were simply shot down by guns. This groundfire forced the pilots to increase their attack altitude to around 15,000ft (4572m), though the NVA soon acquired new weapons which could reach them. By 1967, North Vietnam had acquired one of the most lethal air defence systems anywhere in the world, mainly as a result of Soviet-supplied SAM weapons and related technology. The mainstay missile of the NVA was the SA-2 Guideline, a medium-range, radio-command guided SAM with an effective ceiling of around 69,000ft (21,000m). The SA-2 was directed to its target by the ground-based Fan Song radar guidance systems which transmitted target data via a computer across a UHF link. The SA-2s tended to be deployed in dedicated SAM sites each consisting of six missiles, a command centre, Spoon Rest (an early-warning radar) and Fan Song radar units, and various maintenance and transport groups.

The SAM missiles were a serious danger to US aircraft. One common SAM application practised by the North Vietnamese was to fire an initial missile which had the effect of forcing the attacking plane to a lower altitude whereupon a salvo launch would be

ABOVE: TWO GRUMMAN A6-A INTRUDER BOMBERS UNLOAD HIGH-EXPLOSIVE OVER NORTH VIETNAM. THE INTRUDER WAS AN INVALUABLE ASSET TO THE US MILITARY IN THAT IT HAD ADVANCED ATTACK AVIONICS AND POSSESSED A GENUINE ALL-WEATHER CAPABILITY.

LEFT: A DOUGLAS A1E SKYRAIDER DROPS NAPALM ON AN NVA STAGING POST ALONG THE HO CHI MINH TRAIL. ALTHOUGH A GROUND-ATTACK AIRCRAFT, SKYRAIDERS ALSO NOTCHED UP MIG KILLS IN VIETNAM.

Right: North Vietnam 1966. A farmer on a rice plantation in the Red River Delta hands over his shift, and his gun, to his relief. Much of the adult population of the DRV had defence responsibilities.

initiated. For the US pilot, the primary defensive action was to make a sudden turn beyond the missile's manoeuvrability. However, the Americans also developed an impressive range of anti-missile equipment. One simple but effective technology was 'Chaff': thousands of silver-foil strips which interfered with enemy radar signals were dispersed into the air by F-4s and A-7s to provide a protective flight corridor for attacking aircraft.

Above: Arming a B-52 bomber ready for Arc Light strikes over South Vietnam and Laos.

More sophisticated counter-missile technology existed in a range of ECM equipment. The Douglas EB-66 Destroyer was able to jam early-warning and SAM radar with conflicting signals, though between 1967 and 1968 more individual fighters and fighter-bombers started to carry their own ECM pods. A more aggressive anti-radar measure was the AGM-45A Shrike anti-radar missile. When launched from a Wild Weasel – a dedicated anti-missile and ECM strike aircraft – it flew down the tracking beam of an enemy target-acquisition radar, thus the enemy's lock-on basically brought destruction upon itself. The innovative North Vietnamese soon mastered the Shrike, however, by using a different radar system to locate the enemy's position and only switching on the target-acquisition radar at the very last minute to fire the missile; it would then be switched off immediately to avoid a Shrike lock-on.

THE NORTH VIETNAMESE AIR FORCE (NVAF)

In addition to the North Vietnamese air defences, the US pilots also faced their counterparts in the North Vietnamese Air Force (NVAF). In 1967 North Vietnam fielded an air

PRECISION-GUIDED MUNITIONS

During Rolling Thunder, almost all the ordnance dropped over North Vietnam was of the conventional 'dumb-bomb' type – that is bombs guided only by the release trajectory of the aircraft. Because of the general inaccuracy of these munitions, US scientists developed munitions which actually had a directable glidepath. The first of these 'precision-guided munitions' (PGMs, or so-called 'smart bombs') was the Walleye electro-optically guided bomb. This utilized a standard 850lb or 1000lb (390kg or 450kg) bomb fitted with a TV camera in the nose and flight-adjustable tail fins. Once released, the pilot received TV screen images transmitted from the bomb's camera and could use them to assist him in guiding the bomb straight to the target. These were first used in 1967 by the US Navy against the Thanh Hoa bridge – which had previously survived thousands of tons of conventional bombs – and straight away a hit was achieved. Yet the Walleye required the pilot to hold his jet's course for over 15 seconds of level flight, something which made him very vulnerable to anti-aircraft fire. A less risky alternative was the Paveway laser-guided bomb (LSB), first used by the US Air Force in 1968. This again used the standard bomb with steerable fins, but in this case it was fitted with a laser-seeker in the nose. When a target was illuminated by a laser-designator unit, mounted on either the attacking aircraft, another aircraft or from a ground unit, the released bomb would fly down the reflected beam directly to the target. The results were impressive and ensured that over 80 per cent of such bombs landed within 30ft (9m) of the target (dumb bombs often fell up to 500ft/150m from their target.) The final stage of development was 'fire-and-forget' technology which gave the Walleye camera the capability to memorize the target area and guide itself without pilot control. The introduction of PGMs dramatically improved the operational success of US bombing throughout the war.

AN F-4 PHANTOM WITH LASER-GUIDED BOMBS.

force of around 80 fighters, mostly MiG-15s, -17s, -19s and -21s. Although some of the aircraft, such as the MiG-15, were rather dated, MiGs as a whole were manoeuvrable and powerful aircraft; and, in the North Vietnamese context, they usually had the advantage of operating over their own territory acting in conjunction with SAM sites. Admittedly, as the war progressed the odds stacked against the NVAF got dramatically higher as US technology and standards of training progressed (the US Navy pilots of the Top Gun school, for example, ultimately achieved a kill ratio of 12:1). Yet the NVAF still inflicted losses heavy enough to be taken very seriously. In 1967, for instance, a long series of attacks on North Vietnamese airbases saw 52 MiGs destroyed, but they in turn shot down 11 F-105s and nine F-4s.

BELOW: A CANBERRA BOMBER OF THE ROYAL AUSTRALIAN AIR FORCE JETTISONS A 500LB (227KG) BOMB DURING A DAYLIGHT PRECISION ATTACK.

DESTRUCTION BEGINS

Rolling Thunder's bombing of North Vietnam commenced on 2 March 1965. Actual control rested with the US president, for this was to be no unrestricted campaign. Johnson had to keep public opinion on his side, for the bombing of a developing country by a superpower might seem excessive to

The US air forces were never allowed a free hand to choose their targets during Rolling Thunder. To this day, many veteran pilots blame the failure of the campaign on the restrictions imposed by government-controlled target lists.

RIGHT: THIS US AIR FORCE RECONNAISSANCE PHOTOGRAPH SHOWS MIG-17 FIGHTERS BASED AT PHUC YEN AIRFIELD ONLY 20 MILES (32KM) NORTHEAST OF HANOI.

BELOW: THE FIRING OF NORTH VIETNAMESE SURFACE-TO-AIR MISSILES CAUGHT ON CAMERA BY A RECONNAISSANCE AIRCRAFT ON 5 JULY 1966.

many. The JCS themselves initially advocated the '94 target list', a comprehensive campaign of destruction against the North starting with airfields and finishing with its industrial base. Johnson, however, could not countenance such a wide destructive scope, instead selecting individual targets from the list and permitting a steady escalation in the type of target available.

The early sorties mainly targeted infrastructural objectives, particularly roads and bridges which were essential for VC/NVA supply routes. One of the biggest of these strikes was the Thanh Hoa bridge across the Song Ma River. This road and rail freight crossing was pounded by some 700 sorties of strike aircraft dropping massive amounts of conventional ordnance. It is revealing, however, that all this effort only damaged it and did not destroy it. That feat was not accomplished until later, in April and May 1972, by using the advantages of new bomb technology: 2000lb and 3000lb (900kg and 1360kg) laser-guided bombs demolished the bridge in a few precision strikes (though during Rolling Thunder electro-optically guided bombs heavily damaged the bridge in 1967).

Thanh Hoa was also the scene of the war's first aerial dogfight on 4 April 1965 when four F-105 Thunderchiefs and their escort of F-100 Super Sabres came under surprise attack from four MiG-17s. It was the MiGs day of victory as they quickly downed two US

Left: A US airman lies dead on the wreckage of his aircraft in a rice paddy in North Vietnam.

aircraft, though three MiG-17s were also destroyed by F-105s later that day. Further revenge was taken on 17 June when four US Navy F-4s from USS *Midway* engaged four MiG-17s, destroying two of them with Sparrow AAMs. Thereafter all aviation branches of the US armed forces started to notch up regular 'kills'. Interestingly enough, while the US was applying advanced AAM technology, a high percentage of kills still came as a result of cannon fire (F-4s initially had no gun fitted, despite the performance of F-105s using only their cannon).

CONCILIATORY OVERTURES

By the end of 1965 Rolling Thunder was eliciting greater levels of national protest in the US, focused particularly around the universities. Johnson had tried to bring the North Vietnamese to the negotiating table in April by offering a multi-million dollar development programme for the Mekong River region in exchange for a cessation of military activities. This failed, and Ho Chi Minh issued a list of his own demands which were unacceptable to the United States. Johnson made another attempt at a peaceful resolution by initiating a break in Rolling Thunder over Christmas 1965–66. This was contentious; key military figures such as General William Westmoreland, the commander of MACV (Military Assistance Command, Vietnam), argued that the hiatus would allow North Vietnam to rebuild its capabilities.

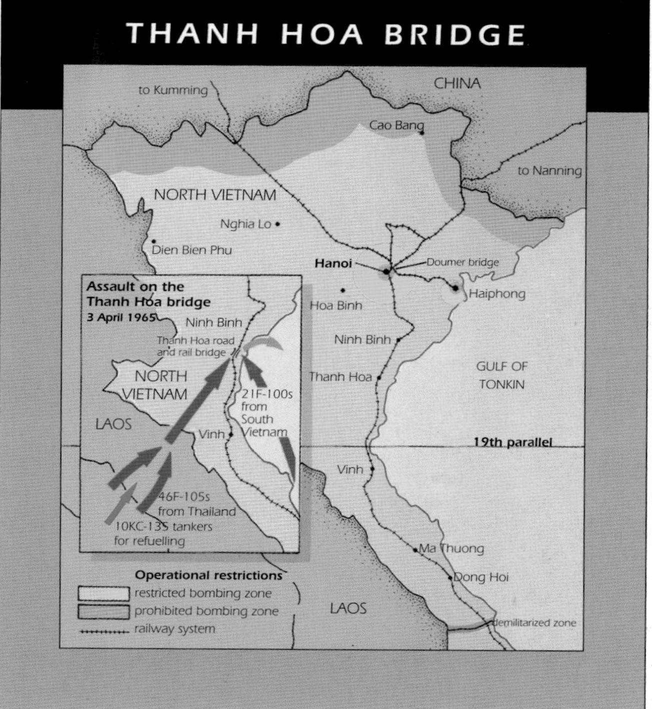

RIGHT: NORTH VIETNAMESE PEASANTS INSPECT A DOWNED US VOUGHT F-8 CRUSADER.

The conciliatory measures achieved nothing, and operations were resumed with a new level of intensity in 1966. Missions now included Boeing B-52 Stratofortress strikes against NVA infiltration routes in Laos, though these aircraft had also been pursuing tactical bombing in South Vietnam since 1964 in so-called Arc Light strikes. This policy of steady escalation advanced the number of sorties to around 10,000 a month in 1966, near the logistical limit of US operations under the existing political restraints. Advances in radar, bomb-targeting and surveillance were enabling more accurate locating of enemy targets. Furthermore, major destruction was being wrought upon North Vietnam's infrastructure. The oil depots at Haiphong, for instance, were almost entirely destroyed in 1966. These depots contained around 90 per cent of North Vietnam's oil storage facilities,

RIGHT: A THREE-AIRCRAFT CELL OF B-52S UNLEASH 750LB (340KG) AND 1000LB (450KG) BOMBS AT A VIETCONG TROOP CONCENTRATION NEAR BIEN HOA. SUCH WAS THE DESTRUCTIVE POWER OF THESE STRIKES THAT A MINIMUM OF THREE MILES (5KM) BETWEEN THE BOMB ZONE AND ALLIED TROOPS WAS RECOMMENDED.

A CAPTURED US PILOT.

PILOT RESCUE AND CAPTURE

The strength of North Vietnam's air defences made the rescue of downed US pilots a huge enterprise in its own right. Massive logistical effort went into locating and retrieving men who had received years of expensive aviation training and possessed valuable information about US technologies. The physical rescue itself would be done by helicopter, usually a Sikorsky HH-53C or a Bell UH-1 Huey, but they worked in tandem with a whole train of other rescue aircraft and ground personnel. Rockwell OV-10 Bronco reconnaissance aircraft, for instance, maintained contact with the survivors and directed ground or river patrols and artillery support. ECM aircraft such as the Lockheed EC-121 Warning Star protected the rescue aircraft from SAMs, and refuelled fighter and strike-support aircraft. With such a large presence dedicated to each downed pilot, rescue mission losses could be high and might result, in turn, in their own need for rescue.

Many of the pilots who were shot down were captured alive by the enemy – in fact some 586 USAF pilots were captured or went missing between 1962 and 1973. Their propaganda and intelligence value generally saved them from being killed when caught and instead they were taken to one of a number of prisons in or around Hanoi. The most infamous of these was the Hoa Lo prison in the centre of Hanoi, popularly known as the 'Hanoi Hilton', but there were other equally brutal compounds such as those at Cu Loc and Son Tay.

Horrifying torture was a daily reality for around 80 per cent of US airmen. North Vietnam's amendment to the 1957 Geneva Convention stated that war criminals were outside the jurisdiction of the convention's codes, and US airmen were categorized as 'war criminals'. The torture was sustained over many days, even weeks, to break down the pilot's resistance; it was common for prisoners to be tied in excruciating positions and left like that in filthy conditions for extended periods, often resulting in permanent deformities or injuries. Apart from military intelligence, a typical goal of such torture was to produce a filmed 'confession' condemning the US actions for propaganda purposes. This was eventually achieved in many cases, though the ideological language used in these speeches usually betrayed the forced nature of their extraction.

though after the bombing oil storage was redistributed to smaller sites across the country, a tactic which showed how quickly North Vietnam could overcome the impact of massive single-site air strikes even when executed effectively.

DISAPPOINTING RETURNS

In 1966 US military advisers had to admit that Rolling Thunder was having a minimal impact on the chain of supply from North Vietnam to the South, especially as it was estimated that only 60 tons (61,000kg) of supplies had to get through to keep the Vietcong active militarily. Alternative counter-measures started to be suggested, including the building of the 'McNamara Line' a physical barrier across the key points of NVA infiltration. Government-commissioned reports gave further credence to the plan as a way of moving away from the air campaign, and McNamara himself advocated putting $1 billion into the project. Work started on the line in early 1967, but Rolling Thunder was to push on for another 18 months.

Notwithstanding alternatives, a reappraisal of Rolling Thunder at the end of 1966 maintained the steady escalation – indeed sortie numbers would actually reach over 13,000

US air operations in Vietnam were one of the most expensive elements of the war. Over 2200 US aircraft, each valued at millions of dollars, were lost between 1962 and 1973 and the price tag for USAF operations between these years came to a staggering $3,129,900,000.

RIGHT: A ROAD BRIDGE IN NORTH VIETNAM DESTROYED BY AN ACCURATE US AIR ASSAULT. THE AREAS AROUND SIGNIFICANT BRIDGES WERE OFTEN SOME OF THE MOST HEAVILY BOMBED DURING ROLLING THUNDER AS THE US ATTEMPTED TO SEVER NVA SUPPLY LINES TO THE SOUTH.

BELOW: US BOMBS EXPLODE AROUND A RAIL BRIDGE IN NORTH VIETNAM. CONVENTIONAL BOMBING OF SUCH TARGETS WAS VERY INEFFICIENT AND HUGE AMOUNTS OF ARMAMENT WERE EXPENDED FOR FEW DIRECT HITS.

a month during 1967. It was recognized, however, that a vital part of the future success was the destruction of the North Vietnamese Air Force. Ironically, the USAF had no order to destroy the planes on the ground, so Colonel Robin Olds of the 8th Tactical Fighter Wing conceived and launched Operation Bolo. This was essentially an attempt to lure the North Vietnamese fighters into the air where they could be destroyed.

On 2 January 1967 a large force of F-4C Phantoms took off and assumed the pattern of a group of F-105s on a bombing raid. The North Vietnamese took the bait, sending up a pack of MiGs which then fell foul of the Phantoms' AIM-7 and AIM-9 missiles; seven MiGs in total were destroyed that day.

Following this action, the US target list was expanded, including airbases at Kep, Kien An, Hoa Loc and Phuc Yen, military bases around Hanoi and across to the Chinese border, and more of Hanoi's industrial sites. The Thai Nguyen steel plant, a great symbol of pride for the North Vietnamese, came under continual attack for around four months, slashing production. The Paul Doumer bridge over the Red River in

Few bombing targets in North Vietnam actually had any overall significance to the North's prosecution of the war. Even when large industrial targets around Hanoi were destroyed, war production continued throughout North Vietnam's rural areas.

LEFT: THE NEWLY BUILT THERMAL POWER STATION IN UONG BI, NORTH VIETNAM, AND ITS SURROUNDINGS, TOTALLY DEVASTATED BY US AIR RAIDS.

BELOW: BOMBS DROPPED FROM AN A4-C SKYHAWK FALL TOWARDS A ROAD BRIDGE IN NORTH VIETNAM IN JULY 1966.

Hanoi was destroyed on a number of separate occasions throughout the year. Yet as has already been noted, by 1967 the North Vietnamese air defences had achieved a much greater competency and the loss figures for USAF planes in that year came to 294.

The escalations during 1967 set the tone for the rest of Rolling Thunder. The bombing and destruction continued almost unabated, though public concern was growing in the United States and throughout the world that the Vietnam War was now getting out of hand. Around 52,000 North Vietnamese civilians died in Rolling Thunder and many civilian and military figures started to question such destruction when all the analysis indicated that Rolling Thunder was in no way achieving its initial objectives. The

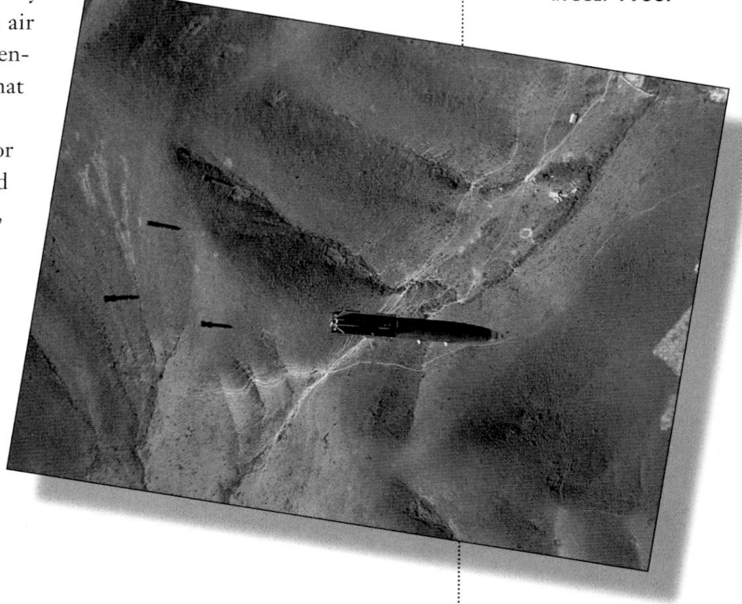

MIKOYAN-GUREVICH MIG-19

The introduction of the Mikoyan-Gurevich MiG-19 in the mid 1960s added a supersonic dimension to the North Vietnamese Air Force. The first successful prototype, the I-350M, was introduced in 1952, with the production-model MiG-19F following shortly afterwards. Improved models soon followed, including the MiG-19PM, a supersonic, air-to-air missile armed fighter which provided excellent levels of manoeuvrability and speed. Armed with two or three 30mm NR-30 cannons and 1100lb (500kg) of ordnance, the MiG-19PM could achieve maximum speeds of 960mph (1540kmh) generated by its two Wopen-6 turbojets and climb at 30,000ft (9150m) per minute. Although production of MiG-19s ended in 1958 in the Soviet Union, and 1961 in Czechoslovakia, they found their way into the North Vietnamese arsenal to counteract Rolling Thunder. All MiGs operating in Vietnam were vulnerable to the more sophisticated US aircraft and weaponry, yet only eight MiG-19s were shot down by the USAF during the war compared to 61 MiG-17s and 68 MiG-21s. In some measure these figures reflect the difference in numbers of aircraft available, but they also indicate the superb performance of this potent fighter.

A MiG-19 in Czechoslovakian Air Force colours.

three-year campaign saw over one million tons (1,100,000,000kg) of ordnance dropped, yet the chain of North Vietnamese men and supplies getting through to the South actually increased over the period of the bombing. US intelligence figures showed that whereas only 35,000 NVA were believed to have infiltrated South Vietnam in 1965, by late 1967 that number had climbed to 150,000. Furthermore, the Vietcong and NVA could pursue the war with only a fraction of the logistics required by the United States; so even if the supply chain was reduced to a mere trickle it had little discernible effect on the level of combat being experienced in the field.

Right: Female VC members shelter in Northern air raid trenches, 1968.

The sheer scale of Rolling Thunder meant that its costs were astronomical and some calculations estimate that $12 was spent for every $1 of damage inflicted. By the end of 1967 alone aircraft worth $900 million had been lost. Thus as it became clearer that the damage being inflicted upon the enemy was not seriously impairing their prosecution of the war, Rolling Thunder became untenable.

Under such military and financial analysis Rolling Thunder had no future. On 31 March 1968 Johnson suspended any bombing above the 20th parallel and on the 31 October Rolling Thunder ceased. After that point only reconnaissance and retaliatory actions were allowed. The cessation of bombing was part of the bargained agreement with Democratic Republic of Vietnam officials, who in turn committed themselves to refrain from both artillery attacks on South Vietnamese cities and infringements of the DMZ.

ABOVE: TWO OF THE 25 B-52S WHICH BOMBED A VIETCONG CONCENTRATION AND TRAINING AREA SOME 30 MILES (48KM) FROM SAIGON ON 7 JULY 1965.

For by 1968 the US government was seeking a way out of the war. As well as the air war, the US and its allies had been fighting a vicious three-year war on the ground. Air power would continue to make its presence felt throughout the rest of the Vietnam War, particularly in South Vietnam, Laos, Cambodia and again in North Vietnam during the Operation Linebacker raids of 1972. Yet from 1968 the American policy was that of steady contraction rather than steady escalation. The aircraft of the US Air Force, US Navy and US Marine Corps had inflicted truly dreadful punishment upon North Vietnam and any location into which its soldiers strayed. However, the casualties did not erode either communist morale or efficiency, a fact which the North Vietnamese demonstrated with their 1968 invasion of South Vietnam.

LEFT: REPUBLIC F-105 THUNDERCHIEFS ROLL INTO THE ATTACK. THE 'THUD' WAS SAID OFFICIALLY TO HAVE ACQUIRED ITS NICKNAME FROM THE HEAVY NOISE UPON LANDING; A GRIMMER SUGGESTION WAS THE SOUND MADE BY A SAM MISSILE HITTING THE TARGET.

Chapter 4

Search and Destroy

Troopers of the 1st Cavalry (Airmobile) Division jump from their UH-1D Iroquois helicopter during a search and destroy mission in Quang Ngai province. 'Search and Destroy' was to become the dominant, and controversial, US ground-war strategy during the first years of the conflict in Vietnam.

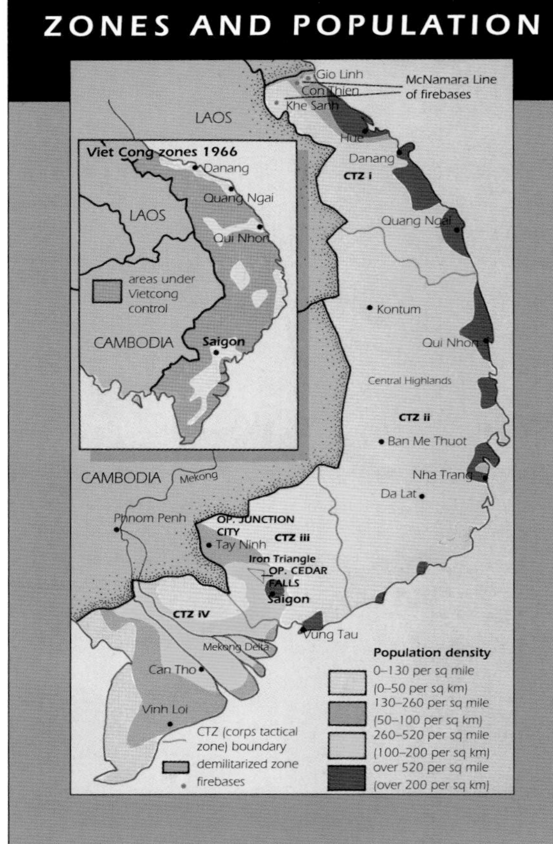

By 1965, the Army of the Republic of Vietnam's (ARVN) war against the Vietcong was a disaster in the making. South Vietnam's unstable governments crippled military effectiveness, something that would not start to be resolved until General Nguyen Van Thieu and Air Force General Nguyen Cao Ky took control in mid-1965. Militarily, the ostensible ARVN priority was the protection of roads, districts and military bases from Vietcong infiltration. Although it later had superb units such as the marine and airborne divisions, in 1965 the army was ineffective and demotivated, using what US advisers disparagingly called 'search and avoid' tactics. The force was blighted by appalling wages, food shortages, corruption and criminality, resulting in an ineffectual army which by mid-1965 was losing the equivalent of an infantry battalion each week. On 30–31 May alone, for example, the 1st Battalion of the ARVN 51st Regiment lost over 390 killed after an ambush by the Vietcong's 1st Regiment near Ba Gai, just to the south of Chu Lai

South Vietnam's social policies were no better than its military ones. The 'strategic hamlets' programme was replaced by the 'new life hamlets' programme, a simple continuation of community relocation which proved no more popular. Not until 1967, when the US set up Civil Operations and Rural Development Support (CORDIS) programmes, would pacification be properly coordinated and judged.

In the absence of a competent South Vietnamese military, the US took matters into its own hands. On 8 March 1965, 3500 US Marines of the 9th Marine Expeditionary Brigade (9 MEB) made a major amphibious landing at Danang. The marines were quickly reinforced in subsequent landings and expanded to become III Marine Amphibious Force consisting of the 3rd, 4th, 7th and 9th US Marine regiments and based in

RIGHT: A VITAL STRAND OF US STRATEGY WAS TO WIN THE SUPPORT OF THE CIVILIAN POPULATION OF SOUTH VIETNAM. HERE A TEAM FROM THE US MEDICAL CIVIC ACTION PROGRAMME (MEDCAP) TREAT LOCAL PATIENTS IN A MOBILE CLINIC.

BOOBY TRAPS

A SOLDIER USES HIS BAYONET TO UNEARTH A VIETCONG MINE.

Probably the most basic VC booby traps were those employing excrement-smeared spikes. These would be located in either concealed pits or holes into which the victim would fall or tread, the result being a pierced foot and leg. Otherwise, the spikes were attached to bamboo whips or rocks and released by tripwire which either sprung or swung into the victim. The excrement on the end of each spike would almost always result in blood-poisoning if the skin was broken. Yet the Vietcong's guerrillas were also masters in turning commonplace munitions into devastating anti-personnel devices. One of the simplest was the 'toe-popper', a bullet buried right up to its tip with the primer sitting on a nail as a firing pin. The bullet would simply go off if trodden on. Grenades were frequently used in booby traps linked up to tripwires set across jungle trails or streams, attached to stakes at helicopter landing zones, or detonated by remote control. Standard Soviet or Chinese anti-personnel mines were also used in grassy areas, including 'Bouncing Betty' mines which jumped out of the ground when trodden on before exploding at chest height.

The booby-trap war had a terribly demoralizing effect on US and allied troops. US patrols could lose several men to booby traps without encountering a single Vietcong soldier in combat. The injuries inflicted by them were terrible, with the traps often being deliberately designed to maim rather than kill. The mental strain of operating in an area likely to contain booby traps was extreme, and there is no doubt that they were as effective as a form of psychological warfare as much as they were one of normal combat.

the northern 1 Corps Tactical Zone. These deployments were significant because dedicated combat troops were now expanding the 23,000 US personnel already in South Vietnam, and by the end of 1965 this number would reach 184,300. So what was the strategy and intention behind this escalation?

STRATEGIES

In early 1965 the commander (1964–68) of MACV, General William Westmoreland, and the US ambassador to South Vietnam, General Maxwell D. Taylor, presented the strategic options for escalation to President Johnson. Westmoreland wanted to raise five divisions of international troops and deploy them across the DMZ and along the border with Laos, with one US division in the Central Highlands to counter the build-up of an NVA division in that area. Westmoreland wanted authority to pursue direct aggressive operations against the VC/NVA, otherwise, he argued, the ARVN would probably collapse within a year. Taylor's recommendation was more subdued (if only because his previous proposal of an invasion of North Vietnam was rejected). He proposed an enclave strategy in which troops gathered around population centres and coastal sites, protecting areas of military and social value while the ARVN fought the communist insurgents elsewhere. Units would be permitted to patrol in a 50-mile (80km) radius around their enclave, and engage the enemy if warranted.

Search and Destroy was a strategy of overwhelming firepower. The US brought immense resources of infantry and field weaponry into Vietnam and it was hoped that the Vietcong insurgents would be defeated by the sheer scale of this destructive capability.

Above: US Marines from the 3rd Marine Division use the M60 machine-gun, affectionately known as the 'Pig', during a mission on a Vietnamese hillside. Firefights could be a daily occurrence during S & D operations.

Taylor won the argument with the president. For Johnson, Taylor's plan meant escalation without belligerence and, much to Westmoreland's annoyance, III Marine Amphibious Force was distributed to various enclaves along the Vietnamese coastline at Danang, Phu Bai and Chu Lai.

Initial contact between US and VC/NVA units was limited. The VC focused its efforts on the ARVN, trying to crush it before US commitments developed further. The US soldiers, consigned to their designated areas, were limited in what they could contribute. Thus on 20 April, Johnson, McNamara and General Earle G. Wheeler (Chairman, Joint Chiefs of Staff), among others, met in Honolulu to discuss tactical escalation. Westmoreland requested an additional nine US battalions plus one battalion from Australia and three from South Korea (a non-US investment of 7300 soldiers). The proposal was put into effect under the umbrella of SEATO agreements, and ultimately Australia, New Zealand, South Korea, Thailand and the Philippines would all contribute soldiers to the war in Vietnam. South Korean forces alone would number nearly 48,000 men by the end of 1967, and by the end of 1969 there would be 7000 Australian troops in action. Westmoreland was in charge of all US air and ground forces in South Vietnam, while the bombing of North Vietnam fell under the jurisdiction of the C-in-C Pacific, Admiral S. Sharp.

With escalation approved, there also came a vital shift away from the enclave strategy. The VC were avoiding US positions and hitting the ARVN units, so on 8 June Johnson approved the use of US troops in more active counter-insurgency combat operations in support of South Vietnamese forces. By the end of June this policy had widened to the point where US troops could be applied in any situation considered necessary to strengthen the relative position of ARVN forces. Effectively, Westmoreland could now pursue his tactical cornerstone – 'Search and Destroy'.

SEARCH AND DESTROY MISSIONS

Search and Destroy (S & D) is an old and simple military doctrine. Its basic premise is that if you inflict a great enough level of attrition on enemy forces, there comes a point when the enemy is unable to make good its losses and has to terminate military activity. This point, called by Westmoreland 'the crossover point', was the primary objective of the US ground and air operations in South Vietnam from the end of June 1965.

Search and Destroy was not just Westmoreland's strategy, it was further advocated by the JCS in August 1965 and on 7–8 February 1966 Robert McNamara and Dean Rusk also gave their official sanction. The strategy is often portrayed as the unimaginative limit of US strategy in Vietnam. This is a superficial representation. Throughout the war, Westmoreland committed over 50 per cent of all US troops to pacification duties, while S & D was consciously chosen as the best way to defeat the VC/NVA in the field. Yet the emphasis on enemy 'body counts' led to US units often making inflated kill claims or, on occasions, the accidental or deliberate killing of civilians. Furthermore, massive US firepower created such indiscriminate destruction that it further aggravated the South Vietnamese population, not to mention its adverse effects on world opinion through the reporting of it in the global news media.

Search and Destroy had at its disposal vast resources of weaponry. US patrols carrying high-velocity M16 rifles, M60 machine-guns, fragmentation grenades, C4 plastic explosive and Claymore anti-personnel mines (capable of discharging 700 metal balls with lethal anti-personnel effect), could also radio in devastating support fire from 105mm and 155mm howitzers situated at firebases throughout South Vietnam. The same radios could be used to command the awesome air power of the USAF, US Navy, US Marines and Vietnamese National Air Force (VNAF). Air power included

BELOW: AIRMOBILITY. A SOLDIER FROM THE 1ST CAVALRY (AIRMOBILE) DIVISION GUIDES A UH-1 HELICOPTER INTO A JUNGLE CLEARING.

JUNGLE CONDITIONS

As well as fighting a war, US and allied soldiers also had to struggle with the unforgiving jungle. Each soldier would be carrying between 50lb and 70lb (23 to 32kg) of equipment in temperatures of around 40 degrees Centigrade with humidity at 80–90 per cent, consequently heat exhaustion became a perennial and occasionally lethal problem. Clothes and boots would also rot under the effects of sweat. During the monsoon season the rains would become so torrential that the ground turned to almost impassable mud, breathing could became difficult and flash floods and mudslides could sweep entire units away to their deaths.

Many operational areas contained virgin rainforest which had to be hacked through by machete, and cuts from sharp foliage and thorns soon became infected in the humid climate. Yet one of the worst problems encountered was that of the wildlife. With 131 species of poisonous snake, including lethal varieties of krait, cobras and vipers, and many scorpions, medical evacuations for animal poisonous bites and stings became commonplace. But a problem few could avoid was that of insect attack. Mosquitoes were a constant bane, and hacking through the jungle disrupted bees and hornets which could deliver hundreds of excruciating and potentially fatal stings. Biting ants and leeches made their own contribution to the soldier's misery, the latter attaching themselves to his skin when streams were forded, and causing a nasty infection unless removed correctly.

A JUNGLE OPERATION.

BELOW A CH-47 CHINOOK WITH SUPPLIES IN OPERATION PICKETT, 1966.

enhanced attrition planes such as the AC-47 gunships which could spray 100 cannon rounds per second into the jungle, while B-52s dropped awesome payloads on the countryside (with great accuracy, too, when coordinated with the Combat Skyspot system which allowed ground radar units to actually direct the bombers to target and initiate bomb release). With a simple request from troops on the ground, US aircraft would swoop in and deliver a withering array of destructive materials, including napalm, phosphorus bombs, cluster bombs, defoliants, air-dropped mines and cannon fire.

Of course, Search and Destroy would have been impossible without helicopter airmobility. By the end of the war, US helicopters would have flown a total of 36,125,000 sorties in every role from ground-attack to medevac. Entire units became fully airmobile; the 1st Cavalry (Airmobile) Division became the first division capable of full airborne deployment. S & D missions depended absolutely on helicopters for the rapid deployment by air of troops to areas of engagement.

The most dangerous time for the helicopter was putting down in an operational landing zone (LZ), often the focal point of enemy groundfire and US artillery and bombing. Flawless fire-control between air and artillery units was essential.

Once the VC/NVA had experienced the lethality of US firepower, they started to operate in very close proximity (called 'hugging the belt') to US troops so as to negate the use of American artillery and air power. In this position they could inflict small but continually increasing casualties on their opponents, and operational data from 1966 reveals that 88 per cent of US/VC contact was initiated by the VC.

The weaponry available to the VC/NVA in the South did not begin to compare with that of the US. In the early years, French firearms from the earlier conflict were common, yet soon Soviet AK-47 and Chinese Type 56 assault rifles had been distributed widely and gave the guerrilla forces a personal firepower equal to that of the US soldier. Yet what the Vietcong lacked in technology it made up for in brutal innovation, and booby traps became ubiquitous (see boxes, pages 57 and 62). The Vietcong proved to be an especially frustrating enemy to fight. Elusive and resilient, it would briefly engage US, ARVN and allied troops before disappearing into the dense foliage or dropping underground into one of the

ABOVE: A US SOLDIER, BURDENED WITH AN M14 RIFLE, BODY ARMOUR AND PACK, TIPS WATER OVER HIMSELF IN AN EFFORT TO STAVE OFF THE POTENTIALLY LETHAL EFFECTS OF HEAT EXHAUSTION.

LEFT: THE JUNGLE MADE NAVIGATION DIFFICULT, AND UNITS OFTEN RELIED ON OBSERVATION AIRCRAFT FOR ACCURATE POSITIONING. HERE TWO US SOLDIERS PLOT THEIR LOCATION.

Search and Destroy required body counts to prove that it was working. This had several undesirable effects, such as the counting of civilian deaths as Vietcong fatalities and a poor public image for US military operations.

RIGHT: TWO VIETCONG SUSPECTS ARE LOADED INTO A US JEEP BY AMERICAN SOLDIERS OF THE 173RD AIRBORNE BRIGADE.

many networks of tunnels which it built throughout South Vietnam (particularly in the laterite soil areas north of Saigon).

The unequal firepower between the US and VC/NVA forces would often produce kill ratios of 13:1 in favour of US troops after each major encounter. Yet the VC/NVA strategies were often more about political rather than military attrition. Like the war against the French, the North Vietnamese understood that the loss of a single American life would have greater political implications than the loss of one of their own.

TUNNEL NETWORKS

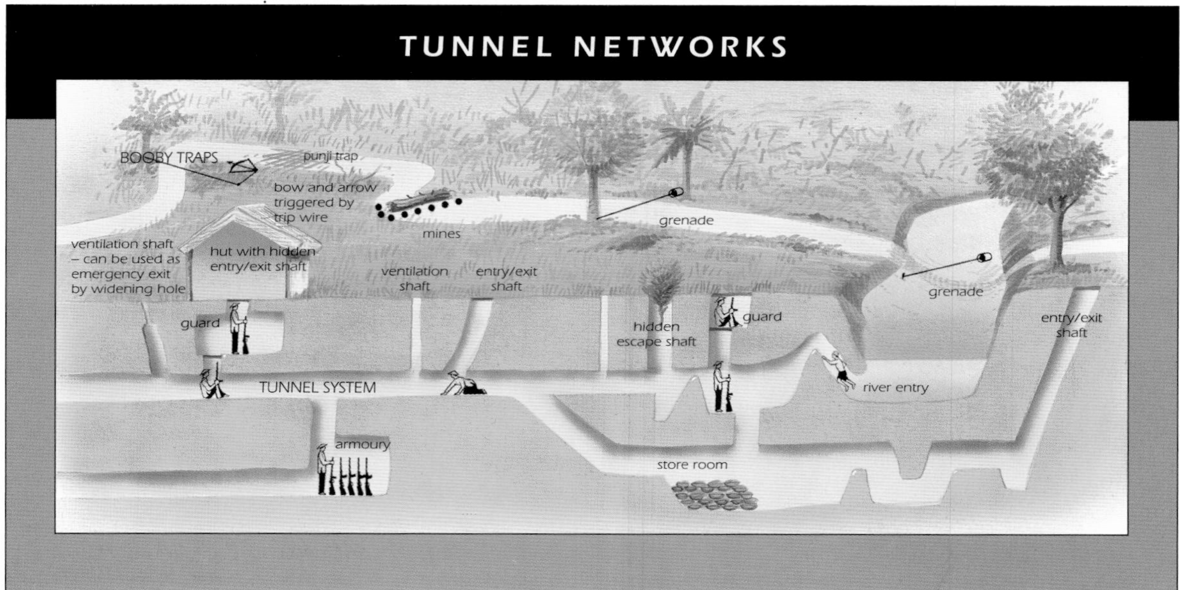

OPERATION STARLITE AND THE BATTLE OF IA DRANG

Search and Destroy continued until 1972 on a local unit level, yet it also gave rise to major operations between 1965 and 1968. The first of these actions was Operation Starlite launched in August 1965 in Quang Tri province close to the DMZ.

On 15 August information was received that 1500 members of the Vietcong's 1st Regiment were based around the Van Truong peninsula, 12 miles (19km) from Chu Lai. It was decided to trap the Vietcong in a three-directional attack using an amphibious landing, helicopter deployment and land assault of 4000 Marines from around Danang and the helicopter weaponry of the 1st Cavalry (Airmobile) Division. Starlite began on 18 August. All the attack routes were heavily contested from the very start and it quickly became a protracted and violent operation. Yet eventually American firepower prevailed and 614 VC were killed in contrast to only 45 US servicemen. The first major test for S & D seemed to have been successful, albeit not anywhere near as easy as imagined.

BELOW: HAVING BEEN DEEP INTO A VIETCONG TUNNEL NETWORK, A SOLDIER IS PULLED OUT BY HIS COMRADES.

The next month brought a further major land battle, this time in response to the build-up of an North Vietnamese Army division in the Central Highlands. In early to mid-October, the US Special Forces camp at Plei Me attracted several NVA attacks which were repulsed by US air strikes and ARVN actions. However, a concentration of NVA remained in the Ia Drang Valley and Westmoreland decided to act with force.

The battle of Ia Drang lasted from 23 October to 20 November. In a classic S & D mission, the 1st Battalion, 7th Cavalry Regiment were deployed by helicopter to Landing Zone (LZ) X-Ray, unaware that it was surrounded by about 2000 NVA soldiers. The US troops fought straight from the helicopter doors and became entrenched in a confusing, close-quarters battle in the Ia Drang jungle. Their precarious position was abated by awesome B-52 strikes carried out by aircraft flown from Guam – the first use of B-52s in tactical coordination with ground troops – which pounded NVA consolidation points on Chu Pong Mountain for over six days. Further US support came with reinforcements from the 7th Cavalry Regiment's 2nd Battalion. These too were airlifted to X-Ray but ordered to advance two miles across land to LZ Albany. En route they were ambushed by three NVA battalions and 155 US soldiers were killed. Massive US firepower again restored the situation and pushed the NVA out from Ia Drang and over the border with Cambodia, leaving behind some 3500 NVA dead.

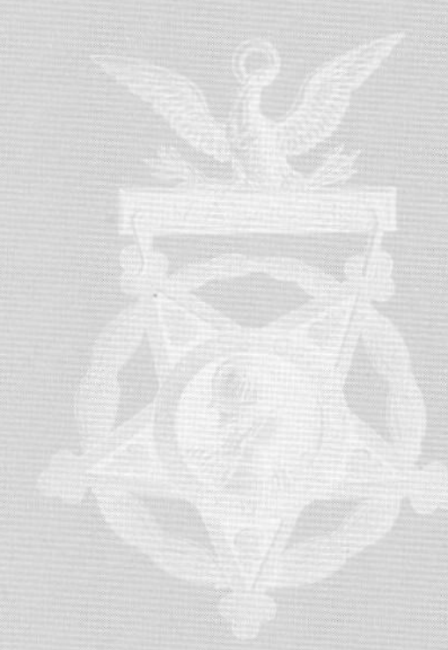

KOREAN FORCES

The Republic of Korea's (ROK) soldiers were first deployed in South Vietnam in August 1964, generally in non-combat roles such as engineering and medical support. Yet over the subsequent years more than 47,000 ROK troops served in South Vietnam, mainly being given responsibility for suppressing communist activity in the coastal districts of II Corps Tactical Zone stretching from Cam Ranh to Qui Nhon in Binh Dinh province. South Korean soldiers brought with them a keen sense of anti-communism and proved to be truly excellent soldiers. Elite units such as the Capital (Tiger) Division and the 9th (White Horse) Division pursued decisive Search and Destroy operations against Vietcong-dominated areas, often using a brutality which attracted international controversy. Torture and killing of prisoners was commonplace among ROK units, though this was balanced by genuine sensitivity to the needs of local communities and a very disciplined approach to combat operations (many ROK soldiers even learnt Vietnamese to enable them to have better contact with the local populace). Acting effectively under their own jurisdiction, the ROK soldiers controlled Binh Dinh province with greater success than almost any of the provincial military group of the war, partly because their cruelty inspired a great deal of fear among VC personnel.

Ia Drang cost the lives of 300 US soldiers. It illustrated some of the problems of airmobility, especially the high costs incurred at contested LZs, and also the difficulty of effectively coordinating artillery when in close-quarters combat. The kill ratios, however, could not be denied, and attrition seemed a proven strategy. But in response to this, from now on the VC/NVA tactics changed. More and more they avoided outright conflict and frustrated many US operations by simply disappearing into the jungle and conserving their numbers. This would in some senses become the undoing of the S & D strategy, as communist units would often be severely damaged but rarely completely destroyed.

SMALL AND LARGE ENCOUNTERS, 1966–67

Major S & D deployments escalated rapidly in 1966 and there were also growing confrontations between the US Marines and NVA soldiers around the DMZ (see Chapter 6). That year, 18 large-scale operations resulted in an estimated 50,000 VC/NVA dead. It was also a year in which S & D became more multinational. The ARVN started combined S & D manoeuvres with US troops aided by the reasonable stability of the new South Vietnamese government of Nguyen Cao Ky and Nguyen Van Thieu. From January to March 1966, for instance, US Marine, US Army and ARVN units conducted operations Double Eagle I and Double Eagle II against large VC/NVA units in Quang Ngai province. Meanwhile, South Korean forces were in charge of pacifying the coastal districts from Qui Nhon to south of

BELOW: US TROOPS ARE AIRLIFTED OUT IN THE WAKE OF AN S & D DEPLOYMENT.

LEFT: ARVN TROOPS PACK THE INTERIOR OF A C-130 TRANSPORT AIRCRAFT EN ROUTE TO OCCUPY A MILITARY OUTPOST IN SOUTH VIETNAM.

BELOW: SUPPLIES ARE AIRLIFTED INTO A US FIRE-SUPPORT BASE (FSB) NEAR PLEI KEN NGO IN THE CENTRAL HIGHLANDS. HELICOPTERS WERE THE LIFELINE OF US GROUND FORCES IN VIETNAM.

Cam Rahn. They did this with brutal efficiency, and units such as the Capital (Tiger) Division and the 9th (White Horse) Division became especially feared by the VC/NVA. Their ruthlessness had its results, however, and their assigned area became one of the best controlled provinces in Vietnam.

From June 1966, Australian soldiers were engaged in counter-insurgency (COIN) operations in Phuoc Tuy province, southeast of Saigon. The use of the Australian SAS and their previous experience of COIN warfare in Malaysia made them particularly effective in this role. Australian troops fought relatively few major set-piece battles, an exception being the victory gained by D Company of the Royal Australian Regiment over the Vietcong's 275th Regiment at Long Tan. But even so, by the time the last Australian soldiers withdrew from Vietnam in December 1972, 496 of them had been killed and 2398 wounded.

The biggest operations remained in the hands of the US forces. A landmark action was Operation Attleboro conducted between 14 September and 25 November 1966, when US troops attempted to crush the VC's 9th Division in War Zone C in Tay Ninh province. War Zone C stretched from the Cambodia border to northeast Saigon, and previous US operations in the area had forced much of the 9th Division over into Cambodia, though at heavy cost to the US. However, by November the VC was massing again in the province. Attleboro was undeniably a large-scale operation: 22,000 US and ARVN soldiers were heavily supported by artillery and Arc Light strikes. The first unit into action was the US 196th Infantry Brigade, a generally inexperienced unit which took severe losses against the

Search and Destroy and the US attempts at social welfare did not sit easily together, and all too often the consequences of the former undid the benefits of the latter.

RIGHT: SOLDIERS EXPLORE A HUT DURING OPERATION THAYER IN OCTOBER 1966

BELOW: PREPARATIONS FOR OPERATION MASHER.

veteran VC. More US battalions had to be dragged into the province before the area was subdued with 2000 enemy dead for the cost of 155 US soldiers killed and 494 wounded.

Despite the extent of the victory, in their post-battle analysis of Attleboro many US officers admitted that the VC/NVA controlled the ebb and flow of the battle, often engaging in limited actions before escaping to Cambodia and reforming themselves for later battles.

A TWOFOLD STRATEGY

S & D was used in a twofold strategy from 1967, first to destroy existing VC/NVA bases and create 'pacified areas', and second to attack build-up and infiltration points in order to stop the establishment of further VC/NVA outposts. Particularly contested areas

included the Central Highlands, which saw bitter confrontations between US forces and the NVA's 1st and 10th divisions, and the Iron Triangle, the southern area between Ben Suc and Ben Cat bordered by the southern flow of the Saigon River. The Iron Triangle had been a VC-dominated area since 1965, and huge B-52 raids there had failed to uproot them. Operation Cedar Falls (8–26 January) was to be a classic 'hammer and anvil' action aimed at destroying the Iron Triangle opposition (see box, page 68). The 2nd Infantry Brigade and the 196th Light Infantry Brigade would act as the anvil in positions south of the Saigon River, while US airborne, cavalry and infantry units attacked as the hammer from the north into the Iron Triangle. Ben Suc fell to the 2nd Infantry Brigade on 8 January while the 173rd Airborne and 11th Armoured Cavalry moved out from Ben Cat and, on 9 January, the 3rd Infantry Brigade pushed into the dense forest at Than Dien.

The battle was slow and bloody. To hold captured ground, US bulldozers cleared vast swathes of jungle behind the advance. By the end of the operation, 750 VC were dead, but 2711 acres of cleared jungle did nothing to assist the aims of the pacification programmes. Huge areas of Vietnam were becoming increasingly devastated by the war. Operations Thayer II and Pershing in mid-1967, for instance, saw over 140,000 artillery shells and 2,500,000lb (1,130,000kg) of explosives, including 500,000lb (227,000kg) of napalm being dropped into the coastal Binh Dinh province. The political fallout from the environmental impact of these operations almost counteracted the military benefits, as they presented the

ABOVE: AUSTRALIAN SOLDIERS WITH ARMOURED PERSONNEL CARRIERS DURING OPERATIONS IN SOUTH VIETNAM. THE AUSTRALIANS HAD SUCCESS IN THE PACIFICATION ROLE, CONTROLLING MUCH OF PHUOC TUY PROVINCE THROUGH SUPERB ABILITIES IN JUNGLE WARFARE LEARNED PREVIOUSLY IN PLACES SUCH AS MALAYA.

OPERATION CEDAR FALLS

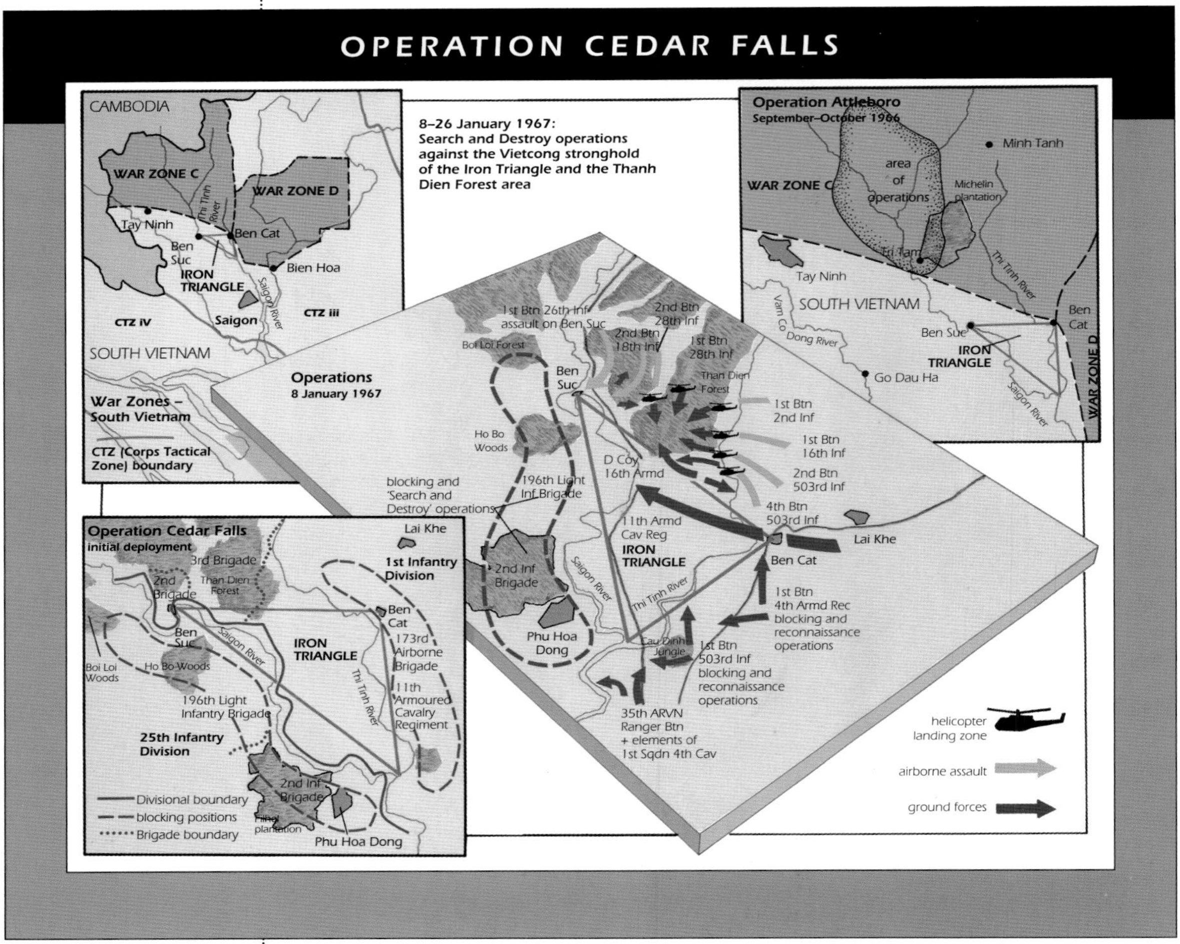

8–26 January 1967:
Search and Destroy operations against the Vietcong stronghold of the Iron Triangle and the Thanh Dien Forest area

War Zones – South Vietnam
CAMBODIA
WAR ZONE C
WAR ZONE D
Tay Ninh
Ben Suc
Ben Cat
Bien Hoa
IRON TRIANGLE
Saigon
Saigon River
Thi Tinh River
CTZ IV
CTZ III
SOUTH VIETNAM
CTZ (Corps Tactical Zone) boundary

Operation Attleboro
September–October 1966
area of operations
Minh Tanh
Michelin plantation
Tri Tam
Tay Ninh
SOUTH VIETNAM
Vam Co Dong River
Go Dau Ha
Ben Suc
Ben Cat
IRON TRIANGLE
Thi Tinh River
Saigon River
WAR ZONE C
WAR ZONE D

Operations
8 January 1967
1st Btn 26th Inf assault on Ben Suc
2nd Btn 28th Inf
2nd Btn 18th Inf
1st Btn 28th Inf
Boi Loi Forest
Ben Suc
Thanh Dien Forest
1st Btn 2nd Inf
1st Btn 16th Inf
2nd Btn 503rd Inf
4th Btn 503rd Inf
Ho Bo Woods
D Coy 16th Armd
196th Light Inf Brigade
blocking and 'Search and Destroy' operations
11th Armd Cav Reg
IRON TRIANGLE
2nd Inf Brigade
Saigon River
Thi Tinh River
Ben Cat
Lai Khe
1st Btn 4th Armd Rec blocking and reconnaissance operations
Phu Hoa Dong
Cau Dinh Jungle
1st Btn 503rd Inf blocking and reconnaissance operations
35th ARVN Ranger Btn + elements of 1st Sqdn 4th Cav
helicopter landing zone
airborne assault
ground forces

Operation Cedar Falls
initial deployment
Lai Khe
3rd Brigade
2nd Brigade
Thanh Dien Forest
1st Infantry Division
Ben Cat
Ben Suc
Saigon River
IRON TRIANGLE
173rd Airborne Brigade
Boi Loi Woods
Ho Bo Woods
Thi Tinh River
11th Armoured Cavalry Regiment
196th Light Infantry Brigade
25th Infantry Division
2nd Inf Brigade
Filhol plantation
Phu Hoa Dong
Divisional boundary
blocking positions
Brigade boundary

US as a careless destroyer rather than a social benefactor. But the US pushed the VC/NVA death toll still higher.

Operation Junction City (22 February–14 May) resulted in over 2700 VC from its 9th Division in War Zone C being killed. The operation used 22 US battalions and four ARVN battalions and included parachute operations by the 173rd Airborne Brigade's 2nd

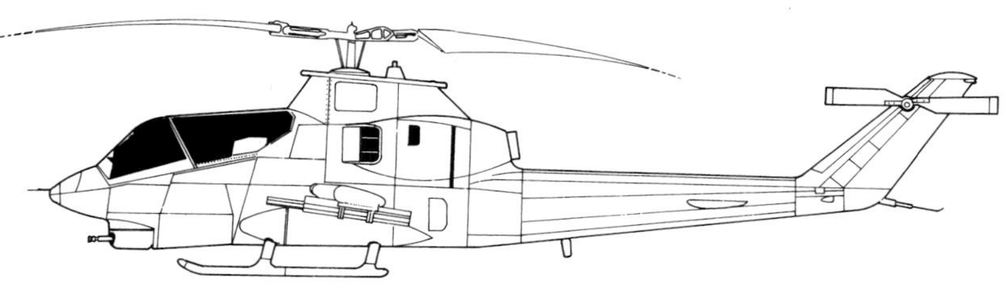

RIGHT: THE BELL 209/AH-1G COBRA GUNSHIP.

An AH-1G shows its firepower.

HELICOPTER GUNSHIPS

In 1962 the idea of the helicopter gunship came to fruition when the Bell UH-1 Huey helicopter arrived for service in Vietnam. Armed with four Browning 0.30in machine guns, two M60 door guns and inboard pods carrying 38 2.75in (70mm) rockets, the UH-1s formally established the principle of the armed escort helicopter. A seminal leap in the gunship was taken in 1967 with the introduction of the Bell 209/AH-1G Cobra. The Cobra was totally dedicated to ground-attack and fire-support roles. It was fast at 200mph (320kmh) and was typically armed with two 40mm belt-fed grenade launchers, up to 76 2.75in (70mm) rockets and two six-barrelled 7.62mm rotary Miniguns. The grenade launchers alone could fire 40mm grenades at the rate of 400 per minute while the Miniguns fired a mixture of ball and tracer rounds at either 2000 or 4000 rounds per minute. The rockets could contain either high-explosive, white phosphorous or flechette (a package of around 500 nails dispersed from the rocket at burn-out). Cobras operated in many roles, especially as support at contested landing zones and as 'Pink Team' squads of choppers working in unison to saturate enemy positions in gunfire. Once the gunship idea became firmly fixed most helicopters in Vietnam received some form of armaments, even aircraft such as the large double-blade Boeing-Vertol CH-47 Chinook acquired grenade and rocket launchers and 0.50in calibre machine guns.

Battalion. It was intended to destroy the 9th Division and the mobile communist headquarters for the South, the Central Office of South Vietnam (COSVN). Yet despite a series of major battles, COSVN escaped (some have doubted its existence at all) and many VC disappeared to fight another day.

THE NVA COMES TO THE FORE

By mid-1967 impressive numbers of VC/NVA troops had been killed without any real strategic gains having been made. Hostile opinion was escalating worldwide and pacification was patently failing. There was also another change in VC/NVA tactics. In April 1967, the influential North Vietnamese theorist Truong Chinh proposed an expansion in large unit NVA actions against the US forces in the north. The intention was to produce the conditions for a general civilian uprising in South Vietnam by drawing US troops away from population centres. Giap was

Below: A UH-1B gunship descends for a rocket attack against an enemy position.

opposed to this strategy, but it won the politburo's support and the approval of the Chinese, who subsequently increased their levels of military aid.

The influence of this strategy was particularly felt by the US Marines in Quang Tri province and around the DMZ (see Chapter 6). By September the NVA was crossing the DMZ and engaging the US troops in artillery duels. NVA artillery units fired 3000 shells alone at the US Marine outpost at Con Thien, an act of aggression to which the US replied with thousands of bombs (part of the US SLAM strategy – 'Seek, Locate, Annihilate and Monitor').

Between October and December 1967 some of the bloodiest battles of the war took place. On 29 October 850 VC of the 273rd Regiment were killed when they attacked Loc Ninh, the ARVN district headquarters 70 miles (112km) north of Saigon. In November, four NVA regiments began an assault on Dak To Special Forces camp near the border with Cambodia. Dak To expanded into a huge battle between the NVA and the 173rd Airborne Brigade, the US 4th Infantry and 1st Cavalry divisions. The NVA troops deployed rockets and artillery in their assaults and the battle climaxed on Hill 875, where a battalion of the 173rd Airborne was totally surrounded by NVA soldiers between 19 and 22 November. The epic battle for the hill was tilted in favour of the Americans only by colossal air and artillery strikes, ending with the NVA having lost a further 1200 men.

ABOVE: VIETCONG PRISONERS TAKEN FROM A TUNNEL COMPLEX DURING OPERATIONS IN THE IRON TRIANGLE, 1967.

RIGHT: SOLDIERS OF THE 173RD AIRBORNE BRIGADE PINNED DOWN ON THE CHARRED AND SHATTERED HILL 878 NEAR DAK TO.

LEFT: SLOW PROGRESS. A US TEAM CLEARS A ROAD IN SOUTH VIETNAM OF ANTI-PERSONNEL AND ANTI-VEHICLE MINES DURING OPERATION PERSHING.

BELOW: A US PATROL PAUSES ALONG A RIVERBED WHILE OTHER TROOPS CHECK OUT THE ADVANCED AREAS DURING OPERATION PERSHING. BECAUSE OF THEIR OPENNESS, RIVERS WERE COMMON SITES FOR AMBUSHES, AND VIGILANCE WAS REQUIRED IN SUCH AREAS.

Despite all the major battles from 1965 onwards, by the end of 1967 a curious situation existed in which both sides believed the war was progressing in their favour. Westmoreland and many US monitors estimated that the 60,000-plus personnel lost by the enemy in 1967 meant that 'the crossover point' had now been reached. Meanwhile, Ho's officers had succeeded in their strategy of drawing US troops away from the main population areas. The significance of this would be fully realized in January 1968, the time of the Lunar New Year celebrations, or Tet, when North Vietnam would launch its first mass invasion of the South.

S & D remained a controversial part of US tactics, and its emphasis on kill-counts led to popular distaste, especially when evidence of US atrocities started to emerge. After the Tet Offensive in 1968, it was realized that three years of attrition had not affected the NVA's prosecution of the war. VC/NVA recruitment was a continual process, and over the years they made good their losses while continually upping the US and allied death toll. S & D was rapidly phased out alongside the steady withdrawal of US troops from Vietnam after 1968. Politically it had been disastrous, and the errors committed during it have put caution at the heart of US military strategy to this day.

602
RESCUE
RESCUE
AB
144628
NAVY

Chapter 5

From the Sea

A carrier-borne A-4C Skyhawk prepares to launch itself on a bombing mission in 1965. The US Navy and Marine Corps occupied a multitude of roles in Vietnam which often put them at the forefront of the fighting on land, air and sea.

Of all the multiple roles the US Navy played in the Vietnam War, the logistical one was probably its most influential contribution. At the height of the war the US had to support over one million US and allied soldiers in South Vietnam who required around 850,000 tons (863,655,000kg) of supplies each month. The vast bulk of this burden – some 95 per cent – fell squarely on the shoulders of the US Navy via the Military Sealift Command (MSC). Sailing from bases across the Pacific, MSC ships maintained full logistical support for all ground troops throughout South Vietnam. It has even been suggested that they were too successful. Some have claimed that incidences of Post-traumatic Stress Disorder (PTSD) were increased when soldiers were airlifted straight from combat to rear areas full of reminders of home. Whatever the case, US Navy logistics built the infrastructure of the Vietnam War, ably assisted by US Navy construction units known as Seebees (from CB for 'construction battalion'). Seebees from the 3rd and 32nd naval construction regiments worked in Vietnam from 1954 onwards, building everything from schools, bridges, roads, ports and depots, and remained much in demand throughout the war.

ABOVE: THE USS *IOWA* FIRES A SALVO FROM ITS MAIN GUNS AT NORTH VIETNAMESE COASTAL EMPLACEMENTS.

The US Navy's logistical involvement in Vietnam went back to the 1950s, and in a very real sense the war proper began at sea. Back in 1962, Chief of Naval Operations Admiral George Anderson advocated a US naval deterrent force around South Vietnam, and by 1964 the US Navy was engaged in two main operational duties, apart from the general security and logistical ones (see also Chapter 2). The first, codenamed 'Op-Plan 34A', was run by the MACV and involved providing the South Vietnamese navy with US and Norwegian fast patrol boats, training advisers and offering US logistical support for covert actions against North Vietnamese coastal installations. The second was called 'Desoto'. This was a US Navy Electronic Intelligence (ELINT) operation, using destroyers off the shores of North Vietnam to gather information on enemy radar sites and coastal bases.

Both operations were conducted in the Gulf of Tonkin, dangerously close to the North Vietnamese coastline. On 2 August 1964 several Soviet-built North Vietnamese Navy (NVN) P6 patrol boats attacked the USS *Maddox* while it ran a 'Desoto' patrol 28 miles (45km) out to sea. One PT boat fired two 25in (533mm) torpedoes to no effect and the attack was subsequently negated by the USS *Maddox*'s own guns and a lightning deployment of four F-8E Crusaders from the carrier USS *Ticonderoga*. These first attacks by the NVN were most likely provoked by an 'Oplan-34' bombardment of the islands of Ho Me and Hon Nieu in the Gulf of Tonkin on 31 July. But whatever the cause, subsequent US claims of PT boat attacks on the USS *Maddox* and its reinforcement, the destroyer USS *C.Turner Joy*, precipitated the Americanization of the war as President Johnson escalated US commitment in response.

FIRE AND INTERDICTION

With the advent of hostilities, US Navy cruisers, destroyers and battleships participated in an offshore bombardment role from 1965, firing against coastal and inland targets in North Vietnam and VC/NVA infiltration and consolidation points in South Vietnam. During Operation Rolling Thunder, for instance, US Navy artillery fired on North Vietnamese bridges, airbases, radar sites and supply routes, and also targeted any shipping attempting to supply forces further down the coast. The most venerable ship to perform fire-support was the battleship the USS *New Jersey*, which between September 1968 and March 1969 shelled NVA positions around the DMZ with over 3000 16in (406mm) rounds and 11,000 5in (127mm) rounds. It was her last major action and she was decommissioned later in 1969. Further extensive use of such naval artillery came in 1972 when, during the invasion that Easter, over 20 ships of the US fleet decimated NVA units advancing down the east coast towards Hue.

Because of the great distances involved in offshore bombardment, the destructive results varied considerably, yet the range of the naval guns and the strategic manoeuvrability of the ships made it a valuable addition to ground-based artillery and air strikes. Yet the

US commitment in Vietnam escalated rapidly once the US Marines landed in March 1965. By the end of that year, over 180,000 US personnel were in Vietnam, an increase of 160,000 men from the beginning of the year.

LEFT: US MARINES RACE THROUGH THE SURF DURING A BEACH LANDING. THE US MARINES WAS EFFECTIVELY THE FIRST MAJOR UNIT OF COMBAT TROOPS COMMITTED TO THE WAR, AND PLAYED A MAJOR ROLE IN DEFENDING THE NORTHERN BORDER.

USS *ENTERPRISE* (CVN65)

In 1965 the USS *Enterprise* (CVN65) arrived in Vietnam, the first combat deployment in the world of a nuclear-powered aircraft carrier. Serving at Yankee Station during Operation Rolling Thunder, the vessel offered a huge operational air capability with its capacity for 24 F-4 Phantoms, 24 A-7 Corsairs, 10 A-6 Intruders and space for up to 40 more surveillance, electronic intelligence and other specialist aircraft. Its displacement at full load was 89,600 tons, over 13,000 tons greater than that of the USS *Forrestal*, and its massive reservoir of aviation fuel meant that air operations could be mounted for 12 days before resupply was needed.

The USS *Enterprise*'s first combat action was on 2 December 1965, launching 125 sorties against Vietcong and North Vietnamese targets, followed the next day with 165 sorties, a US Navy record for the time. In total, she made six combat tours of Southeast Asia from 1965 to 1972, and was also used during the evacuation of Saigon mounted in 1975.

THE USS *ENTERPRISE* FULLY UNDERWAY.

The combination of airborne surveillance, sophisticated radar and rapid-response boat units meant that the US Navy had almost total control over shipping infiltration routes between North and South Vietnam.

US Navy in Vietnam soon found itself in more complex combat roles. Naval supply routes were vital not only to the US; North Vietnam also relied on the infiltration of trawlers along the southern coastline, particularly into the complex and concealing waterways of the Mekong Delta just south of Saigon. An additional destination was Sihanoukville in southern Cambodia, from where transportation was continued by lorry and bike across the border with Vietnam.

After more than 100 tons (101,600kg) of munitions was discovered in a North Vietnamese trawler forced to beach at Vung Ro Bay, north of Cam Ranh Bay, on 16 February 1965, the US 7th Fleet established Task Force 71, a special anti-infiltration force using shallow-draft, heavily armed patrol boats in a stop-and-search role along the South Vietnamese coast and into its rivers.

Such activities, however, were already being practised before 1965; indeed South Vietnam's navy had investigated some 348,000 suspicious vessels from 1963 to 1964. But from 1 August 1965, the US upped the ante with Operation Market Time. Under the control of General William Westmoreland (it subsequently passed to the US Navy), Task Force 71 was redesignated Task Force 115 and the unit used 100 PCF (Patrol Craft Fast) fast boats, 30 WPB (Coastguard Patrol Boat) cutters and 500 armed junks, plus destroyer back-up, to mount interdiction operations from the Gulf of Tonkin to the Gulf of Thailand. Operation Market Time was also assisted by US Navy surveillance aircraft such as the Lockheed P-2 Neptune, Lockheed P-3 Orion and the Martin P-5 Marlin seaplane. These aircraft flew 1012 hours of missions using electronic surveillance to monitor suspicious shipping and conveying their data to the interception vessels. An indication of their success is the fact that out of 50 North Vietnamese trawlers heading for South Vietnam between 1965 and 1972, 48 were either destroyed or captured.

RIGHT: A 2.5-TON TRUCK BACKS ONTO A US NAVY LANDING CRAFT IN SEPTEMBER 1966. THE US NAVY'S ABILITY TO DEPLOY MEN, WEAPONS AND VEHICLES ALONG THE COASTLINE MEANT THAT GROUND FORCES COULD QUICKLY RECEIVE REINFORCEMENTS DURING SEARCH AND DESTROY OR DEFENSIVE OPERATIONS.

Some of the US Navy's most distinctive interdiction operations did not take place on the open sea. The river-laced Mekong Delta was a deeply contested area that could only be negotiated by a 'brown water navy' of specially designed patrol boats (see Chapter 7). These boats could operate in the shallowest of waters and were armed with weapons such as 20mm cannons and 81mm mortars. The contest for the Mekong Delta would go on for much of the war, firstly, from 1966 to 1968, under the jurisdiction of Task Force 116, known as Game Warden, then, from 1968 to 1972, under a joint US-South Vietnamese operation known by the acronym Sealords.

CARRIER OPERATIONS

By the time Game Warden was underway in the Mekong Delta, US carriers were already in Vietnamese waters and being used to launch huge air strikes. The first carrier to reach the region was the USS *Kitty Hawk*, deployed in the Gulf of Tonkin in April 1964. It was soon conducting its first operations, sending out Chance-Vought RF-8A Crusader photo-reconnaissance aircraft on surveillance missions over Laos. On the 6 June it was reinforced in this mission by the USS *Constellation*, the same day as the US Navy lost its first aircraft, an RF-8A shot down by 37mm groundfire over Laos's Route 7.

ABOVE: A US COASTAL PATROL BOAT BOMBARDS THE COASTLINE WITH CANNON FIRE. OFFSHORE FIRE SUPPORT COULD BE COORDINATED WITH GROUND UNIT OPERATIONS, US ARMY ARTILLERY FIRE OR AIR STRIKES.

LEFT: THE USS *ENTERPRISE* MEETS WITH THE SUPPORT SHIP USS *SACRAMENTO* IN THE GULF OF TONKIN IN 1967. SUCH SHIPS WERE VITAL FOR KEEPING COMBAT VESSELS REPLENISHED WITH FOOD, AMMUNITION, OIL AND OTHER ESSENTIALS.

ABOVE: A US NAVY STRIKE AIRCRAFT IS REARMED FOR ONE OF THE THOUSANDS OF BOMBING MISSIONS FLOWN FROM CARRIERS DURING THE COURSE OF THE WAR.

The versatile power of aircraft carriers led to their increased deployment. Other ships, such as the USS *Ticonderoga* and USS *Constellation*, joined the existing carriers, rotating in and out of active service under the jurisdiction of Task Force 77, the overall Asian-sector command structure within the US 7th Fleet. Around Vietnam, two particular operational stations were established: Yankee Station was positioned about 86 miles (140 km) off the coast of North Vietnam, roughly parallel with the area between Danang and the DMZ; Dixie Station, by contrast, was based off the southern coast of South Vietnam, around 90 miles (145km) southeast of Cam Ranh Bay. Yankee Station's aircraft were used especially in Operation Rolling Thunder and in strikes around the DMZ and Central Highlands, while Dixie Station's aircraft could cover the southern provinces, as well as Laos and Cambodia. A typical aircraft carrier could deploy two fighter squadrons, three attack squadrons plus reconnaissance, electronic intelligence and ECM aircraft, and helicopter units. Once the individual weapons systems of each aircraft were factored in it can be seen that aircraft carriers were capable of delivering ferocious firepower in support of the entire spectrum of US ground operations. By the end of 1965 alone, US Navy and US Marine pilots had flown an incredible 56,000 sorties from carriers.

The first carrier combat mission was the rapid response of the F-8E Crusader aircraft from the USS *Ticonderoga* to the attack on the USS *Maddox*. And from that point onwards their operations escalated rapidly. The first missions, operations Pierce Arrow, Barrel Roll, Flaming Dart 1 and Flaming Dart 2 were all retaliatory strikes against North Vietnamese military bases and fuel storage facilities; and in Operation Barrel Roll the targets were NVA logistical vehicles and routes through Laos. However, between 1965 and 1968 Yankee Station's greatest role was during Operation Rolling Thunder, deploying its planes for 12 out of every 24 hours each day.

When Rolling Thunder began on 2 March 1965, the US Navy's first activity was sending out reconnaissance aircraft over North Vietnam, from USS *Ranger* and USS *Coral Sea*. Combat missions soon followed, and throughout March US Navy aircraft delivered serious blows against targets such as the military depots at Phu Van and Vinh Son and between 26 and 31 March radar installations at Cape Ron, Vinh Son and Bach Long Vi.

By the end of May the USS *Independence* had joined the carriers, such was the need for maintaining the scale of the Rolling Thunder offensive. The US Navy was also starting to take losses, and in August two Skyhawks from the USS *Midway* were shot down by North Vietnam's new SA-2 Guideline missiles. This led to Operation Iron Hand, the direct attack of North Vietnamese missile batteries. Using low-level tactics and the new Shrike anti-radar missile, US Navy and US Marine pilots had some success in this role, though attacks against the SA-2s often made the pilots more vulnerable to conventional anti-aircraft fire.

Below: An F-8 Crusader is launched from USS Oriskany for a bombing run over North Vietnam.

In December 1965, US air forces gained governmental permission to attack industrial sites in the Hanoi-Haiphong region and 110 aircraft from USS *Enterprise*, USS *Ticonderoga* and USS *Kitty Hawk* completely destroyed the Uong Bi powerplant and cut almost a quarter of North Vietnam's electrical power. There followed a major period of escalation in the US Navy's campaign, and in April 1966 Yankee Station was shifted closer to the action, only 125 miles (201km) east of Dong Hoi, and operational zones were focused more against the coastal districts of North Vietnam.

Aircraft carriers gave the US forces enormous floating arsenals less than 200 miles (321km) from North Vietnam, and during Rolling Thunder US Navy carrier aircraft flew around 50,000 sorties a year.

US Navy pressure on North Vietnam continued throughout Rolling Thunder, and efficiency was increased in 1967 with the introduction of 'smart bomb' technology when, on 11 March, Walleye electro-optically guided bombs were first delivered, and subsequently used to great effect. Yet losses mounted steadily throughout the campaign. The US Navy lost 283 aviators and over 300 aircraft in combat during Rolling Thunder, with a further 1000 aircraft seriously damaged. Despite further dramatic missions during the Tet Offensive, especially in support of troops around Khe Sanh, the failure to bomb North Vietnam into submission meant that by November 1968 Rolling Thunder was over, yet this did not mean the end of operations for the US Navy and US Marine Corps pilots.

Since 1965, the carrier pilots of Dixie Station had been conducting ongoing combat strikes over South Vietnam and the border areas with Cambodia and Laos. Their main targets were VC units and bases – elusive targets which demanded a good deal of coordination with ground forces and reliable electronic surveillance. The pilots also provided

The two main carrier stations, Yankee and Dixie, covered all of South Vietnam plus target areas in North Vietnam with a powerful operational footprint. A simple radio call from ground troops could bring US Navy aircraft rushing in with ordnance.

RIGHT: AN ARMOURER REFILLS THE BELTS OF MACHINE-GUN ROUNDS IN THE HELICOPTER'S EMPTY MAGAZINE.

reconnaissance, search-and-rescue duties and even support roles for amphibious landings. Yet by August 1966, the large number of land-based air force units effectively rendered Dixie Station redundant and thereafter carriers were sent almost exclusively to Yankee Station.

Yet throughout the war, Laos remained a central target of all carrier forces. In April 1965, the US military divided Laos into two regions: 'Barrel Roll' north of the so-called Ho Chi Minh Trail, and Steel Tiger, the NVA supply route corridor down through the south of the country. US Navy pilots performed thousands of sorties over these regions during the war, especially between November 1968 and February 1972 when they dropped around 700,000 tons (711,245,000kg) of bombs over Laos and South Vietnam.

CARRIER ACCIDENTS

Apart from US Navy aviator losses during Rolling Thunder, the campaign was also blighted by two devastating tragedies on board the aircraft carriers themselves. On 26 October 1966, a magnesium flare ignited on board the USS *Oriskany*, which was then thrown into a storage locker containing around 600 more such flares. The huge fire that resulted ignited ammunition and aviation fuel. Many men trapped below deck died from either burns or asphyxiation and it took several hours for fire-fighting crews to bring the blaze under control. The final death toll was 19 sailors and 25 pilots with a further 38 men injured, and the carrier was out of action for eight months. The second tragedy occurred on 29 July 1967 onboard the USS *Forrestal*. Prior to a major combat mission, with fully armed combat aircraft massed on the deck, a McDonnell-Douglas F-4 Phantom's Zuni missile was accidentally fired and smashed into the fuel tank of an A-4E Skyhawk parked just in front. A huge chain of explosions rushed across the aft deck as bombs, missiles and aviation fuel detonated. Two destroyers and three other carriers were involved in fighting the fire, which took 12 hours to control. In the end, 134 US Navy personnel had been killed, 60 injured and 62 aircraft destroyed. Costly accidents were commonplace in the Vietnam War, the fires on the US carriers were just a small portion of the 10,811 non-combat deaths suffered by the US from 1964 to 1975.

AN F8U-1 CRUSADER CRASHES ON THE DECK OF A CARRIER.

Left: On board the USS *Constellation*, an aviation ordnanceman wheels two Snakeye 500lb (227kg) bombs.

Below: Pilots of A-6 Intruder aircraft check their bomb payloads just prior to taking off from the USS *Ranger* for bombing missions over North Vietnam.

Improved aviation technology in aircraft such as the Vought A-7E Corsair and Grumman A6-C Intruder enabled effective night attacks to be conducted, and thus the application of round-the-clock bombing. Furthermore, in February 1971 the ARVN invaded Laos in Operation Lam Son 719, requiring the support of aircraft from the USS *Hancock*, USS *Ranger* and USS *Kitty Hawk*. Over Laos alone, 130 US Navy aircraft were shot down during the course of the war.

Such operations kept US Navy and US Marine pilots on active service until the famous Linebacker missions of 1972, when they participated in the last air raids of the war against North Vietnam (see Chapter 13). Aircraft carriers remained a feature of the war until its conclusion in 1975, even being used to assist in the evacuation of Saigon, by which time over 1,800,000 US Navy personnel had served in Southeast Asia, with 2600 of them killed and 10,000 wounded.

US MARINE CORPS OPERATIONS

Any analysis of the US Navy's contribution to the Vietnam War would be incomplete without considering its most famous unit, the US Marine Corps. The US Marines were essentially the first dedicated US combat troops to be deployed in Vietnam, put ashore in the amphibious landings of the 9th Marine Expeditionary Brigade (9 MEB) at Danang in 1965. The 9 MEB subsequently developed into the III Marines Amphibious Force (III MAF) which in 1968 numbered 85,881 out of more than 500,000 US Marines who served in Vietnam between 1962 and 1975.

III MAF was mainly consigned to the 1 Corps Tactical Zone in South Vietnam's five northernmost provinces, based in four enclaves at Danang, Phu Bai, Chu Lai and Qui Nhon. Yet with the abandonment of the enclave strategy in mid-1965, the US Marines found themselves heavily

Although the US Marines fought with distinction in Vietnam, the ambiguous nature of the war resulted in the breakdown of discipline and organisation in some units which had not been witnessed in previous conflicts.

engaged in the 'Search and Destroy' (S & D) missions which characterized US ground force operations between 1965 and 1968. As discussed earlier, Operation Starlite was the first such US Marine operation, attacking from land, sea and helicopter on 18 August 1965 against the VC's 1st Regiment in the Van Truong peninsula. One of the first S & D operations of the war, Operation Starlite gained a significant amphibious presence when three US Marine battalions and a Special Landing Force (SLF) battalion were beach-landed near An Cuong before attacking the enemy. Other US Marine units closed the trap on VC forces via three major helicopter landings to the west and an overland assault from the north. The operation was a resounding success with 614 VC killed to only 45 Americans, and it inspired over 70 smaller-scale amphibious operations along the South Vietnamese coast between 1965 and 1969, coordinated between the SLF of the 7th Fleet and the MACV. None were as heavily contested as Operation Starlite, yet the amphibious units remained a useful tool for tactical deployment and reinforcement.

RIGHT: AN F-8 CRUSADER LAUNCHES A MISSILE ATTACK AGAINST A VIETCONG SITE IN SOUTH VIETNAM.

BELOW: US MARINES ENGAGE VIETCONG TROOPS IN A FIREFIGHT NEAR CHU LAI, JANUARY 1966.

The US Marines were involved in many other S & D operations, but they also executed their own distinctive pacification programmes. General Lewis W. Walt, the commander of 1 Corps, and Lieutenant General Victor Krulak, commander of Fleet Marine Force Pacific, both favoured a military approach which involved the active protection of Vietnamese communities from VC infiltration. Subsequently, Vietnamese villages in the 1 Corps area became the beneficiaries of extensive US Marine welfare and medical programmes, with each battalion of III MAF being given its own tactical area of operation (TAOR). Pacification units were expanded in August 1965 with the Combined Action Company (CAC) programme. This programme was based on

ABOVE: US MARINES DEPLOY ASHORE IN LANDING CRAFT IN ONE OF THE MANY AMPHIBIOUS OPERATIONS CARRIED OUT IN SOUTH VIETNAM.

LEFT: DECEMBER 1967. A US MARINE ADVANCES ACROSS A STREAM DURING A SEARCH AND DESTROY MISSION SOUTH OF DANANG. VIETCONG BOOBY TRAPS WERE OFTEN SUBMERGED BELOW THE WATERLINE OF POPULAR CROSSING POINTS.

An F-4 Phantom ready for launch.

THE F-4 PHANTOM

The McDonnell-Douglas F-4 Phantom stands as one of the defining aircraft of the Vietnam War. First production of the Phantom began as the AH-1 attack aircraft in the mid-1950s, but was then developed as an interceptor, the F-4H (F-4A). The performance of this aircraft was startling at the time. Its two General Electric J79-8B turbojets could generate 17,000lb (7711kg) of thrust and a maximum speed of 1500mph (2400kmh). It was armed with up to six AIM-7 Sparrow III air-to-air missiles, or four AIM-9B or -9D Sidewinder AAMs, as well as being able to carry up to 16,000lb (7257kg) of further munitions. It quickly went through several variations to meet US and international requirements, but by the time of the Vietnam War the F-4 II was the standard fighter of the US Navy and US Marines. The USAF was also committed to Phantom use, particularly using the F-4C, F-4D and F-4E in ground-attack, anti-radar and interceptor roles throughout the war.

The F-4 was the ideal multi-role aircraft for Vietnam, and it became the primary deployment aircraft for new 'precision-guided munitions' technology as the war progressed. On 10 July 1965, F-4s shot down two MiG fighters in air-to-air combat, the first of 107 such victories scored by USAF F-4s alone during the course of the war.

mixed units of US Marines and soldiers from South Vietnam's 'Popular Forces' which integrated with Vietnamese communities and thus were better able to perform counter-insurgency operations against the VC.

Below: A flame tank in action, a ferocious weapon to use in a jungle environment.

The Combined Action Program (CAP) in early 1967 took the CAC idea further. Based on the same principles of mixed units, CAP developed broader pacification programmes in addition to anti-VC measures, programmes which included intelligence-gathering, village security and various other forms of civic service. Ultimately CAP was of limited success, particularly because it was often difficult to find suitable personnel to carry it out and there was little backing from the South Vietnam government.

Yet pacification showed the US Marines willingness to integrate with local forces. The S & D operations Double Eagle I and Double Eagle II in January-March 1966 featured combined US Marine and ARVN forces making decisive sweeps against VC/NVA units in Quang Ngai province. The similarly composed operations of Utah/Lien Ket 21 and Texas/Lien Ket 28 in March, aimed at relieving the ARVN outpost of An Hoa, resulted in over 1000 communists being killed.

Perhaps one of the most distinctive duties of the US Marine Corps in Vietnam was the protection of the DMZ (see Chapter 6). From 1967 through to the Tet Offensive, the NVA made regular aggressive incursions across the DMZ which were resisted by the 3rd Marine Division at places like 'The Rockpile', Con Thien, Khe Sanh and Dong Ha. These major battles were conducted using thoroughly conventional tactics of massive artillery fire, decisive air power and massed infantry assaults. The siege at Khe Sanh, in 1967, when a US Marine regiment was surrounded by two NVA divisions, became an epic act of survival which cost the NVA 10,000 dead against the US Marines 205 (see Chapter 9).

The Tet Offensive launched in January-February 1968 brought the various DMZ actions to a climax and forced the US Marines onto the defensive around Danang, while three US Marine battalions also combined forces with ARVN troops to liberate the city of Hue in a treacherous street-by-street battle. The US Marines played a vital part in breaking

Above: The anchorage at Cam Ranh Bay. The supply ships seen here could replenish not only the ground troops, but also the carriers at Dixie Station to the southeast.

Left: Bombs from an A-4 Skyhawk smash around the Phuoc Dinh railroad bridge near Thanh Hoa on 10 September 1967.

The Vietnam War made an insatiable demand on manpower. As the conflict went on, the professionalism of the US Marine Corps found itself increasingly diluted by the newer recruit's inexperience and poor training.

the thrust of the offensive and they fought the NVA back to the border regions with the loss of 4500 soldiers. This action included Operation Meade River, the biggest helicopter assault in the US Marines' history which killed 1200 NVA around the NVA's DMZ bases and even involved a regimental-sized incursion into Laos to attack outposts on the Ho Chi Minh Trail.

The US Marines began 1969 with Operation Dewey Canyon, mounted from 22 January to 19 March. This huge deployment sent the entire 9th Marine Regiment into the Da Krong Valley in Quang Tri province where they killed 1355 NVA and captured over 525 tons of weaponry.

Yet 1969 also marked the beginning of the steady withdrawal of US troops from Vietnam, and the US Marines were no exception. The DMZ and 1 Corps operations were transferred to the authority of the US Army and ARVN, and the 3rd US Marine Division, once the most active of units with over 120 actions to its name, was sent to Okinawa while 1st US Marine Division continued in combat duties in Quang Nam province. In 1970, the US Marines still accounted for around 5000 VC/NVA dead, but by June 1971 III MAF had been almost entirely withdrawn from combat –

ABOVE: A US MARINE IMMERSED IN THE JUNGLE DURING A COMBAT PATROL.

RIGHT: A US MARINE CORPORAL SETS FIRE TO A VIETNAMESE HUT DURING OPERATION PRAIRIE III IN MARCH 1965.

though small guard units and US Marine advisers stayed on in limited numbers, with the latter assisting the ARVN during the 1971 invasion of Laos and the North Vietnamese invasion of 1972. Finally, a brigade-strength US Marine force was used in the evacuation of key personnel from both Saigon and Phnom Penh in the last days of the war.

The US Marine Corps lost 14,821 men in Vietnam out of more than 500,000 of its soldiers who served there. A further 86,753 were wounded. The experience had been a punishing one for the corps. Apart from the high levels of casualties, both discipline and motivation had broken down at times as the overall goal of their military efforts was so often lost in the politics of the war. Nearly 50 incidents of fragging – the deliberate killing of one's own officers or fellow soldiers using fragmentation grenades – occurred in 1970 alone within the US Marines. Yet such problems were endemic throughout all forces in the Vietnam War. The war's clash of political, ethnic, cultural and military objectives created a confusing and frequently demoralizing picture for troops on the ground, sea and in the air. As Rear Admiral D.V. Gallery bitingly said in 1965, 'I doubt if Mr McNamara and his crew have any morale setting on their computer.' Yet despite the depressing confusion of the war, US Navy and US Marine units can still list many of their actions in Vietnam as being among their finest moments.

ABOVE: ITS BEAUTY BELIES ITS DANGER – THE INFAMOUS ROCKPILE CAN BE SEEN HERE IN THE BACKGROUND AS US MARINES PATROL A HILL DURING OPERATION PRAIRIE. SUCH HILL WORK REQUIRED BOTH STAMINA AND THE ABILITY TO REACT RAPIDLY TO ANY ENEMY AMBUSHES.

CHAPTER 6

Holding the DMZ

IN A BLASTED HILLSIDE LANDSCAPE, A US SOLDIER TAKES COVER FROM AN NVA SNIPER. AS A FOCAL POINT FOR NORTH VIETNAMESE TROOP CONCENTRATIONS, THE AREA IN AND AROUND THE DMZ SAW SET-PIECE BATTLES WHICH TOOK THE VIETNAM CONFLICT BEYOND COUNTER-INSURGENCY TO THE LEVEL OF CONVENTIONAL WAR.

The DMZ was all that separated South and North Vietnam. With NVA artillery able to fire across this border zone, US forces around the DMZ had to fight an enemy whose firepower could be equivalent, or sometimes better, than its own.

One of the most distinctive zones of combat throughout the Vietnam War must be the area in and around the Demilitarized Zone (DMZ) which separated North and South Vietnam. This was not due to its geography, for its jungles, mountains and rivers were identical to those found throughout Vietnam; instead, what made it unique was the simple fact that it was a mere 6-mile (10km) wide separation between two warring countries. Border zones in wars are always contentious, and during the Vietnam War the South's entire western border with Laos and Cambodia was the scene of both violent battle and huge communist infiltration. The DMZ was different because the NVA could mass itself only a few miles from South Vietnam without a lengthy, logistically difficult journey and without entering a foreign country. The result was that throughout the late 1960s the DMZ became one of the most contested areas of the war, producing battles of conventional scale, weaponry and casualties which were at times reminiscent of those of the two world wars.

THE DMZ

The Demilitarized Zone was established in 1954 as part of the Geneva Accords to act as a military-free buffer zone between North Vietnam and South Vietnam, to be maintained until reunification elections were held in 1956. It evenly straddled the 17th

BEGINNING THE JOURNEY SOUTH.

THE HO CHI MINH TRAIL

The so-called Ho Chi Minh Trail was the dominant communist supply route of the Vietnam War. Snaking down from Hanoi, it cut through the jungles of eastern Laos to southern Cambodia, bringing North Vietnamese supplies and troops into South Vietnam and providing launch-off points for full-scale NVA incursions and invasions.

Work began on a north-south communication route in 1959, when supply columns (known as Group 559) used narrow tribal trails through eastern Laos to supply VC insurgents in South Vietnam. As the supply movement grew, rest stations, supply depots and medical facilities were built along the route and the track was tenaciously expanded by youthful construction units called Special Youth Shock Groups in order to take wheeled vehicles rather than just bicycles and men. By 1964, the trail had begun to mature as a sinuous network of multiple tracks which became further developed in 1965 after the introduction of Soviet and Chinese road-construction machines.

Few accurate figures exist for the quantities of men and materiel which passed down it during the course of the war. Figures for 1968 estimated that up to 100,000 NVA soldiers (along with thousands of tons of supplies) penetrated the South via the trail that year, compared to 10,000 in 1964. Naturally, the Ho Chi Minh Trail attracted US air strikes throughout the war, making Laos one of the most bombed countries in history. But although the US caused tremendous casualties among the supply columns, it never completely stopped the activity along the trail.

LEFT: A CESSNA A-37 IN ACTION OVER THE DMZ. THE STRENGTH OF NVA FORCES IN THE AREA MEANT THAT US AIR POWER WAS OFTEN DECISIVE, SLASHING NVA TROOP STRENGTH IN HUGE BOMBING RAIDS AND SAVING MANY US UNITS FROM ENCIRCLEMENT, DEATH OR CAPTURE.

parallel across the entire northern border of South Vietnam and any military occupation or incursion from the forces either side of the divide was prohibited. But when the elections were not held and war began both the US and South Vietnam recognized that the DMZ afforded opportunities for North Vietnamese infiltration and offensive build-up.

The US found the DMZ a frustration as much as anything else. In both 1966 and 1967, as battles started to rage within South Vietnam's northernmost provinces, some military planners argued that the forcible occupation of the DMZ was a strategic necessity. The DMZ, however, was a military and political tightrope: occupation of it could be perceived as a step towards an actual invasion of the North, something which would have escalated Cold War tensions between the US, USSR and China. Consequently, both presidents Johnson and Nixon rejected such suggestions.

Yet this reticence did not avoid the DMZ becoming a combat sector. From July 1966 US Special Forces made temporary (and secret) incursions up to the 17th parallel on reconnaissance missions, and US and South Vietnamese strike and bomber aircraft would regularly pound NVA positions within the narrow band of the DMZ. One of the US forces' greatest concerns was how to stop the NVA using the area to infiltrate combat personnel into the US

SUPPLYING THE VIETCONG

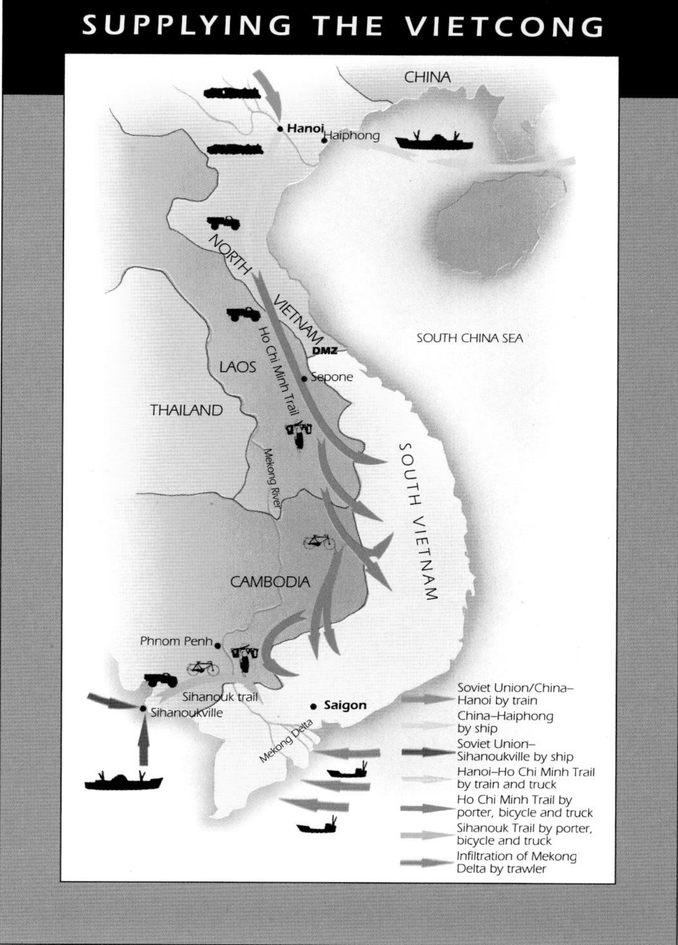

RIGHT: A CH-54 TARHE SKY CRANE AIRLIFTS IN A 105MM M101A1 HOWITZER TO A US FIRE SUPPORT BASE (FSB) SOUTH OF THE DMZ. BECAUSE OF THE TERRAIN AROUND THE DMZ, MANY FSBS WERE ISOLATED OUTPOSTS THAT WERE UTTERLY DEPENDENT UPON AIRBORNE SUPPLIES.

BELOW: FIRE SUPPORT. A M-107 175MM HOWITZER PUMPS SHELLS INTO NVA TARGETS. CROSS-BORDER ARTILLERY DUELS WERE COMMON, THOUGH THE US HAD THE ADVANTAGE OF AIR SUPREMACY.

1 Corps zone (consisting of South Vietnam's five northernmost provinces: Quang Tri, Thua Thien, Quang Nam, Quang Tin and Quang Ngai), which was occupied by two US Marine divisions and assorted ARVN forces. Because of US ground surveillance, NVA infiltration through the DMZ was almost entirely of personnel rather than supplies; once NVA troops were across the border they received supplies which had been infiltrated from Laos, usually in Quang Tri province.

By 1966 concerns over DMZ infiltration took a new turn. Between January and May infra-red, night-vision-equipped aerial reconnaissance missions over the DMZ had revealed regimental-sized NVA troop concentrations distributed throughout the zone. The build-up was primarily due to the effectiveness of US bombing over the Ho Chi Minh Trail in Laos, with the NVA seeking a safer infiltration route. Yet intelligence gained from a captured NVA officer also revealed aggressive intentions towards Quang Tri province, with the potential for full-scale NVA attacks against the province or even an invasion of the South.

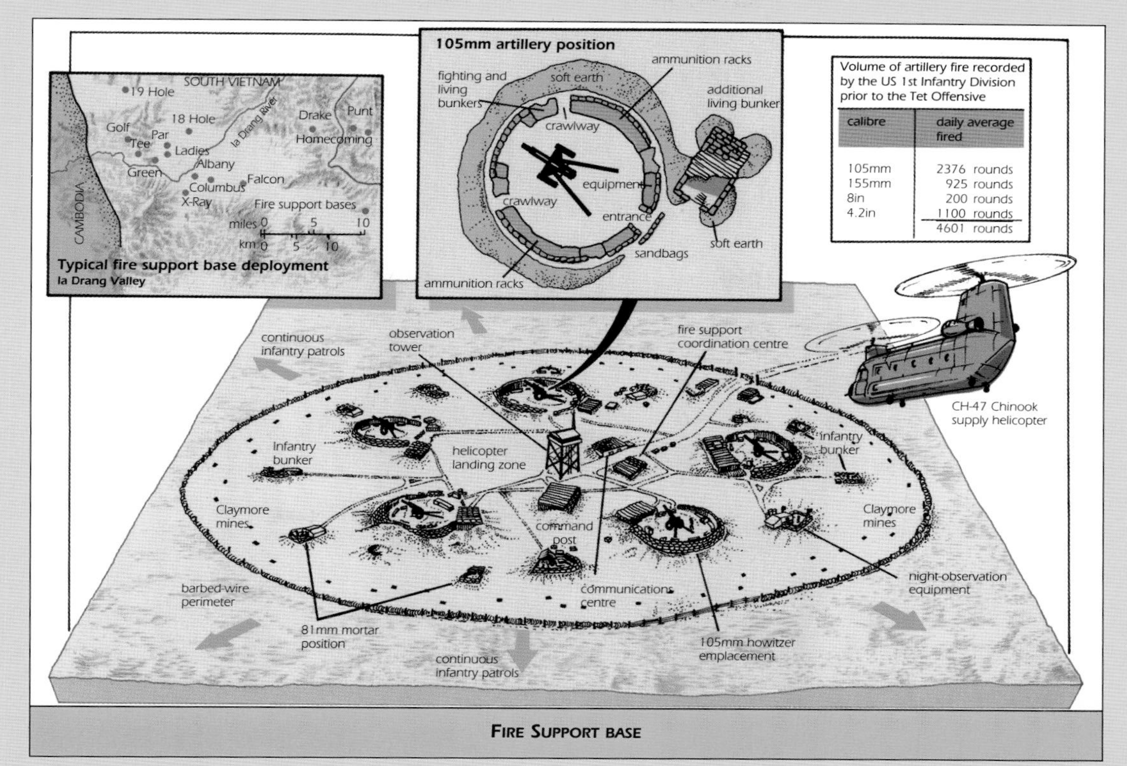

calibre	daily average fired
105mm	2376 rounds
155mm	925 rounds
8in	200 rounds
4.2in	1100 rounds
	4601 rounds

FIRE SUPPORT BASE

US FIREBASES

The Fire Support Base (FSB) was one of the US forces' central strategic emplacements during the battles around the DMZ, and indeed throughout the Vietnam War. The establishment of such a base would usually start with a helicopter deployment or troop ground assault to secure an appropriate elevated natural feature, after which batteries of 105mm and 155mm guns were heli-lifted to the site and construction of the FSB would begin. A typical FSB would consist of a fire-coordination centre and command post in the middle of the base, around which would be sited the howitzer emplacements and 81mm mortar emplacements (the latter for more defensive roles). FSB security was formidable. Around the barbed-wire perimeter fence would be a ring of Claymore mines, while inside the base multiple bunkers containing machine-guns, grenade launchers, recoilless rifles and infantry units would serve as protection against ground attack. FSBs were generally used to support S & D or defensive operations in their area. If a US infantry or US Marine unit required artillery support, its radio transmission officer (RTO) would relay target coordinates back to the FSB, which would reply with smoke shells to find the target before loading with high-explosive. FSBs were essential to the conducting of US ground operations, though from 1968 the power of the NVA's own artillery made them increasingly vulnerable and embattled places to be.

THE McNAMARA LINE

In preference to direct combat measures, US strategists devised several logistical and barrier tactics to counter the NVA manoeuvres. US Marine bases and Fire Support Bases (FSBs) were strengthened just below the DMZ, and two new airfields were built around Hue into which troop and armour reinforcements could be flown. Yet the most

RIGHT: MANNING A 0.50IN CALIBRE MACHINE-GUN AT A SECURITY POST.

BELOW: A C-130 TOUCHES DOWN AT THIEN NGON ON A RESUPPLY MISSION.

unusual measure proposed was one in 1966 by Professor Roger Fisher of the Harvard Law School who suggested the construction of a 160-mile (257km) long, 10-mile (16km) wide barrier system running from the coast of South Vietnam just south of the DMZ to Tchepone in Laos. This would be built in a specially defoliated strip and would consist of military emplacements, minefields, trench systems, barbed-wire fences and various other prohibitory constructions. The idea reached the ears of Robert McNamara who subsequently gathered together a group of tacticians and scientists in mid-1966 to discuss its feasibility. McNamara's imagination was caught by the proposal, despite Westmoreland's scepticism, and in 1967 building work began on the so-called 'McNamara Line'.

An updated version of France's De Lattre Line, the McNamara Line was envisaged as having a robust barrier of fences and watchtowers with the hi-tech addition of electronic monitoring devices. In the end very little of this deterrent was built.

The McNamara Line was to be a physical barrier of electrified fences and watchtowers with a string of FSBs positioned just south of it. McNamara's military scientists also invented a fantastic range of monitoring devices, including seismic detectors, voice-activated recorders and motion detectors that were meant to pick up any attempted NVA breaches of the line (it was even proposed to develop a variety of monitor to be disguised as dog excrement).

In the event, the line never achieved any real substance: only 10 miles (16km) of it were built outwards from the South Vietnamese coast, and progress was incredibly slow because of NVA shelling and attacks. Furthermore, it was soon realized that like the De Lattre Line of the French in the 1950s, the McNamara Line tied down too many soldiers in its construction and maintenance while not necessarily preventing communist infiltration (the NVA could simply go round the line through Laos). By 1968, when NVA attacks were already being made against targets like Khe Sanh below the proposed line, the project was abandoned. The only way to stop the NVA would be by force.

Areas of the DMZ were so pulverised by US forces that they looked like scenes from World War I: trees blasted to stumps, shell craters altering the contours of hills, the dead lying unburied and the constant, violent noise.

LEFT: US VESSELS OFF DANANG, ONE OF THE KEY NAVAL LANDING POINTS FOR RESUPPLYING TROOPS IN THE DMZ.

BELOW: THE CH-54 TARHE SKY CRANE WAS ONE OF THE US FORCES MORE MUSCULAR AIRCRAFT. HERE IT LIFTS A RIVER PATROL BOAT, BUT IT COULD TRANSPORT EVERYTHING FROM ARTILLERY PIECES TO VEHICLES.

FROM THE NORTH

From 1966, the NVA started to commit regimental-sized units into the DMZ for both cross-border infiltration and attack purposes. Despite the strength of the US forces facing them, the narrowness of the zone allowed the NVA to utilize their extremely potent artillery systems to the full. Perhaps the most effective weapon in their arsenal was the Soviet-made (or Chinese copy) M46 130mm howitzer. It could outrange most US artillery pieces, delivering up to six high-explosive, fragmentation or armour-piercing shells a minute to a range of 18 miles (29km). In addition, the NVA employed Chinese-made 107mm and 122mm high-explosive rockets with ranges of five miles (8.5km) and 10 miles (16km) respectively. Such hardware would be acutely important in the battles around the DMZ, as the confrontations often involved huge cross-border artillery duels which escalated the casualty figures.

The first significant contests between US and NVA forces in the DMZ were not, however, set-piece battles but US clearance sweeps. Operations New York, between February and March 1966, and Swift Saber, in June, were small- to medium-scale missions throughout the northern provinces which returned mixed results: Swift Saber resulted in only one or two enemy killed in the area 10 miles (16km) northeast of Danang, while New York took out an entire VC battalion from their underground bunkers in the Phu Thu peninsula. Yet these actions were general counter-measures against the communist presence in the north rather than specific attacks on NVA units moving through the DMZ. This would all change with the reconnaissance information indicating NVA units within the DMZ itself.

The fight around the DMZ achieved exactly what the North Vietnamese wanted it to achieve, drawing US troops away from population centres and preparing the ground for a major invasion.

RIGHT: AIRBORNE DEPLOYMENT COULD TAKE US TROOPS STRAIGHT FROM SAFETY INTO THE MIDDLE OF A FIREFIGHT. HERE A CH-47 DEPOSITS SOLDIERS ONTO A MOUNTAIN RIDGE LANDING ZONE.

By spring 1966 NVA forces, including the NVA's 324th Division, began to cross the Ben Hai River running through the middle of the DMZ and build up in Quang Tri province. With thousands of communist soldiers pushing down into the South, the US responded with Operation Hastings between 15 July and 3 August, followed by Operation Prairie I in early August (Prairie I would be the first of four S & D missions in Quang Tri and the DMZ area between August 1966 and May 1967). Both operations turned into enormous firefights that fully characterized the nature of combat around the DMZ. Hastings involved III MAF and the 1st ARVN Division pitted against the 90th, 803rd and 812th regiments of the NVA's 324th Division. Following a heli-lift of two battalions of US Marines into the combat zone, Hastings quickly descended into a series of extraordinarily vicious close-quarter actions, particularly in the Song Hgan Valley just two miles (3km) south of the DMZ. Losses quickly mounted on both sides: the US Marines lost 126 men and the ARVN 21, but more than 800 NVA were killed and 200 guns and 300,000 rounds of ammunition captured. Operation Hastings was essentially a success, but the depth of the fighting had surprised many. The terrain around the DMZ also made combat particularly demanding. The mountainous Mutters Ridge, that stretched between hills 484 and 400 and offered a gathering spot for bunkered NVA mortar operators, and the soon to be infamous hill named 'The Rockpile' became focal points for repeated exchanges of artillery and clashes between fighting patrols, especially once the latter had become established as a prominent American FSB.

BELOW: US RANGERS ADVANCE AFTER BEING AIR-LANDED IN A HELICOPTER INSERTION MISSION.

Operations Prairie I and II generated an NVA death toll in excess of 2000. In total, the four Prairie operations throughout Quang Tri province would take the lives of over 500 Marines and wound another 3167 by the end of their run in May 1967. Yet it was during 1967 that a change in Hanoi's strategic vision started to affect the battles in and around the DMZ. North Vietnam's peripheral strategy, aiming to draw US forces away from population centres in preparation for an invasion of

US SURVEILLANCE METHODS

A key US surveillance objective in Vietnam was the detection and monitoring of enemy troop movements down the Ho Chi Minh Trail and throughout South Vietnam. The primary tool for this work was the air-dropped sensor, the most common of which was the ADSID, or Air-Delivered Seismic Intruder Detector. This 3ft-long (1m) heavily camouflaged bomb-shaped device was dropped along enemy supply routes by US jets or helicopters, where it buried itself in the ground up to its fins and left a 4ft-long (122cm) antenna – disguised as a plant – above the ground. Once deployed, the ADSID monitored acoustic and seismic patterns in its locality and transmitted the information to US aircraft such as the Beech Model A-36 Bonanza or Lockheed EC-121 Warning Star. If the data indicated enemy truck or troop movements, the data would be fed to artillery units or strike aircraft.

ADSID was just one of several air-dropped sensors, the others being Acousid, Spikebuoy and Acoubuoy, the last two providing sonar data. However, despite the $800 million-plus that was spent in surveillance programmes such as Operation Igloo White from 1966 to 1971, the devices were not a great success owing to problems interpreting data and the exposure of monitor aircraft to anti-aircraft fire. More immediately successful was the rapid development of the personnel radar and night-vision technology.

A Rockwell OV-10 Bronco on patrol.

The AN/PPS-5 radar could detect people at up three miles, while night-vision scopes, such as the AN/TVS-4, had an image intensification range of nearly one mile. Of course, efforts at innovation also brought a fair share of failures. One notable example was the XM2 airborne personnel detector, nicknamed the 'people-sniffer', which could detect human odours from a helicopter-mounted platform. Naturally, such a device could not distinguish between friend or foe, or even foe and non-human animal, and it failed to achieve widespread use.

Left: US troops board a Sikorsky S-55 during a DMZ operation. Helicopters were just as essential for evacuation as for deployment, yet the intense fire of the DMZ battles often prohibited the rapid evacuation of both casualties and isolated troops.

South Vietnam accompanied by an uprising, meant that the DMZ became a focal point for NVA activity as an attempt was made to disperse the US forces throughout the north. This would in effect move the Vietnam conflict to the third stage of 'revolutionary war' – large-scale conventional conflict, though by this point such a situation almost existed already around the DMZ.

ESCALATION

Sensing the increased likelihood of combat in the DMZ during 1967, the US command reinforced the immediate area with the 1st US Marine Division which had previously had responsibilities for territories south of Danang to Chu Lai. They and the 3rd US Marine Division manned a string of defensive outposts stretching along Route 9. These outposts, including Khe Sanh, 'The Rockpile', Camp Carroll, Cam Lo, Gio Lihn and Dong Ha, acted as consolidation points for American S & D

ABOVE: SOLDIERS IN QUANG TRI PROVINCE REST AROUND A STACK OF 81MM SHELLS WHICH ARE ARMED AND READY TO FIRE.

RIGHT: US MARINES TAKE COVER FROM A GRENADE DURING THEIR TAKING OF HILL 484 CLOSE TO THE DMZ IN SEPTEMBER 1966.

In 1967 the NVA built up to the Tet Offensive. NVA actions started to become bolder and more aggressive; far more willingness was shown to test out full-blown conventional tactics on US troops.

operations, FSBs and logistics landing bases. Naturally, they started to attract NVA attention. On 20 March NVA artillery units fired around 1200 shells at Con Thien and Gio Lihn, demonstrating the capabilities which would play such a key role in the forthcoming battles.

Khe Sanh, a place whose name would go down in military legend for some of the fiercest battles of the war, was one of the first to attract major NVA troop onslaughts. Some 15 miles (24km) south of the DMZ and overlooking Route 9 which ran across into Laos, this airstrip in western Quang Tri had little initial tactical value, but it did provide some valuable reconnaissance information on NVA troops movements into Laos. In Khe Sanh's vicinity were three hills – 861, 881 South and 881 North – all occupied by the NVA and all of which would, if captured, enable the US to establish more effective control over the infiltration into Laos.

ABOVE: BATTLE-WEARY TROOPS SEARCH FOR VIETCONG BODIES AND SUPPLIES DURING OFFENSIVE OPERATIONS IN JULY 1967.

The Hill Fights, as they were known, or the First Battle of Khe Sanh as it was later called, began on 24 April following an NVA ambush on 16 March of a company of men from the 9th US Marine Regiment. The battle would rage for over two weeks during which time the US Marines took each hill, backed by the explosive support of US Marine Corps ground-attack aircraft and 175mm artillery bombardments from the FSBs. The fight for the hills was truly epic, and by the time fighting concluded on 12 May 160 US Marines had been killed for 570 NVA dead .

Shortly after, Con Thien became the focus of NVA attentions. Some 14 miles (23km) from the coast and only two miles (3km) from the DMZ, Con Thien was to be one of the first outposts of the McNamara Line. As primary construction on the line began in mid-1967, the NVA chose it as the most viable site for a massive infantry incursion to smash the incipient line, threaten the US logistics base at Dong Ha and lay the foundations for a widespread invasion of Quang Tri province.

Although what became known as 'the siege of Con Thien' effectively began in September, heavy fighting was already underway in July as US Marine units attempted to clear the area for the construction work on the line to commence. On 2 July two companies of US Marines were decimated when NVA units trapped them in a storm of artillery, flame-

THE LONG-RANGE DESTROYER – THE M46 FIELD GUN.

SOVIET M46 130MM FIELD GUN

The M46 130mm field gun, or its Chinese copy the PRC Type 59, was the NVA's primary artillery piece from the late 1960s onwards. It could significantly outrange US weapons such as the M101 105mm howitzers and it delivered huge amounts of high-explosive, fragmentation and armour-piercing shells against US positions around the DMZ.

Calibre:	130mm
Weight (firing):	16,975lb (7700kg)
Length:	38ft (11.73m)
Depression/Elevation:	2.5 deg to 45 deg
Crew:	Nine
Rate of fire:	6rpm
Range:	88,550ft (27,000m)

thrower and machine-gun fire, with the survivors only coming through by virtue of a timely US Air Force bombing run over the area. US aircraft (both USAF and USMC) were now heavily committed to destroying NVA formations in and around the DMZ. Arc Light B-52s were central to the action and scythed down massive numbers of the NVA in SLAM missions which delivered over 22,000 tons (22,354,000kg) of bombs on the Con Thien area alone. More attention was paid to coordination between the B-52 missions, naval guns and FSBs. Between 11 September and 31 October, for instance, Operation Neutralize attacked enemy positions 24 hours a day without ceasing and over 900 Arc Light sorties were flown over the DMZ itself.

BELOW: THE CLEARING OF JUNGLE TOOK PLACE ON A MASSIVE SCALE IN MANY THEATRES OF THE VIETNAM WAR.

But this did not stop the NVA maintaining the pressure. Some single outposts received thousands of artillery shells each day, especially with the deployment in early July of long-range 152mm howitzers, and the terrain started to resemble the lunar landscape. Casualty levels were appalling. In actions which followed an assault on an NVA bunker system on 8 July, over 500 Marines were casualties while 1290 NVA were killed.

In September the situation became siege-like when the US Marines at Con Thien experienced attacks from the NVA's 812th Regiment – mounted from southwest of the base. The position seemed increasingly precarious. More US Marines were brought up as reinforcements into

LEFT: A UH-1D HELICOPTER PUTS DOWN IN A DEVASTATED LANDING ZONE AND TAKES US CASUALTIES ABOARD FOR MEDICAL EVACUATION.

BELOW: THE FATIGUE AND MISERY OF WAR TAKE HOLD ON A YOUNG US SOLDIER. IN SOME AREAS MEN EXPERIENCED COMBAT ALMOST EVERY SINGLE DAY.

what was the now incessant barrage of artillery and mortar fire being directed against Con Thien. Offensive action by the US Marines did not break the deadlock, and more casualties were taken in four days of firefights with the 90th NVA Regiment.

Apart from their sheer tenacity, in the end it was brute firepower which saved the US Marines at Con Thien. Bad weather had reduced the number of NVA troop engagements but not of artillery fire: between 19 and 27 September over 3000 103mm and 175mm shells, and 122mm and 140mm rockets, crashed down into the outpost. The US reply was awesome: naval units in the Gulf of Tonkin and land-based artillery units fired a total of over 18,000 shells into enemy positions. This, combined with punishing air strikes, reduced NVA activity to manageable levels, though artillery fire and firefights continued for some weeks.

The action around Con Thien was only one of the many battles fought throughout the DMZ during 1967 as the NVA built itself up to the major invasion and offensives of 1968. S & D operations, such as Operation Hickory, Operation Beau Charger and Operation Belt Tight actually thrust deep into the DMZ itself up to the Ben Hai River; almost all such operations were particularly bloody. In Operation Buffalo, for instance, conducted between 2 and 14 July, the 3rd US Marine Division killed nearly 1300 NVA. In Operation Kingfisher from 16 July to 31 October a further 1117 NVA personnel were accounted for. The two-day Operation Hickory II killed 39 NVA for the loss of four dead and 90 wounded US Marines. Such encounters made the DMZ the bloodiest war zone in Vietnam in 1967. Yet as the year drew to a close, events would prove that despite their enormous losses the NVA were far from defeated.

The intensity of combat around the DMZ produced symptoms of battle fatigue in many soldiers. This included Post-Traumatic Stress Disorder (PTSD) and, because of NVA artillery, shell shock.

Right: Bulldozers clear a combat zone. These machines would often move in the wake of US ground troops, flattening vegetation to deprive the VC/NVA of future cover and freedom of movement.

Below: A soldier mans an M60 machine-gun, multiple ammunition belts at the ready.

THE BUILD-UP TO TET

By the end of 1967 the outpost at Khe Sanh had already seen intensive efforts to destroy its effectiveness, though these efforts had died down during the action at Con Thien. During this respite, the US Marines at Khe Sanh continued the process of building it into a massive logistics base and it was taken up to a strength of three US Marine battalions plus several 105mm, 155mm and 175mm artillery batteries. There were also six M48 Patton tanks and a fearsome display of vehicle-mounted machine-gun and cannon systems. The Khe Sanh plateau is now famous for the 77-day siege which developed there from January 1968, with many journalists comparing it to the 1954 battle of Dien Bien Phu in both its location, terrain and isolation. The comparison, however, falls down on the casualty figures alone: Khe Sanh resulted in 205 US deaths as opposed to the 3000 French who died at Dien Bien Phu. Even so, there was no doubting the severity of the NVA attempts to take the base.

The first indications that Khe Sanh might be under serious threat came in early January 1968 when another communist build-up was detected just to the north. Khe Sanh was reinforced by a further battalion of US Marines (2nd Battalion, 26th US Marines) on 16 January. The full extent of the forces arraigned against them was four NVA Divisions and two artillery regiments, with the elite 304th Division having joined the move by mid-January.

Artillery fire started in earnest on 21 January against the nearby Hill 861 and was followed by human wave assaults up its slopes. These reached dangerously close to the top, but were cut down by strong machine-gun fire from the defenders on top, as well as those on the nearby Hill 881 South. From this point onwards, Khe Sanh was smashed daily by artillery and rocket fire, destroying aircraft, tanks, ammunition dumps and, of course, its human defenders. B-52s kept up a thunderous bombardment of the enemy's positions, while the American forces dug defensive emplacements and vulnerable Fairchild C-123 Provider transport aircraft made resupply flights onto the cratered airstrip.

The siege that followed showed massive endurance on the part of those resisting, but it cannot be understood in isolation from what happened on 31 January when North Vietnam launched the Tet Offensive, the full-scale invasion of South Vietnam (see Chapter 8). The battles in 1966 and 1967 in and around the DMZ had achieved the aim of drawing US forces into positions away from the main population centres which the North hoped could then be drawn into open insurrection against the South Vietnamese government. The DMZ would be opened up fully by the North Vietnamese invasion, yet battles would be fought there throughout the 1960s and into the 1970s. The scale of warfare seen in and along the DMZ prior to the Tet Offensive was at times identical to the massed battles of the Western Front in World War I or the Pacific campaigns of World War II, in terms of the devastation wrought, the casualties taken and the firepower applied. Tet was simply the culmination of these early NVA actions into an open and conventional invasion.

Above: Airmobility in action. A US soldier watches a large flight of UH-1 helicopters take off on a resupply mission. One of the most pressing airborne supply campaigns was that devoted to sustaining the US outpost at Khe Sanh near the DMZ.

Left: An M107 175mm self-propelled howitzer is maintained by its crewman at a US base. It was one of the most powerful guns of the war, capable of projecting a shell over 19 miles (32km).

Chapter 7

The Riverine War

A riverine patrol team goes into action. South Vietnam's rivers were as hotly contested as its jungles during the Vietnam War, and US Navy and US Marine forces developed the unique 'Brown Water Navy' to reclaim the inland waterways from the Vietcong.

THE VIETNAMESE TERRAIN

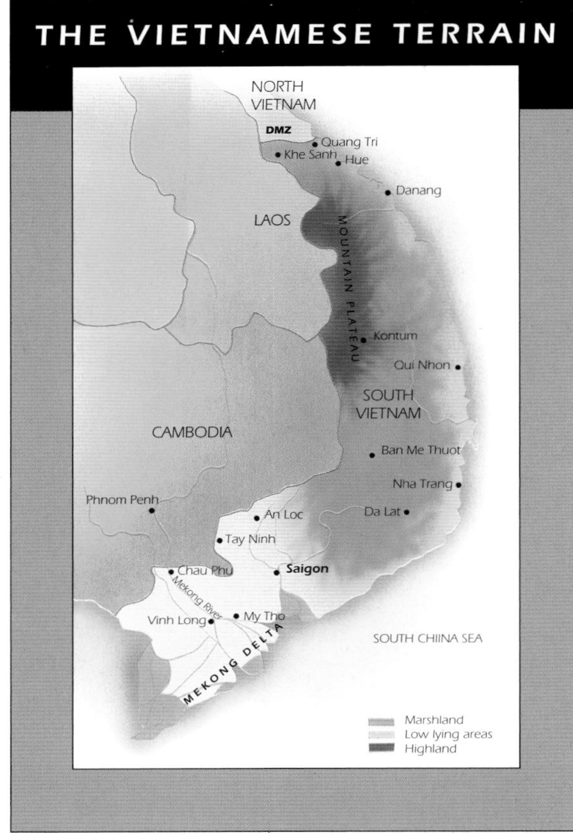

The thousands of miles of waterways that make up the Mekong Delta served as a seemingly inviolable Vietcong stronghold. Supplies flowed down the trackless rivers with ease and the communists drew upon the dense, supportive population for reinforcements. The ARVN dared not enter the hostile area, leaving it a serious threat to the security of nearby Saigon. In 1965 the US Navy created the River Patrol Force (RPF) as a first effort to combat communist domination of the delta. In 1968 and 1969 the US Navy and the Mobile Riverine Force (MRF) of the 9th Infantry Division fought the Vietcong to a standstill in the rice paddies and the fetid water of endless delta swamps. Over time, combined naval, air and land campaigns would do much to wrest control of the Mekong Delta from the communist forces.

The Mekong Delta is perhaps the most important territory in South Vietnam. It is the most fertile rice-producing region in the entire country and is home to more than half the population. The delta was an important area of VC dominance and its 3000 miles (4800km) of waterways made it a thoroughfare for communist supplies. Finally Saigon, the capital of South Vietnam, lies on the northern edge of the delta and relies on riverborne supplies. For these reasons the United States decided that it was of the utmost importance to control the vast network of rivers that make up the Mekong Delta, and in 1965 the River Patrol Force was born.

THE RIVER PATROL BOAT

The war in the Mekong Delta depended upon the versatility of the River Patrol Boat or PBR. This workhorse interdicted enemy supplies, provided covering fire for ground forces and patrolled the wilderness of waterways that was the Mekong Delta. The PBR was usually manned by a crew of four and was equipped with a Pathfinder surface radar and two radios. For armament it sported two twin-mounted 0.50in machine-guns forward, two M-60 machine-guns or grenade launchers amidships, and one 0.50in machine-gun aft. The PBR's fibreglass construction made it light and manoeuvrable – able to slip into many small waterways impassable to other craft – and fast, able to reach speeds of over 25 knots. Its strength, though, was also its weakness for it offered little in the way of protection for its crew and was quite vulnerable to enemy fire. The original PBR, the Mark I, had several operational problems. The vegetation in the Mekong often fouled its engines, and even pulling alongside a sampan for a routine inspection could cause severe damage to the fibreglass hull. As a result a Mark II was introduced in 1966 with an improved engine and more durable aluminum construction. The PBR saw continuous service during the Vietnam War and was the backbone of the riverine war effort.

THE VERSATILE PBR.

THE WAR FOR THE MEKONG

In early 1966 the RPF launched Operation Game Warden with the goal of interdicting the communists' supplies and halting enemy harassment of shipping into Saigon. River Patrol Boats, or PBRs, often based at large Landing Ship, Tanks, (LSTs) floating at the mouths of rivers, set up coordinated river patrols to deny use of the waterways to enemy shipping. Initial efforts were made near the mouths of the Mekong and they met with considerable success. Further upstream, though, success was more limited. Here a mere 140 PBRs patrolled the endless waterways on an irregular basis due to the restriction in

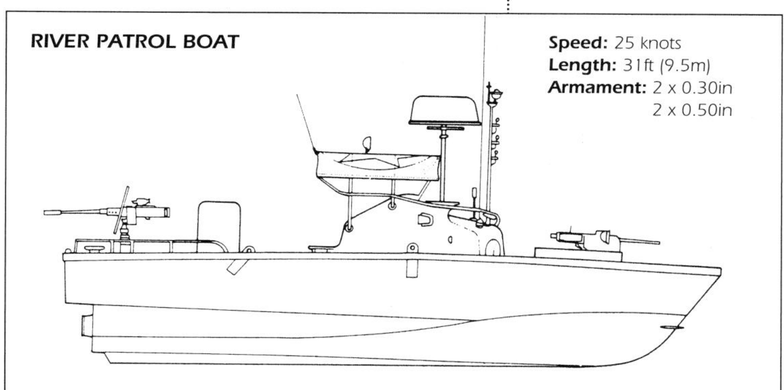

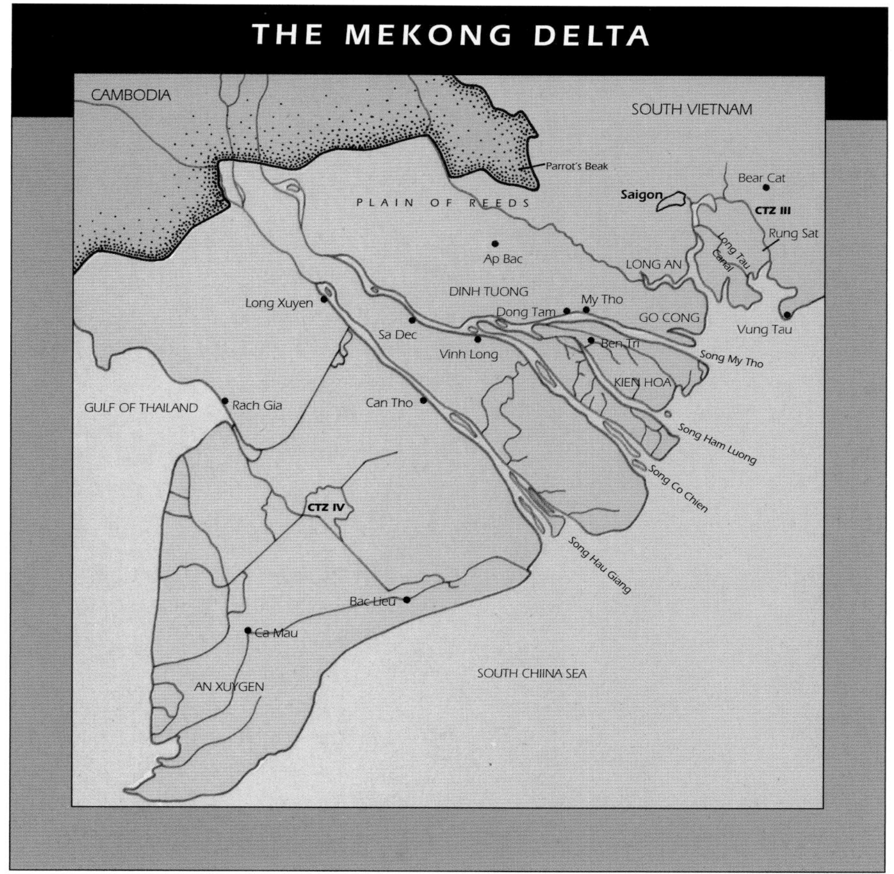

Special river patrol forces were established in Vietnam from the time of the French Indochina conflict, and by 1965 the navy of South Vietnam had built up an offensive-capable river patrol force with in excess of 200 combat boats.

numbers. There were simply not enough PBRs to do the job. Although VC supplies doubtlessly still got through, the results of the river patrols were encouraging. In 1967 alone sailors boarded 400,000 vessels for inspection. As a result the RPF destroyed over 2000 enemy vessels and killed, wounded or captured over 1300 VC – all at a cost of only 39 American lives.

In addition to its patrols, Operation Game Warden sent minesweepers into the rivers near Saigon to clear the area of the seemingly constantly replenished enemy mines. A troublespot was the Rung Sat Special Zone, a tidal mangrove swamp at the entrance of the waterway that led to Saigon. The VC used this inhospitable area to launch attacks on river shipping. In March 1966 US forces, including PBRs, monitor gunboats, helicopter detachments, SEAL Teams and infantry, invaded the VC sanctuary there. The massive 'Search and Destroy' mission resulted in the destruction of several VC base areas and the deaths of some 69 guerrillas. The enemy was soon back in force, though, once again mining the waters and harassing shipping with small arms and recoilless rifle fire. The problem necessitated a more permanent solution.

ABOVE: A MONITOR GUNBOAT FIRES 40MM CANNON SHELLS DURING AN ACTION IN THE MEKONG DELTA, 1967.

BELOW: A US NAVY SEAL TEAM EMBARKS ON A MISSION DEEP INTO VIETCONG TERRITORY.

THE MOBILE RIVERINE FORCE

In an effort to locate and destroy the Vietcong in the Mekong Delta the United States formed the joint army-navy Mobile Riverine Force (MRF). The naval component was called the Riverine Assault Force and provided a mobile floating base for troops. In addition the US Navy provided fire-support through the use of monitors. These armoured vessels bristled with armaments, including 0.50in, 40mm and 20mm gun mounts, two 40mm grenade launchers and a powerful 81mm mortar. The Riverine Assault Force also carried the soldiers into battle using converted landing craft called Armored Troop Carriers (ATC). These craft also carried considerable firepower, including a 0.50in calibre machine-gun, grenade launchers and a 20mm cannon. Some of the ATCs also carried flame-throwers or water cannon for use against enemy bunker complexes. Both US Navy and US Air Force fliers provided the ground missions with air support.

The 9th Infantry Division, recently arrived from the United States, provided its 2nd Brigade and later its 3rd

The Mobile Riverine Force was the product of a shift from stop-and-search operations to a naval version of 'Search and Destroy'. Thus the designers set to work creating a new breed of fast, heavily armed combat craft.

LEFT: US SOLDIERS USE THEIR M16S TO RETURN FIRE FROM THE AREA OF THE SHORELINE. CAUTION ABOUT USING HEAVY WEAPONS WAS SOMETIMES REQUIRED IN THE MORE POPULATED AREAS.

BELOW: A PBR CREW SCANS THE RIVERBANK FOR VIETCONG ACTIVITY.

Brigade to form the ground component of the Mobile Riverine Force. Soldiers began to arrive in the area in spring 1967. These men were often housed on floating base ships, or sometimes in the new divisional headquarters at Dong Tam. Even the creation of the base camp was a massive undertaking, for it was built on a sea of mud dredged out of the Mekong Delta by the largest dredging machines in existence. The 9th Infantry Division, besides providing the ground personnel, also provided artillery support for the riverine war by the use of batteries set up on pontoons floating in the rivers.

STRUGGLE IN THE DELTA

The Mobile Riverine Force found itself involved in bitter struggles against the Vietcong's 263rd and 514th Main Force battalions. The delta was a strong centre of VC support and was vital to its logistic system. ARVN units in the area had never challenged for control, knowing that the VC would fight tenaciously for such an important region. Once construction started on the base at Dong Tam the Vietcong realized that US forces, however, were about to challenge them for control and set about preparing the battlefield to its advantage. The communist forces prepared defensive bunker complexes throughout the region and peppered the area with lethal booby traps. The VC would attempt to discern the direction of a coming American sweep and would then occupy the appropriate bunkers and wait. Sometimes the determined Vietcong waited for days in water up to their necks in their muddy holes just for an American unit to stumble

into an ambush. The VC would hold their fire until the Americans were within a few yards in an attempt to neutralize American air and artillery support. Once they had inflicted as many losses upon the US forces as possible the VC would flee to fight another day.

The men of the 9th Infantry Division quickly developed tactics to deal with the ambush-style warfare practised by the VC in the delta. The Americans were usually landed by ATCs and would run three-day 'Search and Destroy' missions with night ambushes. Generally the Americans kept to the rice paddies to avoid the danger of mines on the dikes. Since each rice paddy dike was a potential VC bunker complex, US troop movement was slow. Upon approaching each dike US forces would send forward a three-man squad to check for the enemy. If the VC were there the lives of the three men were often forfeit and the remaining infantry, who had remained outside the killing zone, could flank the bunkers and call in air strikes. If the three men made it to the dike safely, the advance could continue and another three men were sent to check the next dike, and so it went.

The Mobile Riverine Force fought major battles with the Vietcong in June and July 1967, resulting in over 300 Vietcong fatalities. In addition the soldiers made their way into the Rung Sat to destroy additional enemy bases and supply dumps. The victories were fleeting, though, for the Vietcong still controlled much of the area and received ample help from the peasant population. In September 1967 the VC struck back and ambushed a US Navy convoy southwest of Saigon, damaging over half of the ships and causing more than 80 US casualties. The VC again ambushed a convoy on the Ruong Canal in December 1967, but this time the Mobile Riverine Force was ready. During the heated one-day battle ATCs fought their way through the VC fire and landed soldiers of the 9th Infantry Division on the flanks of the bunker complex. Having compromised the enemy position the MRF went on to win one of its most significant victories by charging the positions and killing nearly 270 Vietcong fighters.

Below: An Armored Troop Carrier's (ATC) firepower included a 20mm cannon, two 0.50in calibre machine-guns and two 0.30in calibre machine-guns.

Above: A French-built South Vietnamese Navy command boat moves through Vietcong-held territory in late 1967.

Stuck out in the middle of a river, bordered by potentially enemy-held riverbanks, a river patrol unit often had to rely on the speed of the boat to put everyone quickly out of the range of any small arms fire.

LEFT: A 7.62MM M60 MACHINE-GUN IS TRAINED ON A DISTANT RIVERBANK IN READINESS FOR ACTION. RIVER PATROLS WERE AS TENSE AND NERVE-WRACKING AS THOSE CONDUCTED IN THE JUNGLE, PERHAPS MORE SO FOR THE MEKONG DELTA WAS HEAVILY POPULATED AND IDENTIFYING FRIEND FROM FOE WAS DIFFICULT.

TET

Throughout Vietnam in 1967 the Vietcong was conserving its strength by avoiding battle and readying itself for the massive Tet Offensive. The same was true in the Mekong Delta. US forces had won several attritional victories, but the scale of the Tet Offensive in the Mekong demonstrates that the US effort had done little to cut enemy supply lines or weaken the enemy in terms of numbers. The offensive caught US and South Vietnamese forces in the delta by surprise. Communist forces attacked and attempted to over-run several important delta cities, including My Tho, Ben Tri and Can Tho. The VC attacks met with fantastic initial success, seizing several important population centres and forcing a crisis upon the American command system in the Mekong Delta.

The speed of the PBRs allowed them to rush to afflicted areas to add their firepower to the defensive efforts. In many ways the patrol boat units were able to make US and South Vietnamese defensive stands in several delta cities successful. Even more importantly, the men of the 9th Infantry Division saved many important places in the delta from disaster. The mobility and strength of the MRF made it the 'fire brigade' in the region, and its actions earned it the Presidential Unit Citation. First the men of the MRF had to battle house by house through the streets of enemy-held My Tho. Having triumphed, the MRF then shifted its rescue effort to Vinh Long, where it battled and defeated some three Vietcong battalions. Finally the MRF had to face Vietcong forces that had encircled

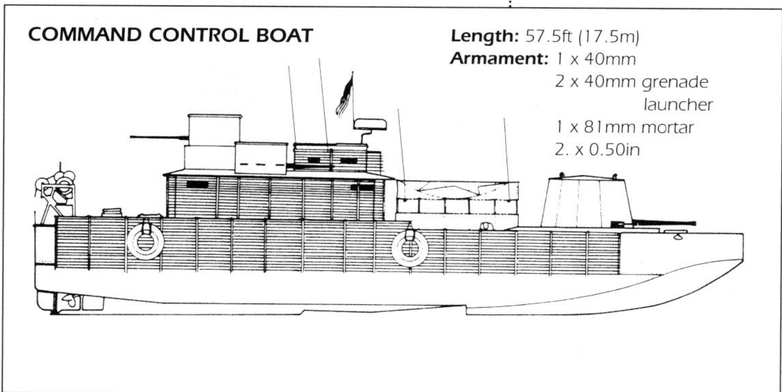

Fording a river.

FIGHTING CONDITIONS IN THE MEKONG DELTA

The Mekong Delta is a flat wilderness of meandering waterways and countless million rice paddies. The war fought in this area of water and mud was dominated by the terrain. US Navy personnel and men of the 9th Infantry Division had to learn to operate in this uniquely hostile environment. In addition the delta is a densely populated area and this placed limits on the usage of firepower for fear of civilian deaths. The Vietcong had a strong presence in the area for many years before US infantry arrived in 1967, and the insurgents had put their time to good use, converting huge numbers of rice paddy dikes into bunker complexes and placing mines and booby traps throughout the area. Infantry could not walk on the dikes themselves for fear of mines, and usually operated in the water-filled paddies. With no cover the infantry had to approach each dike as if the enemy were there in bunkers ready to fight; one slip of concentration could result in a unit being pinned down in the water by enemy fire and wiped out. And in the water lurked mines, snakes and leeches. Men wounded in battle in these conditions required instant medevac, for human waste was used as fertilizer and caused any wounds to go septic very quickly. Conditions were even worse in the Rung Sat Special Zone which guarded the main waterway into Saigon. Troops operating in this area were often in water up to their necks. The conditions in the Mekong Delta were so daunting that even if a unit took no casualties it had to be removed from the field after only three days. Any longer and soldiers would start to become casualties due to the constant immersion of their feet in the polluted water.

the delta's most important city, Can Tho. The MRF had moved from crisis zone to crisis zone and in nearly a month of solid fighting had defeated the Vietcong at every turn. Its actions in the Mekong, though, do not tell the entire story. Elements of the River Patrol Force were called north to aid in the fighting around Hue. These units helped to keep the vital Perfume River open to US traffic during Tet. In the Mekong Delta the MRF alone killed over 1000 Vietcong during the struggles that made up the offensive. These losses, added to others suffered throughout South Vietnam, dealt the VC a crippling blow and helped enable US forces to take the offensive themselves in 1969.

As the Americans and South Vietnamese prepared to press their advantage, the Vietcong launched a series of mini-Tet Offensives in the delta region. Attacks on the cities of Cai Lay and Saigon were both blunted by massive 9th Infantry Division counter-attacks which resulted in some 700 enemy casualties. During July and August 1968 the MRF pursued the defeated enemy throughout the Mekong Delta, winning a series of victories that pushed the VC ever closer to their bases in Cambodia. A testament to the changing fortunes in the delta war was a US incursion into the U Minh Forest. This nearly impenetrable swamp had long been an uncontested Vietcong stronghold, for it lay so far to the south that US and South Vietnamese forces dared not enter. However, the weakening of Vietcong power in the region made an attack there possible. In fierce fighting US forces caused several hundred enemy casualties and did a great deal of damage to the VC's local infrastructure. Although the U Minh Forest would remain a VC stronghold, the allied incursion indicated how the tide of war had turned in the Mekong Delta.

LEFT: US GROUND TROOPS ENTER THE WATERLOGGED TERRAIN OF THE RUNG SAT ZONE. TROPICAL DISEASES AND ENEMY AMBUSHES WERE EVER-PRESENT DANGERS IN SUCH REGIONS.

BELOW: SOLDIERS FROM SOUTH VIETNAM SINK UP TO THE WAIST IN THICK MUD WHILE BRINGING IN A BOAT. SUCH CONDITIONS MADE CLOTHES ROT QUICKLY AND INFECTED ANY WOUNDS.

SEALORDS

In the wake of the Tet victory General Westmoreland was anxious to press the American advantage in the war and pursue and harass the defeated enemy. In the Mekong Delta this strategy took the form of the programme known by the acronym SEALORDS – Southeast Asia Lake, Ocean, River and Delta Strategy. The ambitious offensive plan called for US and South Vietnamese naval and ground forces to cut enemy supply lines from Cambodia and to destroy their base camps deep in the jungle. There was a fundamental change in the structure of the riverine forces, though – US military strategists believed that the 9th Infantry Division would be better used if it were no longer attached to the MRF. For that reason, in June 1969 the 9th Infantry Division left the MRF, meaning that SEALORDS would be much more of a traditional naval operation and ground forces would be co-opted when needed.

In 1969 the American and South Vietnamese naval forces were at the height of their strength in the Mekong Delta. At this time the River Patrol Force numbered some 258 patrol and minesweeping boats, and the 3700-man Riverine Assault Force (which would now handle many of the ground duties) possessed 184 monitors and transports. A squadron of 25 armed helicopters and 15 fixed-wing aircraft augmented the force. In

OPPOSITE BOTTOM: TOTAL FIREPOWER. JUST THE STERN OF THIS PATROL BOAT CONTAINS SUFFICIENT WEAPONRY TO DEVASTATE A SWEEP OF SHORELINE; ARMAMENTS INCLUDE 40MM GRENADE LAUNCHERS, A BROWNING 0.50IN CALIBRE MACHINE-GUN AND M60 MACHINE-GUN.

US tactics in the Mekong Delta became increasingly successful, especially after the Tet Offensive. During the SEALORDS operations, any VC unit which decided to ambush a river patrol would be faced by ruthless navy, infantry and helicopter counter-measures.

RIGHT: A PATROL AIR CUSHION VEHICLE (PACV). THESE VERSATILE MACHINES, KNOWN AS THE 'SHARK-MOUTHED RAIDER', BLURRED THE LINES BETWEEN LAND AND RIVER BY BEING ABLE TO PURSUE AN ATTACK IN SWAMPLAND AND PADDY FIELD WITH MULTIPLE MACHINE-GUNS AND GRENADE LAUNCHER.

addition five SEAL teams worked with it. To this powerful armada South Vietnam's navy added some 655 assault craft and patrol boats. All other operations in the Mekong took second place when SEALORDS became effective in late October 1968.

In the first phase allied forces established patrols and electronic barriers on waterways parallelling the border with Cambodia. This operation called for the opening of canals from the Gulf of Thailand to the Mekong River that were deep inside Vietcong-controlled areas, and were vital to the communists' logistic system. Patrols had never ranged so far from US bases before, but, luckily, organized resistance was light. The same cannot be said of operations north and west of Saigon. Here US and South Vietnamese naval forces moved up the Co Tay River in an effort to interdict supplies coming from the pivotal 'Parrot's Beak' section of Cambodia. Such a move would disrupt the communists' supply route to the areas near Saigon and into the Plain of Reeds. The Vietcong fought back by mining the rivers and ambushing patrol boats, but US forces were employing a new, effective strategy that kept losses to a minimum. The patrols were powerful, all-arms units. The PBRs were augmented by the firepower of monitors, and most patrols had ATCs along with an infantry component capable of dealing with most Vietcong attacks. Finally attack helicopters circled overhead waiting to pounce upon any enemy guerrillas as soon as they showed themselves. These naval units were fast moving, powerful and able to respond to almost any threat. The weakened Vietcong dared not attack such patrols very often for fear of heavy losses. By early 1969, then, the MRF had managed to

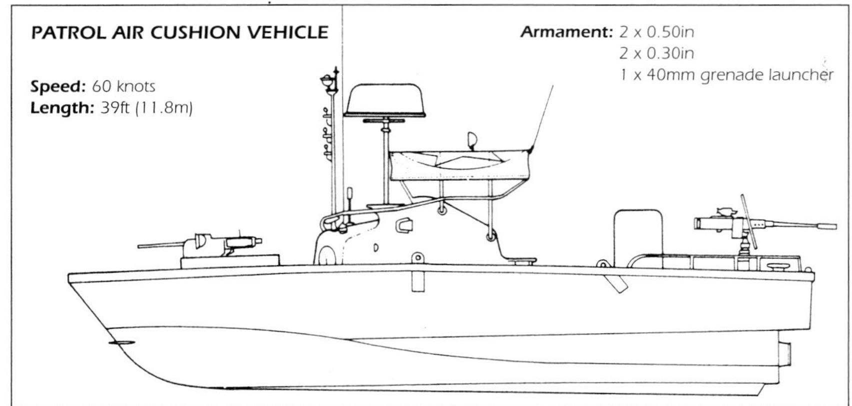

implement a very effective supply interdiction barrier from north of Saigon to the Gulf of Thailand.

After the successful interdiction effort allied forces struck the Vietcong in their sanctuaries of the U Minh Forest and the Ca Mau peninsula. These remote areas had no South Vietnamese governmental presence and served as vital Vietcong territories and base areas. From 7 to 18 April, sea, air and ground forces struck the Vietcong strongholds in a massive operation dubbed Silver Mace II. The Vietcong, true to form, avoided contact with the superior firepower of the MRF, but lost valuable bases. In addition South Vietnamese forces established a permanent presence in the area for the first time. No longer would the remote southern reaches of the Mekong Delta remain an uncontested Vietcong-held area.

SEALORDS, in just under a year of operation, had placed tremendous pressure on the Vietcong in the delta. Communist supplies and reinforcements fell dramatically. Its base areas were no longer secure and allied forces for the first time remained behind to contest control of the area with it when its forces resurfaced. Communist losses to the new style of naval warfare were staggering. Over 500 tons of vital supplies had been lost; in addition some 3000 communist soldiers were killed and 300 were captured. Against this total US and South Vietnamese forces involved in the campaign lost but 186 killed and 1450 wounded. The United States and South Vietnam seemed to be winning the delta war.

ABOVE: THE RIVERBANK BURNS AFTER COMING UNDER ATTACK FROM A RIVERINE ASSAULT FORCE.

LEFT: US NAVY SEALS GO INTO ACTION FROM THEIR ASSAULT RIVER PATROL BOAT (ASPB), 50 MILES (80KM) SOUTH OF SAIGON. DURING THIS RAID AGAINST AN ENEMY BASE, 40 OR 50 BUNKERS WERE DESTROYED AND 51 VIETCONG TAKEN PRISONER.

US NAVY SEALS

The US Navy SEALS derive their name from their environs of operation: 'SEa, Air or Land'. They were formed in 1962 at President Kennedy's direction to provide an elite amphibious and infiltration force for use in covert or deep-penetration missions. Skilled in all the various aspects of counter-insurgency, these highly motivated navy commandos operated in completely self-dependent units which could remain isolated in enemy terrain for days, only to appear suddenly to apply maximum destructive force to a Vietcong unit or base.

The 211-man SEAL Team 1 was based at Coronado, California, and fielded 12 14-man platoons. At any given time usually five of these platoons were in South Vietnam from 1966 onwards. Three of them were normally based at Nha Be and worked with other units in the riverine war as Detachment Golf. In early 1967 SEAL Team 2 became active and fielded platoons at Can Tho. Although active throughout Vietnam, much SEAL work took place in the Mekong Delta where their dextrous handling of riverine patrol boats and first-class combat skills made them ideal for clandestine surveillance and intelligence-gathering operations or aggressive reconnaissance. They fought the enemy relentlessly in a light, mobile war utilizing surprise and speed to great effect.

A SEAL TEAM WITH A SOUTH VIETNAMESE PRU.

The SEALS took on almost any kind of mission, including day and night ambushes, soundlessly beaching their rubber boats on riverbanks near VC strongpoints. The SEALS, almost invisible in their face paint and camouflage, struck terror into the hearts of their enemies. In Operation Bold Dragon III in September 1967, for example, SEAL units attacked a VC bunker base on Tanh Ding Island, entirely destroying it and an arms production plant with demolition charges. Many southern operations were conducted alongside South Vietnam's Provincial Reconnaissance Units (PRUs), specially selected groups of Vietnamese counter-terrorist soldiers drawn from sources which ranged from ARVN troops to military prisoners.

Other operations included the elimination of VC 'tax inspectors', the underwater recovery of the bodies of US aircrew, and even, it is believed, operations within Haiphong harbour in North Vietnam itself. Some of the most ambitious SEAL missions were POW rescue attempts. Several times SEAL teams broke into highly secret and heavily guarded VC base camps in attempts to free American POWs. However, they were never able to locate American POWs, although the SEALS did succeed in liberating nearly 50 ARVN POWs. The mobile and versatile US Navy SEALS, in part due to their unbroken string of success in Vietnam, still form an elite quick strike unit within the United States armed forces.

Night-time was one of the most dangerous periods of operation for river forces. While two-craft units moved in the daytime, at night six boats would work in a pack over their 12–14 hour patrol.

INTO CAMBODIA

The incursion into Cambodia by US and South Vietnamese troops in April 1970 offered SEALORDS a wonderful opportunity. On 9 May, after the incursion had given ground forces over a week to drive off any major enemy units, a combined US-Vietnamese flotilla entered Cambodia bound for Phnom Penh. Along the way the naval force destroyed all communist-owned craft and thus seized control of the upper reaches of the Mekong River from the communists. The task force numbered over fifty ships, including Patrol Boats, Attack Boats and Strike Assault Boats. Once again naval airpower circled overhead and South Vietnamese marines provided ground punch. By the end of the first day of the operation South Vietnamese forces had seized control of the river all the way to Phnom Penh. Further south US and South Vietnamese forces launched a combined

LEFT: A DETACHMENT OF THE MRF DISEMBARKS RAPIDLY DURING AN AMPHIBIOUS LANDING ALONG THE MY THO RIVER ON 26 SEPTEMBER 1967.

BELOW LEFT: A US NAVY UNDERWATER DEMOLITION TEAM SOLDIER PREPARES A DEMOLITION CHARGE ON A VIETCONG BUNKER.

BELOW: US NAVY SEALS GET HELI-INSERTED FURTHER INLAND PRIOR TO SETTING UP AN AMBUSH POINT FOR UNWARY VIETCONG.

assault on Neak Luong, a strategic communist transit point along the waterway. US forces, operating under political restrictions, were not allowed past Neak Luong and had to exit Cambodia by 29 June. The South Vietnamese, though, remained behind on this most important of rivers to continue to interdict supplies at their source. In addition the South Vietnamese began an evacuation effort that removed several thousand ethnic Vietnamese from Cambodia. Like the Cambodian incursion in general, the naval operation was very effective in seriously disrupting the communists' supply efforts and base camps. Along with the overall success of SEALORDS, then, the Cambodian incursion left the South Vietnamese in a very strong military position in the Mekong Delta and the United States felt able to increase the speed of its withdrawal from the Vietnam War.

The successes of the 'Brown Water Navy' brought large tracts of South Vietnam out from Vietcong control and into the hands of US and local South Vietnamese forces, the latter gaining valuable riverine experience as the US began to pull its units out.

RIGHT: CAPTURED VIETCONG ARE ESCORTED AWAY BY MRF UNITS, LUCKY NOT TO BE AMONG THE HUGE VC DEATH TOLL INFLICTED BY THE RIVERINE FORCES.

VIETNAMIZATION

Even before the Cambodian incursion, the Vietnamization policy of President Richard Nixon began to affect the war in the Mekong Delta. As a result the US Navy implemented the process it termed ACTOV (Accelerated Turnover to the Vietnamese) in early 1969. As the US Navy withdrew its men from the theatre it turned over control of the riverine fleet and its logistic establishment to the South Vietnamese navy. US forces, though, realized that the South Vietnamese, many of whom were raw recruits raised by a recent military expansion, needed a great deal of training to operate and service the American equipment. In addition, though the South's navy had performed admirably in the Cambodia incursion, neither its morale nor its leadership skills were very high. Thus the Naval Advisory Group sought to train the South Vietnamese to take over the riverine war for themselves. At first the naval personnel were integrated into the crews of American ships for training, and once the South Vietnamese crew was sufficiently trained the US crew rotated home. In this way hundreds of ships, and eventually all of the riverine operations, were slowly turned over to the control of the South Vietnamese.

BELOW: A US SOLDIER OF RIVER DIVISION 51 FIRES A FLAMING ARROW INTO A FORTIFIED VIETCONG BUNKER ALONG THE BASSAC RIVER.

In early 1970 the US withdrawal necessitated the turnover of most of the interdiction campaign in the Mekong Delta to the South Vietnamese. In addition a combined US-South

Vietnamese naval force launched Operation Blue Shark, the last significant operation undertaken at least in part by US forces in the delta. Blue Shark was an attack operation designed to destroy or disrupt the remaining VC infrastructure in the mangrove swamps at the mouth of the Mekong River and along the islands upriver towards Cambodia. The lightning raids, augmented by deadly attacks carried out by SEAL teams, often caught the normally vigilant Vietcong by surprise and did great damage to the communists remaining supply and command network.

By April 1971 the role of the US Navy in SEALORDS had ended, leaving the South Vietnamese in charge of the effort to control Vietcong supply efforts in the delta. From a high of over 38,000 personnel, the US naval presence in and around South Vietnam had fallen to less than 15,000. Also in early 1971 the US Navy transferred the last of its riverine force, some 293 PBRs and 225 assault craft to the Vietnamese. The number of personnel in the South's navy had risen dramatically to make good the process of Vietnamization, from only 18,000 in 1968 to 32,000 at the beginning of 1971.

In addition the US Navy turned over most of its major riverine bases to the South Vietnamese. Some American naval aircraft units and SEAL teams remained behind to aid the South Vietnamese in their continuing efforts to police the Mekong Delta, but by 1971 the riverine war had in the main passed to the South Vietnamese. In fact the Mobile Riverine Force and the Riverine Assault Force were the first two major US commands deactivated through Vietnamization.

BELOW: ARMORED TROOP CARRIERS (ATCS) DOCK ALONGSIDE A SUPPORT SHIP FOR REPAIR AND RESUPPLY ON THE SOI RAP RIVER. RIVERINE OPERATIONS REQUIRED SMOOTH LOGISTICAL BACKING TO MAINTAIN THE REGULAR PATROLS.

LEFT: A RIVER PATROL PASSES A CIVILIAN BOAT NEAR THE CITY OF CA MAU. FOR PACIFICATION TO BE EFFECTIVE, IT WAS VERY IMPORTANT THAT THE PATROLLING TROOPS DID NOT DISRUPT THE NATURAL LIFE OF THE RIVER FOR LOCAL CIVILIANS. CURFEWS WERE OFTEN PUT IN PLACE AND THE RIVERS PURSUED MORE AGGRESSIVELY DURING THE NIGHT-TIME HOURS.

RIGHT: A PATROL AIR CUSHION VEHICLE (PACV) CUTS ACROSS MARSHLAND AND DEMONSTRATES OFF-RIVER CAPABILITIES OF USE IN PURSUIT OPERATIONS.

BELOW: A COBRA GUNSHIP PULLS AWAY AFTER ROCKETING A VIETCONG POSITION IN THE MEKONG.

The efforts of the US Navy and the 9th Infantry Division can be judged among the most successful during the entire American involvement in the Vietnam War. Before the advent of the River Patrol Force and the Mobile Riverine Force the Mekong Delta had been an area of uncontested Vietcong control. ARVN forces did not enter the area, and much of the local population favoured the communists. By 1969, though, its control over much of the area had been shattered. The losses that the Vietcong had suffered kept the Mekong Delta rather quiet, and certainly ended the threat to

RIGHT: AN RPB OF US NAVY RIVER DIVISION 514 TRANSPORTS MEMBERS OF THE SOUTH VIETNAMESE FORCES ALONG THE VINH TE CANAL EN ROUTE TO SETTING A NIGHT AMBUSH IN OCTOBER 1969. BY THAT POINT A PRIORITY OF US NAVAL FORCES WAS TO TRAIN UP LOCAL TROOPS READY TO TAKE OVER.

A UH-1 HELICOPTER LAUNCHES A ROCKET ATTACK.

THE BATTLE OF 19 JUNE 1967

One of the worst battles faced by US forces in the Mekong Delta was that encountered by the 2nd Brigade of the 9th Infantry Division on 19 June 1967. US intelligence had located elements of the VC's 5th Nha Be Battalion and the 263rd Main Force Battalion. The US 2nd Brigade was sent to investigate. As the US forces slowly made their way through rice paddies and towards the enemy, they found themselves caught in the open, having walked into a 'U'-shaped ambush. Enemy forces had allowed the Americans to approach to within a few yards before they opened fire. Small arms and three 0.50in calibre machine-guns opened up on 'A' Company from point-blank range, causing nearly 80 per cent casualties within minutes. The company was pinned down and had no retreat. Nearby 'C' Company then found itself under attack and pinned down as well, unable to go to the aid of 'A' Company. US forces worked quickly to call in supporting fire from artillery and US Navy gunboats. As the situation worsened the codeword 'Broken Arrow' went out. This meant that an American unit was being over-run and every combat aircraft in the area had to come to its aid. Air strikes pummelled the VC positions, but they were impervious to all but a direct hit. During the melee a few brave medevac pilots attempted to remove wounded from the 'C' Company area, but were shot out of the sky. Under cover of bombing and artillery fire the men of 'C' Company eventually made their way to the bunker complex. They knew that the air strikes would not drive the VC away, it would require an infantry frontal assault on the bunkers themselves. Reminiscent of World War I the men charged forward and gained the top of the bunker complex. Everywhere the VC emerged from their underground bunkers and spiderholes, but they were now in the open and American forces gunned them down. In the battle some 255 Vietcong and 75 Americans were killed and 150 Americans were wounded. As usual, after the battle US forces returned to their base and the Vietcong returned to the area to wait for the Americans once again.

Saigon from that area. In the final analysis the communists would have to advance on Saigon from the north in a traditional land assault. In the last campaign of the war South Vietnam's President Thieu relinquished control of the north of his country, envisaging Saigon and the Mekong Delta as the place where he and his loyal forces could hold out indefinitely. For by then the delta had been transformed from a threatening, enemy-held area to a secure, government-controlled one through the efforts of the riverine forces.

CHAPTER 8

The Tet Offensive

A TEAM OF US SOLDIERS CARRY AN M40A1 160MM RECOILLESS RIFLE INTO ACTION DURING THE TET OFFENSIVE. TET WOULD SIGNAL THE BEGINNING OF THE END OF US INVOLVEMENT IN THE VIETNAM WAR, DESPITE THE US INFLICTING A HUGE DEFEAT ON THE COMMUNIST FORCES.

Tet was meant to be a time of holiday and celebration. With many South Vietnamese troops on leave and security at its slackest, North Vietnam chose this as the ideal moment to invade.

By 1968 the communists had accrued such losses in the Vietnam War that they were willing to gamble everything on a massive offensive designed to end the war. The goal of the Tet Offensive was to launch a surprise attack on the urban areas of South Vietnam, hopefully sparking an uprising that would force the United States to exit the conflict. Although the series of attacks met with some initial success, the Vietcong actually suffered a debilitating countrywide defeat at the hands of superior US firepower. The defeat, though, eventually turned into victory, for this most important event of the Vietnam War caused American resolve to crumble.

By late 1967 the Vietnam War had reached a turning point. For over two years United States forces had been involved in battles designed to 'find, fix and finish' Vietcong and North Vietnamese forces. These battles had achieved a high 'body count' and both President Johnson and General Westmoreland truly believed that the US was winning the war. However, there were cracks beginning to appear in the American body politic. From the campuses of California to Washington, D.C., anti-war protests became more numerous and more violent, and the public watched the growing spectacle of divisiveness on their television newscasts nightly. The protests and their attendant media coverage were of great concern for Johnson, and he decided to retaliate by launching a publicity campaign to allay American fears about the war. Towards this end Johnson called upon several trusted officials, including ex-presidents Truman and Eisenhower, to endorse his actions in Vietnam. Johnson even enlisted Westmoreland himself to assure the nation that the United States was indeed winning the war. Westmoreland played his role with alacrity, assuring his fellow citizens that the end of the war was within sight. Indeed he claimed that the battles of attrition had so weakened the enemy that North Vietnam would be unable to launch any significant military operations in the coming year. Once again the administration had promised its people a victorious war. However, like so many promises made during the conflict, it was a hollow one. The truth of the matter would nearly rend the divided nation asunder.

BELOW: US ARMOURED PERSONNEL CARRIERS OF THE 173RD AIRBORNE BRIGADE CONDUCT A SEARCH OF PHU LOC VILLAGE IN MAY 1968, ON THE HUNT FOR NVA SOLDIERS IN THE AFTERMATH OF THE TET OFFENSIVE.

LEFT: A VIETCONG SUSPECT IS QUESTIONED BY US INFANTRY DURING A SWEEP OPERATION. THE TET OFFENSIVE WAS A TERRIBLE TIME FOR THE VIETCONG, SLASHING ITS NUMBERS AND LEAVING IT MASSIVELY WEAKENED AS A MILITARY FORCE.

BELOW: US AIRBORNE SOLDIERS WITH M16 AND M60 WEAPONS ENGAGE NVA SOLDIERS IN A FIREFIGHT NORTH OF PHU BAI.

While the United States dealt with issues of internal unity, the North Vietnamese had reached their own turning point of sorts. The battles of attrition had indeed cost the Vietcong and the North as a whole a heavy price. The losses had been so devastating that Ho and Giap despaired of the ability of their nation to see the war through to ultimate victory. As a result Giap and the North Vietnamese leadership decided to eschew the ideal of protracted war and to gamble on a single, great military victory in 1968. Giap, though, realized that the US retained the edge in firepower, and still hoped to avoid a pitched battle. In the finest revolutionary tradition, the Northern leadership believed that a grand military assault against the imperialist

TUNNEL WAR

The Vietcong constructed tunnel systems both to avoid contact with American forces and to launch surprise assaults against them. Vast underground complexes covering hundreds of miles reached from Saigon to the border with Cambodia. The Cu Chi district, some 25 miles (40km) from Saigon, contained the most extensive systems in South Vietnam – over 100 miles (160km) of tunnels connected most villages and contained storage areas, training sites and even hospitals. The tiny, dark tunnels themselves were too small to allow entry for most Americans. Thus emerged the 'Tunnel Rat' – slim soldiers armed only with a pistol and a flashlight whose job it was to confront the Vietcong in its subterranean hideaways. The Vietcong defended its territory well with booby traps, including poisonous snakes and spiders. A favourite defensive tactic was to wait in an alcove and while the American lowered himself into the tunnel, fire one shot into his groin. It would take the remaining Americans several minutes to extricate the wounded soldier, allowing the defender to flee and exit the system using camouflaged, secret tunnel openings/exits. In the tunnels of Cu Chi the communists planned for the Tet Offensive and gathered troops for the assault on Saigon. Without its hidden mazes below ground it is doubtful that the Vietcong would have been able to attack Saigon in any meaningful way in 1968. For their part the Americans did all they could to destroy the networks. The use of 'Tunnel Rats', though important until the end of the war, only helped destroy the occupants and not the tunnels themselves. Several Boeing B-52 raids struck the Cu Chi area, but the tunnels and their inhabitants proved resilient and the Vietcong threat remained. Finally the United States resorted to a wholesale destruction of the Cu Chi district to eliminate the threat. Massive Rome Plows were used to destroy the forests in the area and to bulldoze over the numerous tunnel entrances and exits, entombing any defenders inside them.

STRONG NERVES WERE REQUIRED WHEN OPERATING UNDERGROUND.

RIGHT: THE TET OFFENSIVE SAW OVER 1000 US SOLDIERS AND OVER 2500 ARVN SOLDIERS KILLED IN ACTION. HERE THREE US MILITARY POLICE DEFEND THEIR POSITIONS AT THE ENTRANCE TO THE US EMBASSY IN SAIGON, NEXT TO THE BODIES OF TWO US SOLDIERS.

oppressor would spur a popular uprising against which US firepower could not compete. Even if the uprising failed to materialize it was hoped that South Vietnamese morale would crumble and that the United States would rethink its involvement in a war of rising cost. The detailed planning for the offensive was left to General Pham Hung.

LEFT: ARVN RANGER SOLDIERS FIRE AT VIETCONG POSITIONS AROUND SAIGON DURING TET. THE VC HOPED – BUT WERE TO BE DISAPPOINTED – THAT SOUTH VIETNAM'S CIVILIANS WOULD OVERTHROW THEIR GOVERNMENT DURING THE OFFENSIVE.

THE PLAN FOR TET

The preparatory phase of the great offensive began in 1967. During that year NVA and Vietcong attacks lured US forces deep into the countryside, leaving the defence of the cities in the hands of the less capable ARVN. Operations around Dak To and Khe Sanh formed part of this vast diversion (see pages 68–71). With the Americans gone, General Hung hoped to launch a rapid attack against light ARVN resistance and seize control of cities all across South Vietnam. A general, people's uprising would then occur before US forces could react in time.

The second phase of the operation was fraught with danger. Nearly 84,000 NVA and VC forces had to make their way to staging areas near the South's major cities, the heart of American control. The soldiers utilized tunnel networks, jungle trails and winding rivers to inch towards their objectives. If the movement of such forces was discovered, superior US firepower could destroy the offensive before it began. Although the US command noticed increased activity along the Ho Chi Minh Trail and were wary of a coming battle, they remained ignorant of the overall plan. The result was a logistical and intelligence miracle. Using only their feet and their wits the VC and NVA had gathered their forces and stood ready to launch a surprise assault on every major city in South Vietnam.

The attack itself was to take place when the South Vietnamese and US forces least expected it – the Tet Lunar New Year. This most important Vietnamese holiday was an occasion for a celebratory ceasefire. The ARVN had sent many of its soldiers home to

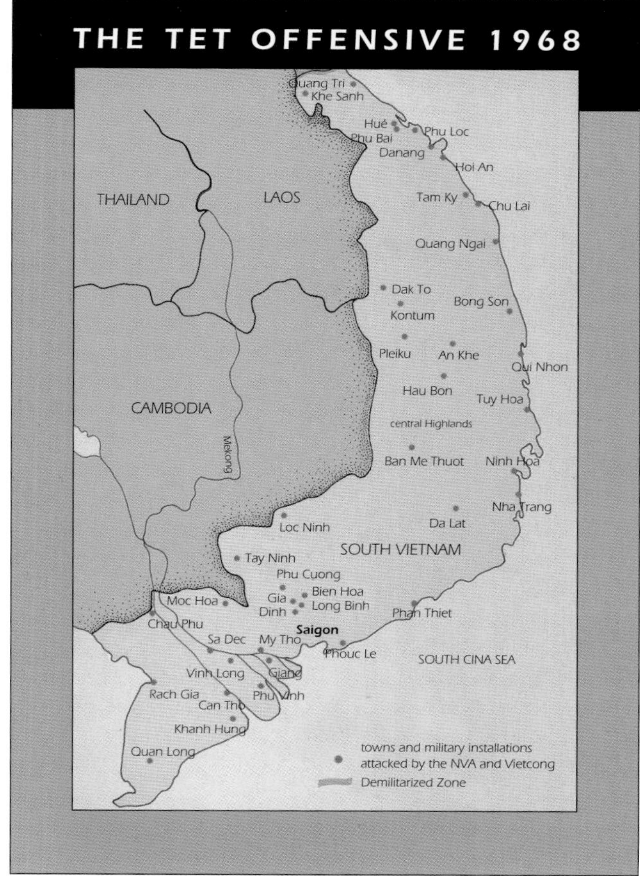

The entire length of South Vietnam was engulfed by the NVA attacks during Tet, reaching from Quang Tri in the far north to Quan Long near the southern tip.

RIGHT: US AMBASSADOR ELLSWORTH BUNKER IS SHOWN THE AFTERMATH OF THE EMBASSY ATTACK.

BELOW: ONE OF THE MANY VIETCONG DEAD WHO LITTERED THE GROUNDS OF THE US EMBASSY.

enjoy it. US commanders, though they expected something, thought that any major enemy assault would take place at the US Marine base at Khe Sanh. The NVA had been massing forces around that isolated base for some time, and both Westmoreland and Johnson feared that Giap would try to achieve a great victory there just as he had at Dien Bien Phu against the French. No one in the US command structure expected urban assaults of the magnitude of the Tet Offensive. The world's great superpower had been tricked.

THE ATTACK ON SAIGON

Early on the morning of 30 January 1968 the NVA and VC launched their offensive against the South's urban centres. One of the main, if rather symbolic, objectives was the American Embassy compound in Saigon. VC sappers blew a hole into the wall that

Above: During the battles and bombings in Saigon, many US personnel found themselves temporarily engaged in combat or medical roles. Here the wounded are taken away after the US Embassy attacks.

surrounded the embassy. Once inside the courtyard they opened fire with automatic weapons and rockets. The VC, though, never managed to gain entry to the building proper. US Military Police battled with the commandos for over six hours and eventually killed them all. The VC had penetrated to the centre of the most secure place in the whole country and attacked the very symbol of American power. General Westmoreland rushed to the scene of the victory and held a press conference amid the rubble of the battle. Standing near the bodies of dead VC, Westmoreland again assured the American people that the situation was in hand and that the enemy had suffered a major defeat. To many American television viewers, though, the surroundings belied Westmoreland's optimism. The assault on the embassy had been a military defeat for the VC; yet they had achieved a major psychological victory.

In the wake of the embassy assault, communist forces attacked targets all over Saigon. A total of 35 battalions was dedicated to the operation, with 11 designated for attacks in

the city centre. The city itself was the bustling heart of South Vietnamese life and more than three million lived in the conurbation. Although many of the inhabitants were desperately poor the city remained the centre of control by and support for the South Vietnamese government. The communists decided not to combine their forces in a traditional attempt to conquer the city; the attacks were designed to cause terror and provoke a revolution. To that end small units struck separately at sensitive targets citywide. The targets were chosen for maximum symbolic meaning. A small suicide squad attacked the heavily defended Presidential Palace. Similar units struck the headquarters of both MACV and the ARVN, as well as the government radio station. Some of the most ferocious fighting took place at the massive Tan Son Nhut airbase. Surprised American troops found themselves attacked from three directions simultaneously. In the dark confusion reigned as the Vietcong fanned out into the facility. Every US soldier who could grabbed a weapon and defended themselves in the vicious fighting. When morning arrived, helicopters, bombers and tanks arrived to rescue the beleagured defenders and destroy the attacking forces.

Throughout Saigon the Vietcong had achieved initial surprise. However, the ARVN troops, leavened with US support, fought doggedly and drove the attackers off with heavy losses. The attacks in and around the capital, then, were all military failures. The VC achieved none of its tactical goals and suffered prohibitive losses. In addition, in this most important of places, the hoped for general uprising did not take place. There would be no

Below: The bodies of dead Vietcong litter the Saigon streets while shocked ARVN soldiers take a brief rest from the fighting.

AMERICAN NURSES IN VIETNAM

The Veterans' Administration counts 11,000 women as having served in Vietnam. It estimates that some 80 per cent of them served as nurses. Although, technically, women never saw combat during the war, the hospitals in which they worked often came under fire; indeed, it resulted in the deaths of eight American women and the wounding of dozens more. All the nurses were officers and served a one-year tour of duty in an unforgiving 'men's only' environment. The nurses undertook their mission of mercy with great care and unfailing strength. The combat soldiers looked upon nurses as admirable and tough. US troops were only exposed to death for short periods, but nurses faced death and mutilation each day as new batches of wounded boys, usually only 19 years of age, came under their care. They had to aid doctors in surgery, comfort young patients who learned they would never walk again, and hold the hands of the dying. Stress levels were extremely high, and often resulted in burn-out and lingering trauma for the nurses. Upon returning home nurses faced the same adjustment problems that most veterans did. They were lost and alone in a society that had come to dislike them and their war. The problems for nurses, though, were often even greater than those faced by men. In one case a nurse veteran named Lynda Van Devanter attempted to join a veterans' march after the war. The march organizer would not allow her to participate, saying that she was not a true veteran no matter where she had served. It was 1982 before the Veterans' Administration even acknowledged that women were Vietnam veterans. Now, though, the role played by nurses and the toll that it took upon them has become better understood. To many combat veterans it was the nurses who were the heroes of Vietnam

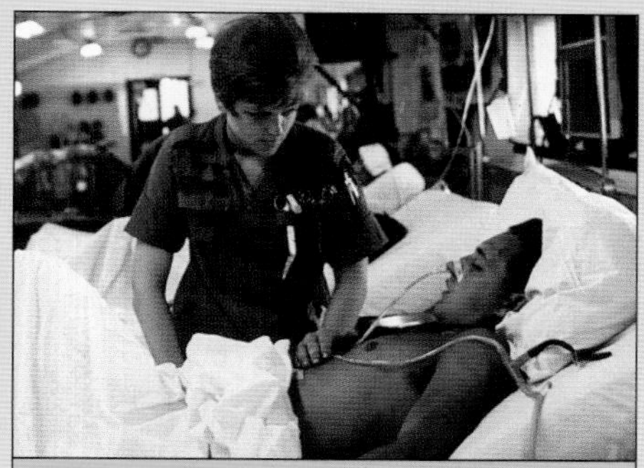

A NURSE TREATS AN INJURED US SERVICEMAN IN A FIELD HOSPITAL.

revolutionary wrath displayed on the part of the people, and the 'imperialist oppressors' would not be driven into the sea. The assault, though, did cause considerable damage In their efforts to drive the attackers away US and ARVN forces had been somewhat indiscriminate in the use of their firepower. As a result there were civilian casualties and many thousands were left homeless. The mood in Saigon darkened as well. Inhabitants of the city had always felt somewhat removed from the fighting and believed that their government, with the considerable aid of the Americans, could protect them. That illusion had been shattered. The public confidence in a regime already maligned for graft and impropriety now plummeted.

LEFT AND BELOW: AN INFAMOUS INCIDENT DURING TET WHEN A VC OFFICER WAS LED AWAY ON CAMERA THEN EXECUTED BY POLICE CHIEF GENERAL NGUYEN NGOC LOAN.

The Vietcong and NVA offensive during Tet was impressive in scale. Yet by attacking across the length and breadth of South Vietnam they had overreached themselves and could not hold on to their gains.

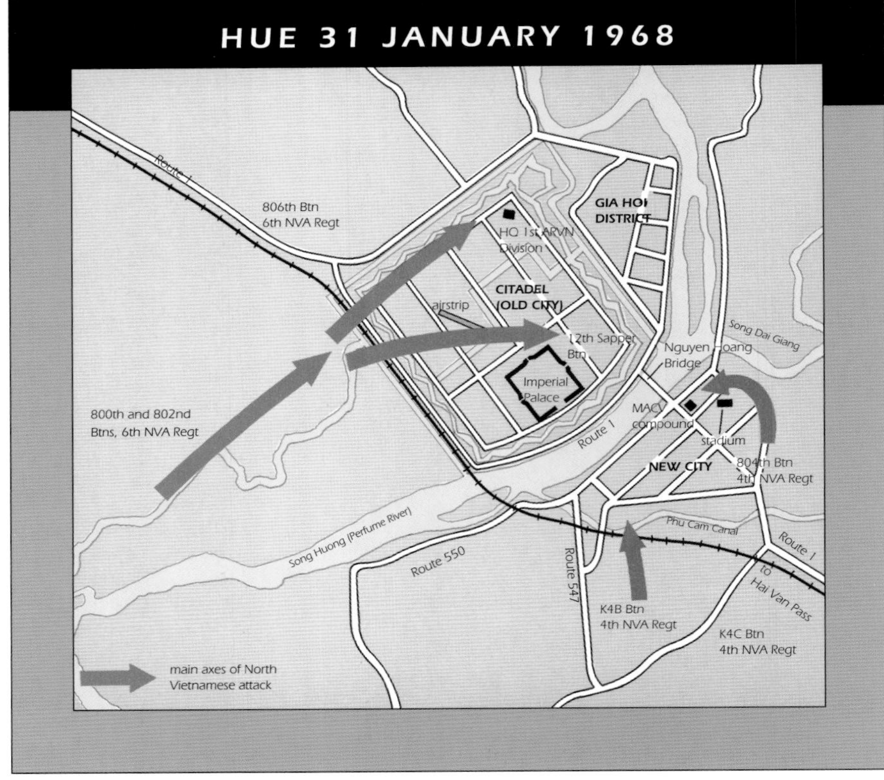

BELOW: A NIGHT VISION OF TET. CIVILIAN CASUALTIES WERE HIGH AS NVA, US AND ARVN SOLDIERS FOUGHT HEAVILY IN TOWNS AND CITIES ACROSS THE COUNTRY.

STRUGGLE IN THE MEKONG DELTA

The Vietcong dedicated much effort during the Tet Offensive to the decisive Mekong Delta region, a traditional VC heartland. The vast, marshy area was the scene of a true insurgency with the VC operating from within the population, and it was felt that the ideal of causing a massive revolution stood its best chance of success there. The Vietcong attacked thirteen of sixteen provincial capitals in the Mekong Delta during Tet. The ARVN forces in the region initially performed poorly and some ARVN commanders even went to the extreme of not answering their telephones during the struggle so they would not be asked to make decisions. To save the situation US forces rushed in and drove off the Vietcong. With the full weight of US firepower deployed, civilian losses were quite high with very conservative estimates put at over 8000 casualties and 200,000 made homeless. The Vietcong suffered heavily as well, losing nearly 6000 dead.

THE IMPERIAL CITY OF HUE

The Tet Offensive reached its ferocious climax in the city of Hue. Situated on the coast north of Danang, the historic and beautiful city had once served as the imperial capital of Vietnam. The Perfume River divides the city into two halves. North of the river lies the walled Citadel, the older and more populous part of Hue. The modern New City occupies the land south of the river. As the respected imperial capital, Hue enjoyed a special place in the hearts of most Vietnamese and the VC and NVA had left the city untouched. It was an open city – until the morning of 31 January 1968. At 3:30a.m. a barrage heralded an invasion by nearly 8000 communist troops. Surprise was complete and within hours the VC and NVA forces had seized the entire Citadel and much of the New City as well. Hue was the only city that the communists would capture and hold during Tet. The struggle to retake the city would last over a month and stands as the bloodiest single battle of the Vietnam War. During it Hue would be destroyed and the war would change irrevocably.

The American reaction to the attack reflected their inability to grasp the reality of Tet. The US Marine command at Phu Bai, a few miles south of Hue, dispatched a single company of US Marines to make contact with an American advisory force that had been surrounded. The US Marines, against heavy odds, actually achieved this feat. They next sent two platoons across the Perfume River into the Citadel and into direct contact with nearly an entire division of VC and NVA. The Americans were repulsed with heavy losses and reported contact with a sizeable enemy unit. The magnitude of the problem now dawned upon the US command. Hue had to be retaken at all costs and before the battle ended it would involve three US Marine and 11 ARVN battalions.

ABOVE: HOUSE-TO-HOUSE FIGHTING IN BIEN HOA. US SOLDIERS FROM THE 101ST AIRBORNE DIVISION CONDUCT AN ARMOUR-SUPPORTED SEARCH FOR VIETCONG SNIPERS HOLED UP IN THE CITY.

URBAN WARFARE

In the initial fighting the US was reluctant to use its firepower to full effect lest it destroy Hue. The ferocity of the fighting, though, forced a change. The plan was for the US Marines to retake the New City while the ARVN recaptured the historic Citadel. ARVN

Hue was devastated. Once the use of US artillery and air power was sanctioned in the battle, high-explosives from land, sea and air tore the heart out of the once beautiful colonial city.

RIGHT: AN M60 GUNNER SHOOTS UP A STREET TO PROVIDE COVERING FIRE FOR ADVANCING TROOPS.

BELOW: RECOILLESS RIFLES WERE OFTEN FIRED AT VERY SHORT RANGE DURING THE BATTLE IN HUE.

and US Marine forces found themselves locked in a house-to-house, room-to-room battle more reminiscent of Stalingrad than the jungle warfare to which they had become accustomed. The on-the-job training in urban warfare was very difficult and costly, for the communists were determined to stand and fight, causing as many casualties as possible. As a result the US Marines advanced a scant four blocks on a very narrow front in six days of fighting and the ARVN made scarcely a dent in the defences of the Citadel. The decision was then made to unleash the might of US firepower upon the city, reducing much of it to rubble as a result. There had been no time to evacuate civilians, so many became innocent victims of the titanic struggle. Still the communists held firm, determined to defend the shattered buildings to the end. The fighting was savage and often hand-to-hand.

By 9 February the US Marines had cleared the New City of all but a few isolated snipers, leaving behind a charnel house of corpses and shattered buildings. In the Citadel, though, the battle raged on. It had become apparent that the ARVN would need aid to recapture the hereditary capital. As a result the 1st Battalion, 5th Regiment of the US Marines crossed the Perfume River to join the fray. All the while the enemy fought on with a bitter resolve. The battle continued until the ARVN forces finally raised their flag over the Imperial Palace on 24 February. Even then pockets of NVA continued to resist, mainly in the Gia Hoi area of the city.

Once the Citadel had fallen, the NVA did not attempt to hold the vulnerable Gia Hoi area. Again the military decision was sound, but in the meantime the NVA had converted much of the district into a hellish collection of mass graves. Some communist forces, however, fought on until the bitter end, and it was 2 March before Hue was entirely liberated. During the month of fighting, in addition to the thousands of civilian deaths, over 8000 soldiers had perished and 75 per cent of the population had been left homeless. Many of the once proud citizens of Hue simply wandered among the rubble and the corpses, unable to comprehend what had happened. The city had been destroyed, but it was 'free'.

The final act of the great Tet Offensive took place at the remote US Marine base of Khe Sanh (see pages 146–148). Communist forces had been encroaching on the isolated site for months. Giap hoped that the impending threat to it would help lure American troops away from the cities, and he had been correct. Some 40,000 NVA and VC surrounded barely 6000 US Marines and the coming battle there was supposed to form the final stage of Tet. After the popular uprising, Giap reasoned that such a Dien Bien Phu-style victory would force the United States out of the conflict.

ABOVE: ARVN MARINES IN THE MEKONG DELTA MOVE INTO THE JUNGLE ON A 'SEARCH AND DESTROY' MISSION AGAINST AN ENEMY SUPPLY ROUTE IN NOVEMBER 1968. VIETNAMIZATION WAS STARTING TO TAKE EFFECT AND ARVN SOLDIERS WERE THEREAFTER FIGHTING AN INCREASING NUMBER OF THEIR OWN BATTLES.

LEFT: ARVN SOLDIERS IN STREETFIGHTING. URBAN COMBAT WAS A HIGHLY VIOLENT, DISORIENTATING EXPERIENCE; ENTIRE DISTRICTS HAD TO BE CLEARED HOUSE BY HOUSE.

Hue gave the NVA an opportunity to enforce its revolutionary law for a few weeks. It did so in a burst of murder and torture, though these tactics only alienated them further from the people it wanted to inspire as supporters.

BELOW: US MARINES FIRE FROM A WINDOW IN HUE DURING A DANGEROUS AND UNPREDICTABLE SEARCH-AND-CLEAR ACTION AIMED AT REMOVING THE NVA FROM THE CITADEL.

SLAUGHTER AT GIA HOI

During the Tet Offensive the NVA ruled over the Gia Hoi district of Hue for over three weeks. Thus in one tiny part of Hue the communists were able to institute their revolution. In the main, they ruled using terror tactics. It was their time for revenge against those who were deemed to have aided and abetted the 'American imperialist aggressor'. They had lists, supplied by sympathizers, which contained the names and addresses of persons who were part of or supported the South Vietnamese government. Heavily armed NVA officers strode through the streets and announced the names of the suspects using megaphones, asking that they report to the high school. Here the revolutionary provisional government would administer 're-education'. Some did as they were told, and others attempted to hide. Time, however, was on the side of the NVA, allowing them to hunt down 'subversive' elements at their leisure. Once located, the result was the same – death. The most common method of execution used by the NVA was to bind the victims arms at the wrist and then fire one round into the back of their skull. However, when it became clear that Gia Hoi would fall, in an effort to save time many victims were simply buried alive. A conservative estimate is that the communists executed nearly 3000 people during the struggle.

The civilian deaths at the hands of the communists would have an even greater importance. As the war drew to a close Nixon would search for peace with honour. He realized that if US forces left South Vietnam too quickly the resulting communist victory would cause a humanitarian tragedy. Millions of people had supported US forces or the South Vietnamese government. The killings in Hue seemed to indicate that these men and women would be slaughtered. Nixon, for good or ill, used this rationale to extend American involvement in the conflict.

COMMUNIST DISASTER

Once the Tet Offensive, and the attendant fighting at Khe Sanh, had drawn to a close it was apparent that the communists had suffered a crushing defeat. There had been no popular uprising. The people of South Vietnam were, as a whole, unwilling to come to the aid of their brothers from the North. This realization was sobering for the Northern leadership. It meant that the people of the South were not disillusioned with their regime to the point of wanting to wage armed struggle. Also few members of the ARVN had defected and their units fought more doggedly than the communists had expected. In the end, then, it appeared the South Vietnamese government would never topple so long as it retained American support. Ho Chi Minh and Giap had to rely on a military defeat of United States forces in the field to achieve victory. It was a stunning revelation for the communists. From the beginning they believed that they struggled for and alongside the oppressed people of the South. Tet indicated that that was not the case and forced the communist leadership to rethink their strategy and goals.

In starker military terms, Tet had been an unmitigated disaster for the communists and

the greatest single victory of the war for the United States. The American strategy in the conflict had been to 'find, fix and finish' the enemy in a war of attrition. However, VC and NVA forces had always refused to be fixed into battle. When losses became prohibitive they broke off contact, relying on a protracted war strategy to wear down US resolve. Tet changed all of that. NVA and VC forces had offered battle and fixed themselves into place then found themselves at the mercy of American firepower. Of the 84,000 VC and NVA committed to the Tet Offensive, some 58,000 were killed. This represents a fatal casualty rate of a stunning 70 per cent. The slaughter virtually wiped out the Vietcong as an effective fighting force. The remaining cadres had to retreat far into the countryside in an effort to recruit new soldiers. As a result the amount of rural Vietnam controlled by the VC fell dramatically. Thus in several areas the VC no longer ruled the night. In an effort to stabilize the situation more NVA regulars came pouring down the Ho Chi Minh Trail to reinforce units that had been destroyed. The process of rebuilding was painstakingly slow and allowed the South Vietnamese time to rebuild and resupply. The communists would fight on of course, but their defeat in Tet seemed to be comprehensive. Little did they know at the time that their military defeat would transform into an unbelievable psychological victory over the strongest nation in the world.

ABOVE: US MARINES IN HUE TAKE COVER.

BELOW: US TROOPS WARILY APPROACH A GAP IN THE WALL.

ABOVE: ARVN TROOPS ENGAGED IN A FIREFIGHT. HUE AND OTHER CITY BATTLES PROVIDED A MASS OF IMAGES FOR THE MEDIA.

SHOCK IN THE UNITED STATES

General Westmoreland was quite pleased with the American victory in the Tet Offensive and he longed to chase the embattled foe into its hiding places and destroy it. Both he and Johnson trumpeted the news of the victory to the nation. Tet was indeed a great triumph for the American armed forces. Ironically, though, the US public would not interpret the events of Tet in the same way, seeing it as a defeat. Scant months before public figures had assured their country that victory was at hand. The massive-scale surprise attacks of Tet shocked an American public that had been lulled into complacency. The fact that it had taken place at all, and assaulted the very symbols of American authority in the process was a blow to the American national psyche. The Tet Offensive simply made all previous assurances that America was winning the war seem like lies. To be sure the VC and NVA had to give up all of their gains, and suffered heavy losses. However, the attritional nature of the victory was hard for most Americans to understand; their forces had captured no city and had not seized enemy territory. The only signs of victory were masses of enemy dead. It seemed that the North had limitless numbers of men to call upon, and that the war would get ever more serious and costly, and possibly last forever.

The Tet Offensive struck hard at both NVA and Vietcong resources – blows which would take them years to recover from. The Vietcong in particular almost ceased to exist as a coherent military power.

In the wake of Tet Westmoreland was anxious to press his advantage and hoped to win Johnson's support for widening the war in Southeast Asia. General Earle Wheeler, the chairman of the Joint Chiefs of Staff, had other plans. He saw Tet as an opportunity to set right several military wrongs. The US had seriously weakened its forces in Europe and

South Korea in an effort to supply troops for Vietnam. This cannibalizing of existing forces was due to Johnson's reluctance to call up the National Guard and Reserves and place the United States on a full wartime footing. Wheeler journeyed to Vietnam in late February on a fact-finding mission. During his journey he conferred with Westmoreland. The two agreed that to achieve the goals of victory in Vietnam and stability in the rest of the world Westmoreland required 206,000 more men. Wheeler then returned to Washington, D.C., and placed the troop request before Johnson.

The massive troop request shocked members of the administration. Even Robert McNamara, in some ways the architect of the war, was taken aback. How could it be that communist forces had just suffered a crippling defeat, yet Westmoreland needed 206,000 more men? McNamara, who was about to resign for personal reasons, undertook his last act as Secretary of State and advised Johnson against the troop request. Johnson realized the magnitude of Wheeler's call for more troops. Approval of the request would require calling up the National Guard and Reserve and would dislocate the economy. Vietnam would truly become a war; it was time to get 'into' the war or get out. Johnson's decision would be the most important single act during the American involvement in Vietnam.

ABOVE: A WELL-HIDDEN US SNIPER TAKES AIM.

BELOW: AT THE HEIGHT OF THE BATTLE IN HUE, AN OBSERVATION PLANE MAKES A LOW, DANGEROUS PASS.

Media presentation of the Tet Offensive tended to highlight it as a defeat for the US and ARVN forces. The cameras focused on individual tragedies, which to the viewing public became general principles.

WALTER CRONKITE

Vietnam was the television war. Members of the media had almost unlimited access to the battlefields, and often interviewed soldiers in the midst of combat. As a result American citizens witnessed the war, from glorious victory to agonizing death, on television every night. There is an entire school of thought that contends that the media, and its negative portrayal of the war, made the public turn against the conflict and cause the American defeat in Vietnam. While such a statement is far too strong, it is safe to say that the role of the media was quite important, especially during the Tet Offensive. Television crews were on hand as the battle raged in the US embassy compound and viewers were able to witness South Vietnamese police chief Nguyen Ngoc Loan place his gun to the head of and execute a suspected VC terrorist in prime time. The most important television event of the war, though, was less dramatic. Walter Cronkite was the highest rated news anchor in the USA. Americans trusted Cronkite like they trusted no other. In a sense he was America. On his *CBS Evening News*, Cronkite had been a consistent supporter of American actions in Vietnam. With the Tet Offensive, though, things changed. What he saw convinced him that the government's rosy predictions of victory were wrong. On 27 February the nation's most trusted man spoke to an audience of over nine million. He offered the startling revelation that the 'bloody experience of Vietnam' would only end in a stalemate. He closed his broadcast with the following:

'But it is increasingly clear to this reporter that the only rational way out then will be to negotiate, not as victors but as an honourable people who lived up to their pledge to defend democracy, and did the best they could. This is Walter Cronkite. Good Night.'

To the greater American public Cronkite's change of heart regarding the war was more important than battlefield victories or losses. Cronkite had passed judgment on the war; Americans believed him, and public opinion shifted irrevocably against the war. Media influence on the Vietnam War caused the military to make lasting changes regarding reporters' access to the battlefield. The tight control of the media during wars since, complete with managed news conferences, is a direct result of Vietnam.

ENTER CLARK CLIFFORD

For advice Johnson turned to the new Secretary of State, Clark Clifford, a relative newcomer to the ongoing governmental debates regarding the war in the region. Clifford knew the gravity of the situation and took his role very seriously. He formed a task force that began a study of almost every aspect of American involvement in Vietnam. The results of the investigation were frightening, and Clifford realized that American policy in Vietnam was bankrupt:

BELOW: VIETCONG PRISONERS ARE LED AWAY BY ARVN TROOPS. MANY SUCH CAPTIVES WERE SHOT OUT OF HAND.

'I could not find out when the war was going to end: I could not find out the manner in which it was going to end. I could not find out whether the new requests for men and equipment were going to be enough, or whether it would take more and, if more, how much . . . All I had was the statement, given with too little self-assurance to be comforting, that if we persisted for an indeterminate length of time, the enemy would choose not to go on. And so I asked, "Does anyone see any diminution in the will of the enemy after four year of our having been there, after enormous casualties, and after massive

Confusion over policy and commitment to Vietnam affected the morale of US troops not just in Vietnam, but also back in the United States. Militarism in general was often made to feel crude and excessive by the anti-war lobby.

Left: In the aftermath of a battle to capture a VC/NVA-held building in Hue, US Marines light up and try to relax. The multiple impact marks on the walls indicate the ferocity of the fighting, and many US soldiers were left traumatized by the scale of their losses and injuries.

President Johnson was faced with an acute problem: keeping the US in the war was impossible, but rapid withdrawal could lead to the fall of South Vietnam and victory for the communists. The only option was to build up the South to stand alone.

Right: M60 at the ready, a US soldier looks out over a scene of total waste and devastation after days of urban fighting.

Below: A US Sergeant strikes a pose seated on the ornate throne in the old Imperial Palace in Hue.

destruction from our bombing?" The answer was that there appeared to be no diminution in the will of the enemy.'

Clifford was convinced that the American situation was hopeless and set out to convince Johnson not only to reject the troop request but also to begin a gradual American withdrawal. Matters became worse for Johnson when the story of the troop request appeared in the *New York Times*, provoking a firestorm of public protest. Politics also played a role in Johnson's decision. Eugene McCarthy, running against Johnson in the Democratic primary as a peace candidate, almost won the New Hampshire primary. The near victory convinced the much more politically formidable Robert Kennedy to enter the fray. Johnson's war and his presidency were coming apart.

JOHNSON'S DECISION

As Johnson teetered on the brink, Clifford applied the final pressure by gathering together the 'wise men'. This group

of influential advisers, including Dean Acheson and Averell Harriman, informed Johnson that they too were of the opinion that the country should begin to disengage from the war. The news crushed Johnson. As the leader of the free world he had to come to grips with the idea that he had presided over the greatest foreign policy failure in US history. He was the first president to lose a war. On 31 March Johnson spoke to a live television audience. The beaten man informed the public that American policy in Vietnam was to change, and a gradual withdrawal was to begin. His final statement was a bombshell:

'With America's sons in the fields far away, with America's future under challenge right here at home . . . I do not believe that I should devote an hour or a day of my time to any personal partisan causes . . . Accordingly, I shall not seek, and I will not accept the nomination of my party for another term as your president.

The Tet Offensive was indeed the most important development of the Vietnam War. NVA and VC forces had hoped to cause an uprising and win a great victory over the United States. Instead American firepower inflicted grievous losses upon the communists, sending them to inglorious defeat. Ironically, even as despair in Hanoi reached its height, American support for the war unravelled. The US victory was seen as a defeat, and one so devastating that Johnson and his advisers began the tortuously slow process of American withdrawal from South Vietnam. In March Johnson so much as admitted that the war was lost. He then refused to run for another term as president and thus became a casualty of his own war.

BELOW: ARVN TROOPS ADVANCE THROUGH A BURNING TOWN. THE ARVN SUFFERED 2788 KILLED DURING TET, AND THREE TIMES THAT NUMBER IN WOUNDED.

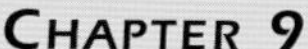

CHAPTER 9

Strategy at the Crossroads

A US SOLDIER ENJOYS A QUIET MOMENT READING A LETTER IN HIS BUNKER. FROM 1968 THE STRATEGY OF VIETNAMIZATION WOULD START TO TAKE EFFECT, AND THE STEADY US WITHDRAWAL BEGAN. THE WAR, HOWEVER, STILL RUMBLED ON.

Many have questioned whether Khe Sanh was worth the effort of its defence. Isolated, with little strategic impact on the NVA, it soon became a symbol of US defiance and, ultimately, defeat.

In the aftermath of the Tet Offensive the Vietnam War focused on the continuing struggle at Khe Sanh. Although both were definitive American military victories the domestic political consensus in the United States crumbled, necessitating a withdrawal from the war – a process known as Vietnamization. In the wake of President Johnson's refusal to run for office, the conduct of the Vietnam War fell to the new American president, Richard Nixon, and his Secretary of State Henry Kissinger. Nixon struggled to balance his hope of 'Peace with Honour' with the increasing demands made by the American public and US Congress to end the country's involvement in Southeast Asia. As both the United States and the North Vietnamese searched for a way out of the conflict the war changed and even spread to Cambodia.

Atop a red clay hill in the jungle near the border with Laos lay the US Marine base at Khe Sanh. It was one of a series of fortified bases near the DMZ designed to interdict the communists' supply efforts and guard the northern border of South Vietnam, its proximity to Laos making it among the most important of its kind. The base sat astride one of the main enemy supply routes and was used to stage covert operations into Laos. As discussed previously, the North Vietnamese planned the attack on Khe Sanh as an integral part of their overall plan for victory in the Tet Offensive.

KHE SANH

Some 6000 US Marines and ARVN Rangers manned Khe Sanh. The main emplacement was surrounded by smaller Special Forces bases and fighting positions which augmented the US Marines' strength. The communists, though, quietly massed nearly 40,000 men in the surrounding jungle, but it did not go unnoticed. US military planners, including a nervous President Johnson, wondered if Khe Sanh could survive the coming onslaught. General Westmoreland had no such misgivings. He hoped that these isolated US Marines would draw the enemy out into the open where massive firepower could be

RIGHT: THE DUSTY STRIP LEADING TO KHE SANH. SET CLOSE TO THE BORDER WITH LAOS, IT WAS HOPED THAT KHE SANH WOULD PROVIDE AN IDEAL BASE FOR INTERDICTING NVA SUPPLY ROUTES DOWN THE HO CHI MINH TRAIL.

Left: Troops scatter for cover as NVA shells rain down into the Khe Sanh base. Two NVA artillery regiments focused their attention on Khe Sanh using powerful 130mm and 152mm weapons.

brought to bear. In his mind any comparison with Dien Bien Phu was faulty, for the US air supply system for Khe Sanh could not be broken.

The NVA siege began on 20 January 1968. A hail of artillery and mortar fire rained down upon the base in an attempt to pound it into submission and destroy its airfield. In doing so, however, the communists had given away their positions and General Westmoreland responded by launching Operation Niagara – B-52 strategic bombers, tactical-bombers and artillery battered the NVA positions with a remorseless, round-the-clock bombardment. This caused heavy casualties among the NVA, but they maintained and squeezed the ring around Khe Sanh ever tighter.

As the NVA closed in they put tremendous pressure upon the surrounding smaller strongpoints. The fighting for these remote hilltops was fierce and sometimes hand-to-hand. Once his forces had neared Khe Sanh General Giap ordered an increase in the artillery barrage upon the base. In its wake on 29 February the NVA 304th Division launched an assault , but the hail of defending fire, coupled with incessant bombing of the attackers, destroyed the 304th in two days of savage fighting before they had even reached the perimeter.

The disaster served to convince General Giap that the American positions at Khe Sanh would not fall to a direct attack. So although the siege continued Giap ordered that the effort to seize the base should halt and he began to withdraw forces from the area. Once again he had misjudged American strength and now realized that there would be no great victory in 1968. While some serious fighting still remained, the US Marines had won their battle. On 8 April a force of US Marines and Air Cavalry troops reached Khe Sanh by ground and lifted the siege after 77 days, marking a substantial victory for American forces. Some 205 American troops had perished, but an estimated 10,000 of the enemy had died. The ground all around had been devastated by the relentless B-52 strikes – in total the equivalent of 10 Hiroshima-sized atomic bombs had been dropped during the course of Operation Niagara.

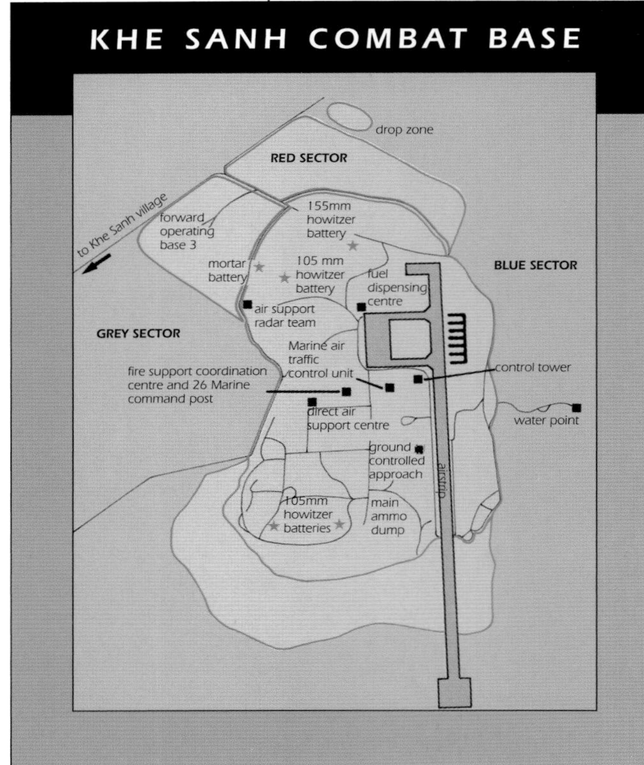

A CHANGING WAR

In the wake of the Tet Offensive both the United States and North Vietnam reconsidered the way in which the war was being fought.

To the North Vietnamese the coordinated offensive actions during Tet constituted a devastating military defeat. However, the public unrest in the United States gave the communists great hope of eventual victory. Thus the North Vietnamese chose to defend and rebuild their strength in the year after Tet. The Vietcong had been destroyed and would need a massive infusion of troops from the North. Everywhere VC and NVA units fled to sanctuary into Cambodia and Laos. The communists still planned attacks, but only of the nuisance variety aimed at causing a maximum number of US casualties for minimal loss. In this way the communists hoped to increase pressure on the United States to exit the conflict.

General Westmoreland and the US command structure saw Tet as a great victory for the Us and its allies and sought to press their advantage. He planned to lock the fleeing VC and NVA into battle and complete the enemy's military destruction, which had proceeded so well in Tet. In addition the US bombing campaign intensified.

While both sides revised their military strategy, they also began peace negotiations. On 13 May 1968 representatives from both sides met in Paris. Talks quickly stalled, however, as each party attempted to negotiate a victorious peace. Thus in the year following the Tet Offensive fighting actually intensified and resulted in the bloodiest year of the war in terms of US casualties. In one sense Westmoreland had played into the hands of the North Vietnamese, for the high casualty rate was to strain the will of an already battered American public to breaking point.

RIGHT: THE AIR CONTROL TOWER AT KHE SANH. THE BASE'S ISOLATION MADE THE GARRISON THERE UTTERLY DEPENDENT UPON AIR SUPPLY, AND THE NVA DID THEIR LEVEL BEST TO SHOOT DOWN ANY AIRCRAFT OR HELICOPTER THAT DARED ATTEMPT THE DANGEROUS LANDING.

Khe Sanh became a magnet for press photographers, camera crews and journalists. With evocations of Dien Bien Phu, Khe Sanh gave the media a drama that was both fascinating and photogenic.

LEFT: THE AIR CONTROL RADAR AND CONTROL TOWER AT KHE SANH, THEMSELVES A TARGET FOR NVA ARTILLERY.

OPERATION RANCH HAND

In 1962 C-123 transport planes, specially modified to carry and spray herbicides, began the US effort to defoliate and thus destroy the jungle hideouts of the Vietcong. Cropland was also targeted to deny food to the insurgents. The operation, called Operation Hades but usually known as Operation Ranch Hand, made use of several defoliant agents packaged in colour-coded crates. The most powerful was the dioxin-based Agent Orange. In a matter of minutes a single C-123 could dispense enough Agent Orange to defoliate 300 acres of land. The results were dramatic and devastating. Plant life quickly became brown and died, leaving behind barren land. US defoliation efforts escalated as the war dragged on, reaching their height in 1967. During that year 1.7 million acres of land were affected, or an area half the size of the state of Connecticut. Pilots of Operation Ranch Hand had lived up to their motto – 'Only you can prevent forests'. Although effective, these environmentally degrading efforts had little tangible military effect and quickly became quite controversial. In 1968 a study indicated that exposure to concentrated levels of dioxin caused birth defects and several other maladies. As more evidence of the health hazards posed by defoliation came to light, the US government slowly scaled back the operation. The last Ranch Hand flight took place in January 1971. In total more than one-seventh of the land area of South Vietnam had been sprayed with defoliant, and the operation has remained controversial since the war because thousands of US veterans – not to mention countless Vietnamese civilians – still suffer the effects of the deadly dioxin in the form of cancer and birth defects

LAYING DOWN AGENT ORANGE.

STRUGGLES IN THE AFTERMATH OF TET

BELOW: THE CHAOS OF KHE SANH. THE SOLDIERS AT THE BASE ENDED UP LIVING IN TOTAL SQUALOR.

Fighting erupted all over South Vietnam as the United States attempted to rout the remaining VC and NVA units. Although some of the battles were large and destined to find a place in history, many more were simply small unit operations. US and ARVN units swept across South Vietnam and engaged in several thousand firefights and minor battles that have largely been forgotten. In April, though, around Saigon, some eighty US and ARVN battalions launched Operation Toan Thang ('Complete Victory'). Their task was to destroy any remnants of the VC units that had attacked Saigon during Tet. The operation, however, met with only limited success, for the enemy was able in the main to make good its escape. That the US-ARVN operation was unsuccessful was shown just a month later in May when the Vietcong began to launch a series of 'mini-Tet' rocket attacks on the capital city.

In the Central Highlands Westmoreland was determined to destroy the NVA staging area located in the A Shau Valley, which posed a threat to Hue. The task of attacking the remote and treacherous valley fell to the 7th Cavalry. Operation Delaware began on 19 April with an air assault on the valley's northern end. The helicopters were met by withering anti-aircraft fire – ten were destroyed and an additional fourteen damaged. Then, to make matters worse, the weather deteriorated dramatically, making resupply of the soldiers on the ground almost impossible. Once the weather cleared, though, it became apparent that the NVA had fled, only choosing to defend a single supply centre in an area called 'The Punchbowl'. The US forces duly managed to seize or destroy large caches of enemy supplies, but by August the area had been abandoned and little lasting damage to the enemy had really been caused. Once the American forces departed the NVA returned to rebuild their staging area and begin the process of resupply.

RIGHT: AN AERIAL VIEW OF KHE SANH BASE. LIKE DIEN BIEN PHU, ITS POSITION IN THE VALLEY FLOOR SHOWS HOW VULNERABLE IT WAS TO NVA ARTILLERY.

LEFT: A CH-34 KEEPS ITS ROTORS TURNING, READY FOR A RAPID TAKE-OFF AS IT TAKES ON TROOPS AT KHE SANH. BY THE END OF THE SIEGE, WRECKED HELICOPTERS AND AIRCRAFT LITTERED THE AIR BASE.

BELOW: A UH-1 GUNSHIP REFUELS AT KHE SANH. AS AN ATTACK AIRCRAFT, SUCH HELICOPTERS MANAGED TO KEEP SOME OF THE PRESSURE OFF THE TROOPS UNDER SIEGE BY SPRAYING NVA LOCATIONS WITH CANNON FIRE AND ROCKETS.

The most intense fighting took place near a village named Dai Do close to the DMZ, where the enemy's 320th Division attempted to sever a critical US Marine supply line. The US Marines discovered this new threat on 30 April and immediately counter-attacked. In a series of running battles lasting for an entire month, US Marines, using landing craft, tanks and naval gunfire, slowly pushed the determined North Vietnamese from their bunkers, tunnels and spiderholes. The fighting was bitter, but in the end the US Marines were victorious and forced the communists to retreat. The month had cost the US Marines 327 dead and 1200 wounded; the NVA, in one of the few times they chose to stand and fight in the year after Tet, lost some 3000 dead. Battles would continue in the area of the DMZ for much of the remainder of the year, leading to the almost inevitable stalemate.

ENTER ABRAMS

In July 1968 General William Westmoreland was succeeded as commander of US forces in Vietnam (COMUSMACV) by General Creighton Abrams, whose unenviable task it was to preside over a war that the nation no longer wanted and the government as much as admitted to be lost. Abrams would find his hands tied by the need to keep casualties low in an effort to avoid trouble on the home front. Also the process of

Above: Taking cover. One of the greatest problems during Khe Sanh was sniper fire, as NVA marksmen would position themselves in the surrounding treelines and pick off individual soldiers.

Vietnamization would slowly rob him of his troop strength. Although traditional Search and Destroy missions would continue under his command, the emphasis of US efforts in the war slowly began to change.

Abrams sought to initiate a 'One War' strategy, which would blend traditional military strikes with increased efforts at pacification of the South Vietnamese countryside. In the Tet defeat the VC had lost control of many villages, and Abrams sought to keep it that way. The plan involved arming South Vietnamese civilians for their own protection. US forces were spread throughout areas of the countryside to help defend loyal villages and their citizens. Additional emphasis was placed on the Chieu Hoi or 'Open Arms' programme, the goal of which was to encourage defection from the ranks of the enemy. Such defectors provided not only valuable intelligence but also a significant morale boost for government forces.

Right: US Marines wait anxiously to be picked up from Khe Sanh by a transport aircraft. They keep their heads down to avoid the blast from mortar and artillery rounds.

The Phoenix Program was probably the most controversial

LEFT: US MARINES HOSE DOWN ONE OF THE MANY AIRCRAFT THAT DID NOT MAKE IT BACK OFF THE KHE SANH AIRSTRIP.

BELOW: WITH CALM RESTORED, A US MARINE CLEANS HIS FIREARM SITTING ON TOP OF ONE OF KHE SANH'S PERIMETER BUNKERS.

element of Abrams's strategy. It sought to eliminate the infrastructure of the Vietcong, and, technically at least, it was run by the South Vietnamese police aided by the CIA. The special teams, often made up of Vietcong defectors, that implemented the programme carried out a wave of assassinations of VC political functionaries at the village level. The violent methods caused controversy, but seemed to be effective in eroding support for the Vietcong in many areas. The success of pacification efforts as a whole, though, is difficult to assess, and the depth of loyalty of the South Vietnamese people to their government would remain in question throughout.

NIXON AND KISSINGER

While the war in Vietnam remained a bloody stalemate, the election process proceeded in the United States. In the wake of Johnson's decision not to run for the presidency the Democratic Party became dogged by in-fighting between its pro- and anti-war elements. The Republican Party stood unified behind Richard Nixon and his brash statement that he had a secret plan to end the war in Vietnam. Nixon won the presidential election in 1968 by a razor-thin margin. He and his chief adviser, Secretary of State Henry Kissinger, then turned to the problem of running the war.

Nixon initially planned to use a 'carrot and stick' approach with the North Vietnamese. The United States softened its negotiating stance at the peace talks in Paris, but intensified its bombing efforts – especially against the Ho Chi Minh Trail. Nixon promised that such

By 1968, Vietnam had become an incredible burden to the US administration. Nixon threatened and cajoled the North, but hostile public opinion in the West limited his opportunities for action.

raids were insignificant compared to those he would unleash if the North did not see reason and agree terms that would allow South Vietnam to remain independent. The communists, though, did not flinch and held firm to their policy of protracting the struggle in Vietnam in an effort to outlast the United States. The North had called Nixon's bluff and he was furious. He longed to retaliate by launching attacks that would dreadfully punish the North, but realized that American public opinion would not allow such action. Nixon had won the election with the promise that he would bring peace; if he instead expanded the war further in search of elusive military victory his political career would be destroyed. His frustration with the situation became clear in September 1969 when he stated, 'I can't believe that a fourth-rate power like North Vietnam doesn't have a breaking point.'

ABOVE: MARINES STORM HILL 881 THROUGH THE DUST, SMOKE AND FIRE OF NVA RESISTANCE.

ABOVE, RIGHT: US MARINES CARRY A 106MM RECOILLESS RIFLE TO THEIR HILLTOP FIRING POSITIONS AROUND KHE SANH, READY TO POUND NVA TROOPS ON HILL 689.

VIETNAMIZATION

Although victory now seemed beyond his grasp, President Nixon could still search for a 'Peace with Honour' that would allow the best chance for South Vietnam to continue to survive after an American withdrawal from the conflict. To achieve that end Nixon hoped to use 'detente' with the Soviet Union and China as a weapon in Vietnam. The communist bloc would have to lessen its support of the North Vietnamese as the price for friendship with the United States. The process of rapprochement between the Cold War's oppositional blocs would be slow, though, and Nixon needed tangible evidence that he was ending American involvement in Vietnam quickly. As a result he turned to a process which carried the tag 'Vietnamization'.

The plan concocted by Nixon and Kissinger called for a gradual withdrawal of US forces from South Vietnam. During this slow process American monetary aid and military training would build up the ARVN to the point at which it could defend South Vietnam without further American military assistance. Finally, before exiting the conflict US forces would launch a number of spoiling attacks to dislocate the infrastructure of the NVA and the VC, thus providing the South with the precious gift of time.

The gradual exit of the United States from the war began in June 1969 when President Nixon lowered the troop ceiling in Vietnam and some 25,000 American soldiers returned home. To counterbalance the American withdrawal, the ARVN and the VNAF received the very latest US equipment, and by 1970 the armed forces of South Vietnam numbered over one million men.

ABOVE: THE MEDIA WAR. HEAVILY ARMED MEMBERS OF AN LRRP TEAM IN THE BIEN HOA AREA TALK TO AN ARMY JOURNALIST.

President Thieu also carried out much anticipated land reform efforts in 1970 in an attempt to solidify support for the Southern regime within the ranks of South Vietnam's peasantry, those most susceptible to the Vietcong's talk of revolution. On paper Vietnamization seemed to be working, for South Vietnam possessed one of the largest, most modern armed forces in the entire world. The gaudy numbers, though, camouflaged fatal morale, economic and leadership weaknesses.

MASSACRE AT MY LAI

On 16 March 1968 men of 'C' Company, 1st Battalion, 11th Infantry Brigade, entered a series of hamlets in Quang Ngai province on a Search and Destroy mission. The hamlets, including My Lai, were known as Vietcong territory. Many soldiers in the US force lost all control and, using rifles, machine-guns and bayonets, murdered an estimated 300 to 400 civilians – men, women and children. In one incident some 70 civilians were herded to a ditch and then mown down with automatic fire. For over a year the army covered up the massacre. It was only in November 1969, due to a report in the *New York Times*, that the public became aware of what had transpired. For another year the story of the events at My Lai gripped the American public as it played out in the courts and in the media. After an investigation, thirteen soldiers were charged with war crimes and crimes against humanity. Of that number only Lieutenant William Calley, a platoon leader of 'C' Company, was convicted. His platoon had killed some 200 of the victims at My Lai and he was sentenced to ten years imprisonment for mass murder. The slaughter repulsed and polarized the United States. Some believed that Calley was merely a scapegoat for the American defeat in Vietnam. Others saw his sentence as mild and hypocritical. Many wondered what other atrocities Americans had committed in the Vietnam War. That the US Army, the defenders of freedom, could commit such an atrocity proved the bankruptcy of the war in Vietnam to too many, and support for the war waned quickly. In the end Lieutenant William Calley served just over three years of his sentence before receiving parole in 1974. He now lives a quiet life as a shopkeeper in Georgia.

THE WAR VISITS A VIETNAMESE HOME.

HAMBURGER HILL

Hamburger Hill was yet another military victory which turned into a political defeat. Search and Destroy had lost its credibility, and US casualties had to be limited in future operations.

During 1969 Abrams continued to implement his 'One War' strategy, and the North Vietnamese continued to avoid major battle. As a result the year was dominated, in the main, by small unit struggles throughout South Vietnam aimed at pacification of the countryside. Some US divisions were even broken up into small task forces whose job it was to patrol the countryside rather than 'seek and destroy' the enemy. In the border areas some larger actions took place aimed at disrupting the communists' supply lines. However, the war was being turned over to the ARVN, and American casualties fell accordingly.

One last, major Search and Destroy mission remained, however. US intelligence had located a renewed enemy build-up in the A Shau Valley, posing a fresh threat to much of the Central Highlands. On 10 May, US and ARVN forces air assaulted into the area to destroy the NVA infrastructure there once again. While searching the entire zone US forces located a series of enemy bunkers dug into the jungle atop Hill 937, later to be known as 'Hamburger Hill'. A single company initially tried to take the hill, but failed to advance through the storm of machine-gun fire that greeted their movement.

At this point the US called in artillery and aircraft strikes against the enemy positions. On 13 May two companies of the 187th Infantry stormed the hill, but were thrown back after intense fighting. Once again air strikes were called in, but a renewed attack on 18 May failed as well. During the epic struggle the heavy shelling and incessant rain turned the hill into an almost impassable wilderness of mud and shattered trees. Men would pick their way forwards, only to slide back down when they lost their footing.

On 20 May no fewer than four battalions attacked and reached the summit, only to find that the NVA bunker system was empty. The communist enemy, having inflicted as much

Right: US Marines fire an 81mm mortar in a mortar duel with the enemy while trying to protect a transport helicopter as it comes into land. The action was part of a search-and-clear operation during September 1968 near the Vandegrift combat base.

Left: Hamburger Hill. US paratroopers of the 101st Airborne Division carrying a wounded buddy wait for a medical evacuation helicopter to arrive. Hamburger Hill was one of the most testing battles in the Airborne's history.

damage as possible on the US forces, had fled during the night. During the struggle, the Americans had lost some 56 dead (compared to nearly 700 NVA dead). After just two nights in possession of the hill US forces were then ordered to abandon their prize, for it was deemed to have no tactical value.

In some ways the example provided by the action at Hill 937 epitomizes the US war effort in Vietnam. In the strategic war of attrition, Hill 937 was clearly a victory for the US; the enemy had been located and routed. But the hill itself had no significance, only killing the men on it had significance, so it was abandoned. Americans, though, found such victories very difficult to understand. It seemed pointless to assault a hill, take losses, and then leave and allow the enemy to take it back. 'Hamburger Hill' received much press coverage in the United States and caused a furore of protest. From down on the streets up to the US Congress demands poured forth that such a battle should never happen again. As a result Nixon ordered Abrams to hold down American casualties in Vietnam. In many ways, then, 'Hamburger Hill' was the final chapter in the American military effort in Vietnam.

Below: A hastily cleared landing strip allows a UH-1D Medevac helicopter to put down and take away wounded from the 101st Airborne Division after injuries sustained in a battle during October 1969.

THE FALL OF LANG VEI SPECIAL FORCES CAMP

A SPECIAL FORCES AND OBSERVATION CAMP SET PRECARIOUSLY IN THE HIGHLANDS OF VIETNAM.

Several firebases, strongpoints and Special Forces' (often known as Green Berets) camps surrounded the US Marine base at Khe Sanh. The Special Forces' locations in the area were part of a series of bases from which Special Forces, in conjunction with local Montagnard tribesmen, guarded the long and vulnerable South Vietnamese border area. From these bases Special Forces units, usually led by US soldiers but manned by Montagnards, 'hopped the fence' on reconnaissance missions into Laos and Cambodia. One such base was located at Lang Vei, a scant five miles (8km) from Khe Sanh. As the NVA began to tighten the siege, the 24 Americans and 500 Montagnards at Lang Vei found themselves surrounded and under constant bombardment and threat of attack. On 7 February 1969 the NVA launched a devastating assault on Lang Vei shortly after midnight. For the first time in the war in South Vietnam the communists made use of armoured warfare, attacking with several Soviet-made PT-76 light tanks. The Green Berets and their Montagnard allies fought tenaciously, using light anti-tank weapons to destroy five enemy tanks, but the NVA tide was irresistible. Communist forces swept over the base and wiped out the defenders in their bunker positions. The NVA used satchel charges, thermite grenades and gas grenades in their assault on the command bunker. As morning came the beleaguered US forces launched counter-attacks and called in air strikes, but Lang Vei had fallen. Some of the survivors were evacuated by helicopter to Khe Sanh, but many had to make the harrowing journey on foot. In the end seven Americans were killed and three were taken prisoner; 200 of the 500 Montagnards were killed.

As the US rationale for the Vietnam War ebbed away, US troops became increasingly demotivated and dispirited. Fighting and dying thousands of miles from home, they felt vilified and persecuted by domestic public opinion.

CRISIS IN CAMBODIA

In 1970 Vietnamization proceeded apace. Nixon was aware that he had to keep his campaign promise of disengaging, especially in a pivotal congressional election year. As a result, over the objections of both Abrams and Thieu, he withdrew an additional 150,000 Americans. Almost at the same time, disaster struck quite unexpectedly in Cambodia. In March, pro-American General Lon Nol overthrew the neutral government of Prince Sihanouk. The new leader ordered the NVA to leave his country and the all-important Ho Chin Minh Trail. The North Vietnamese refused and joined with the Cambodian communist insurgents, the Khmer Rouge, in an effort to destroy Lon Nol and his government.

It was an important moment in the Nixon presidency. He desperately wanted to aid the pro-US Lon Nol regime. In addition his military advisers had pushed for years for an assault into Cambodia to deal with the NVA bases located there. Initially Nixon contented himself with clandestine aid to Lon Nol's government, but he favoured dramatic military aid for the new regime. White House advisers, though, warned the president that such action might be unconstitutional and would certainly spark a firestorm of protest never before seen. In the end Nixon chose a middle ground between inaction and all-out invasion. A force of some 20,000 US and ARVN troops would attack the NVA in the 'Fishhook' and 'Parrot's Beak' sections of Cambodia near Saigon.

LEFT: A JEEP-MOUNTED 106MM RECOILLESS RIFLE IS READIED TO FIRE AT A SUSPECTED VIETCONG POSITION DURING A ROAD PATROL.

BELOW: A REFLECTIVE MOMENT FOR A US PARATROOPER ON TOP OF HAMBURGER HILL, TAKEN AFTER THE HORROR OF DAYS OF COMBAT.

WIDENING THE WAR

Even as this incursion began, Nixon went on television to announce the action. Almost immediately parts of the United States were engulfed in the most serious protest incidents since 1968. It seemed to many that Nixon had broken his pledge to exit Vietnam and was instead widening the war. The protests became violent, most notably at Kent State University in Ohio where four student protesters were shot and killed by the US National Guard. The president, though he had expected protest and had limited the incursion into Cambodia as a result, was livid. He sought to strike back at the protesters, and in so doing began a series of illegal actions against the American people that would result in his demise in the scandal of Watergate (see Chapter 11).

Nixon hoped that the action in Cambodia would accomplish several goals. The surprise assault was designed to catch the NVA unaware and deal them a crushing military defeat. Also US and ARVN forces would destroy the communists' infrastructure there, thus dislocating all NVA planning and ease pressure on the Lon Nol government. Finally the operation would serve as a test of character for

Below: Bell UH-1E helicopters of the US Marines land at Fire Support Base Cunningham, one of the many FSBs heavily in action during search-and-clear operations.

the ARVN. Unbeknown to US planners, though, the communists were well aware of the coming invasion and had made preparations to retreat to avoid undue losses.

On 29 April 1970, ARVN forces, supported by US air power, rolled into the 'Parrot's Beak'. The NVA fell back in the face of the attack. The ARVN for their part seemed only too willing to allow the NVA to escape. On 1 May US and ARVN forces entered the 'Fishhook' region, and the forewarned NVA again eluded decisive battle. In their efforts to achieve victory the US and ARVN forces were once again hampered by limitations placed upon them. Nixon, to reduce protest at home, had directed Abrams to keep casualties low and only invade Cambodia to a depth of 19 miles (30km). Just as so often in the past, then, US forces were frustrated to see the NVA flee just out of their reach into territory that was off limits for political reasons. Nixon also placed a time limit on the operation, ordering Abrams to withdraw all forces from Cambodia by 30 June.

Abrams followed his instructions to the letter, and all US forces exited Cambodia on 30 June. The action had achieved the limited success of dislocating the communists' logistic system. However, decisive victory eluded the Americans. In many ways the episode serves as an illustration for the entire Vietnam War. For several reasons the operation was important enough to undertake, and could have resulted in a clear tactical victory. Political pressure within the United States, though, forced constraints upon it which virtually assured that meaningful victory would prove impossible. After the withdrawal of US forces, the communists duly returned to the area and began to rebuild their logistic system. The principal benefit was that communist planning was disrupted for over a year, giving the flawed process of Vietnamization more time to run its course.

Nixon was certainly dissatisfied with the results of the invasion of Cambodia. Precious little of concrete value had been achieved at the price of social tumult on the home front. He still hoped to achieve an honourable peace that resulted in a viable South Vietnam, though. Towards this end he redoubled his efforts at detente in an attempt to diminish communist support for the North Vietnamese. The quickened pace of Vietnamization, however, meant that Nixon and Kissinger had to achieve results quickly. Another military

In 1969 there were 239 incidents of fragging in the US forces. In 1970 that figure grew to 383, an increase indicative of the collapsing order and morale of the Vietnam forces.

LEFT: AN M48 TANK OF THE 11TH ARMOURED CAVALRY ADVANCES UP A ROAD AFTER DETECTING, AND DESTROYING, A VIETCONG ANTI-TANK MINE.

BELOW: AN AIRBORNE TROOPER GRIMACES IN PAIN WHILE HE WAITS FOR MEDICAL EVACUATION HELICOPTERS TO ARRIVE. SUFFERING INJURIES FOR A CAUSE NO LONGER APPARENT SAPPED THE MORALE OF MANY MEN.

operation, designed to further destroy the Ho Chi Minh Trail and the North Vietnamese logistic system, seemed to be a natural solution.

DECLINING AMERICAN MORALE

The United States had entered the Vietnam War in 1965 with arguably the finest military force in the entire world. By 1970 things had changed. The draft process had filled the US Army with rather reluctant soldiers who were painfully aware that many in their nation had abandoned them and turned against the war. Also by 1970 it had become clear to most American soldiers that the US was withdrawing from the war, and had no real plans to win the conflict. To such men survival, rather than victory, became paramount. Added to this potent mix was an element of racial disharmony. The domestic conflicts between black and white America inevitably had an effect on the army serving in Vietnam. Racial tensions between soldiers were strong, especially in rear areas and sometimes resulted in firefights.

The morale and effectiveness of the US Army in Vietnam fell precipitously during 1970. Units sent out to

Ironically, it was in the last years of the US involvement in Vietnam that the US seemed to find some of its most successful strategies for combating the communists, but they had come too late.

RIGHT: TAKING FROM THE ENEMY. US ENGINEERS CHECK THEIR WAY THROUGH HUNDREDS OF SUPPLY CRATES ABANDONED BY THE COMMUNIST FORCES FOLLOWING AN OPERATION INTO CAMBODIA.

BELOW: A SPECIAL FORCES SOLDIER CHECKS HIS ROTARY-BARRELLED MINI-GUN, CAPABLE OF FIRING 4000 7.62MM ROUNDS PER MINUTE.

find the enemy often preferred to practice 'search and evade' tactics to avoid taking needless casualties. Although such indiscipline did not affect all units, the practice of avoiding battle and disobeying orders became much more common than the military would ever admit.

The US practice of rotating officers out of the field in six months ensured that units prone to morale problems found themselves commanded by young, inexperienced officers. To many men these officers represented a risk to their lives through their inexperience or their efforts to ensure that the unit actually sought out combat with the enemy. As a result the US Army began to suffer from a series of assassinations, or 'fraggings', in which enlisted men attempted to kill their own officers or 'non-coms', usually through the use of a grenade. In 1969 the army reported 96 cases of fragging, and that number rose to an astounding 209 cases in 1970.

Increased drug use also became an indicator of falling morale. Drugs, including marijuana and heroin, were readily available in South Vietnam. In fact the corrupt South Vietnamese government played a major role in their trade. By 1970 drug use was rampant among American soldiers. An exit poll conducted in 1969 revealed that 60 per cent of enlisted men had used marijuana during their tour, and an amazing 35 per cent admitted smoking it over 200 times during their one-year tour of duty. Heroin, though, posed a more serious problem, for not only was it very addictive, it was also cheap. By late 1970 US forces in South Vietnam were suffering two deaths per day from heroin overdose. By 1971 the US Army was forced to admit that 35,000 of its soldiers in Vietnam were heroin addicts. The Vietnam War that had done so much to destroy the consensus on the American home front, was also working to destroy the US Army. This once potent force was, in many ways, falling apart. The damage done to the US armed forces and their image would not be eradicated until the victory in the Gulf some 30 years later.

ABOVE: EVIDENCE OF THE WIDENING WAR. A US ARMOURED PERSONNEL CARRIER CREW STOP FOR A BREAK DURING THE INCURSION INTO CAMBODIA IN 1970, AN ACTION WHICH PROVOKED MASSIVE PUBLIC OUTCRY.

LEFT: A US OFFICER SHOWS NEWSMEN ONE OF THE MANY CARRIAGE-MOUNTED 0.30IN CALIBRE MACHINE-GUNS CAPTURED FROM THE NVA IN CAMBODIA. NVA MATERIAL LOSSES THERE DELAYED THEIR INVASION EFFORTS FOR ANOTHER TWO YEARS.

Chapter 10

The Secret War

Deep in the jungles of Laos and Cambodia, US Special Forces conducted a parallel war to that taking place across the border in Vietnam. The difference in those countries was that if US soldiers were killed or captured, the government would deny the existence of the operations.

The country of Laos, situated between Thailand and Vietnam, became one of the most bombed states of the twentieth century, having been struck by a half-billion tons of US high-explosive between 1964 and 1968.

The first crisis that the United States faced in Southeast Asia was not in Vietnam, but in Laos. The limitations imposed upon the United States by the Geneva Accords dictated that American involvement in Laos, and later Cambodia, would need to be clandestine. Even before American troops splashed ashore at Danang, the CIA and Special Forces had launched a secret war in Laos and Cambodia that would last until 1975. The bitter, often ethnic, nature of the secret war would leave a legacy of hatred and genocide in its wake.

AN UNEXPECTED CRISIS

The nation of Laos, situated between Vietnam and Thailand, occupied a pivotal point in the Cold War strategy of the United States. Even before the French defeat at Dien Bien Phu, the tiny, agricultural nation had become something of a superpower battleground. The Eisenhower administration viewed Laos as the lynchpin of containment, and gave massive military and economic support to the royalist government in Vientiane – even to the point of paying the entire budget of the Royal Lao Army. Opposed to the government was the communist insurgent force known as the Pathet Lao, which received aid from the Soviet Union and China. The neighbouring Vietnamese communists would also come to play an important role in the struggle for control of Laos, especially as the border area became increasingly important to their supply efforts throughout the region.

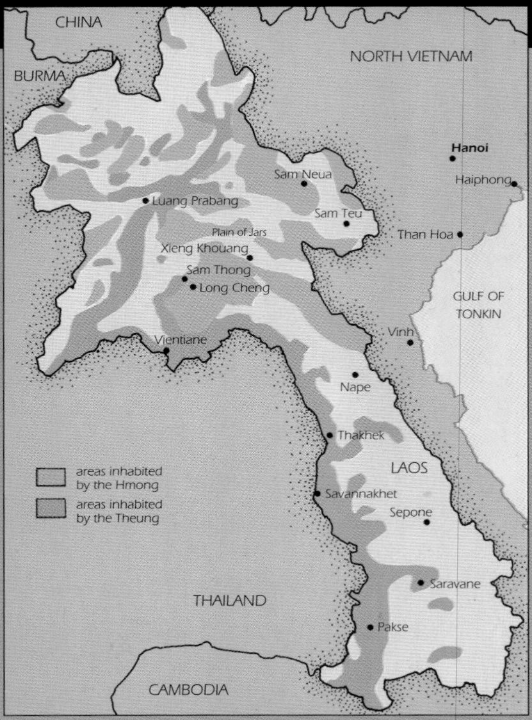

The 1954 Geneva Accords made Laos neutral and forbade superpower involvement there. As a result the growing conflict in Laos had to be waged covertly by both the United States and the Soviet Union. By 1955 Eisenhower's government had decided that Laos was in imminent danger of falling; aid was required to ensure its stability, but the Geneva Accords stood in the way. In an effort to contain the threat of communist expansion yet attempt to remain in compliance with the Geneva Accords the United States created the Programs Evaluation Office (PEO). 'Retired' US military personnel staffed the PEO and were tasked with training and strengthening the Royal Lao Army. By 1959 a total of 428 American advisers were in Laos, beginning the long history of US covert operations in that nation.

ETHNIC DISTRIBUTION IN LAOS

THE KONG LE COUP

A delicate balance had been struck between US- and communist-backed forces in Laos. In 1960, however, that equilibrium was shattered and the nation was dragged into civil war. In April 1960 elections, rigged by the CIA which distributed money liberally, resulted in a government of the political right. The new regime duly struck out against the Pathet Lao. For a young officer named Kong Le the corruption and foreign influence in his country's government was too much to bear. In August the idealistic officer led a successful coup against the pro-American rulers in Vientiane. Le hoped that the resulting government led by Souvanna Phouma would be neutral in nature and help to save his homeland. Phouma, though, soon indicated that he was willing to negotiate with the Pathet Lao and the Soviet Union and forced a crisis in Washington, D.C. The pro-American army under General Phoumi, with PEO advisers and supplied by the CIA, drove Phouma's forces out of the capital. The confrontation between different ideological wings of the Laotian forces shifted to the strategic Plain of Jars. Neither superpower was willing to see its client defeated, and the CIA and Soviet forces conducted massive airlifts of supplies into the area. The superpowers were nearing a clash over the tiny country.

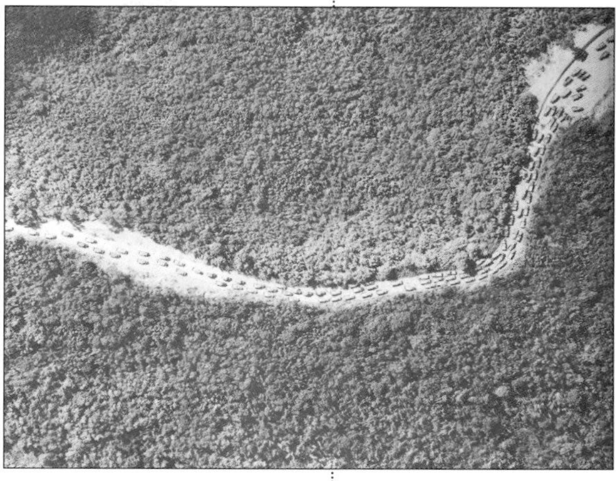

ABOVE: HUNDREDS OF TRUCKS CROWD THE HO CHI MINH TRAIL AS IT SNAKES THROUGH LAOS.

President Eisenhower was keenly aware of the danger posed by the superpower standoff in Laos, but was nearing the end of his term and left the problem to his successor. Before departing office Eisenhower informed the incoming president, John F. Kennedy,

A SPECIAL FORCES TRAINING UNIT.

COMMANDO CLUB

In 1966 the United States once again increased the level of its involvement in Laos. By this time Operation Rolling Thunder had taken a central place in American strategic thinking. However, weather conditions over the north changed quickly and necessitated detailed forecasts to ensure accurate bombing. As a result the US founded a super-secret weather and radar guidance system on the top of Phu Pha Thi Mountain in northern Laos. The mountain was only 20 miles (32km) from North Vietnam and the advanced radar located there could guide bombers to their targets even in the worst of conditions. The operation, codenamed 'Commando Club', also served as a staging area for several CIA commando missions. Usually some 20 Americans, including CIA and USAF personnel, manned the Phu Pha Thi site at any one time. Their radar installation was a virtual fortress. All roads but one to the top of the 5800ft-high (1770m) mountain were heavily mined. Some 300 Hmong and Thai soldiers guarded the remaining road. The important base, and its proof of covert American involvement in Laos, seemed quite safe.

The Vietnamese communists were quite aware of the importance of the radar site, and tried to knock it out by air attack but failed. In March 1968 a sustained ground offensive against the base was launched. The attackers pinned the Hmong defenders into place while an infiltration unit, using hand-held mine detectors, slipped up the 'impregnable' mined roads unnoticed. Once they gained the summit the 18 Americans on duty at the time had little choice but to flee, lowering themselves down the mountain and into a secret cave by means of rope harnesses. For many, though, the exit came too late. News of the assault quickly reached Air America, which sent several rescue helicopters. However, some 11 Americans and the majority of the Hmong defenders were lost.

that Laos was the most important flashpoint in the world. Soon after his inauguration, then, the young president was to face his first crisis. In a public show of support for Laos, Kennedy upgraded the PEO to a Military Assistance and Advisory Group. Losses on the battlefield, though, convinced the United States that its $350 million in aid and nearly 600 military advisers, now operating openly, had done little to make the Royal Lao Army into an effective fighting force. The Pathet Lao guerrillas, supported by a growing infusion of North Vietnamese manpower, had regained the upper hand. The United States had to look for other solutions to contain the advance of communism in Laos. Kennedy received advice from the military to send a force of nearly 150,000 men and tactical nuclear weapons to Laos to crush the insurgency. Kennedy ignored the military's pleas and sought to achieve a diplomatic solution. But while pressing the Soviet Union on the diplomatic front, the US also intensified its covert war in Laos.

THE CIA WAR

Much of the assistance for the US-backed forces in Laos originated in Thailand. There, at Udorn, the CIA air operation, known as Air America, had its base. Supposedly a commercial airline, Air America was staffed by plainclothes CIA agents. Its task was reconnaissance and dangerous covert supply missions into Laos. The CIA established small landing areas, called Lima sites, throughout Laos to support its operations.

Since 1951 the CIA, through a Thai cover organization called the Overseas Southeast Asia Supply Company, had been training the Thai military in

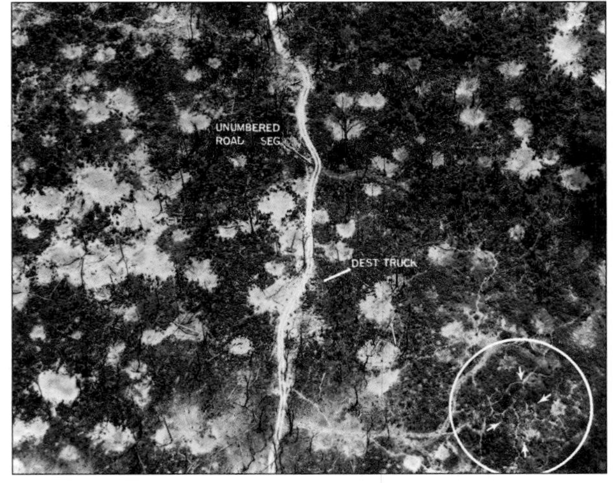

ABOVE: A PILOT OF 23RD TACTICAL AIR SUPPORT SQUADRON DURING A FORWARD AIR CONTROL MISSION TO TARGET ENEMY FORCES.

RIGHT: A US SURVEILLANCE PHOTOGRAPH OF A SECTION OF THE HO CHI MINH TRAIL GRAPHICALLY REVEALS THE DAMAGE DONE BY US BOMBERS.

counter-insurgency techniques. The result of its work was the Police Aerial Reinforcement Units, or PARUs. This highly trained and mobile strike force operated in the vulnerable Thailand-Laos border region against communist insurgents. In 1961 the PARU mission was expanded and Air America carried several CIA operatives and PARU teams into northern Laos for a special covert mission. The failure of the Royal Lao Army had sparked a need for another pro-American military force in Laos.

In the mountain fastness of the northern part of Laos lived members of an ancient culture called the Hmong. With their own language and beliefs, they had resisted absorption into the wider, dominant culture of Laos. Many Hmong regarded the advance of the communists and their promises of revolution as a threat to their independence and way of life. In addition the communists had interrupted the Hmong's lucrative trade in opium. The CIA and PARU teams entered Hmong villages and told them that the communists meant to take their land and offered to help the Hmong defend themselves. By late 1961 the CIA had raised and equipped an indigenous force of over 10,000 Hmong tribesmen. In the south of Laos the CIA recruited from among the Theung tribe in an effort to harass communist supply lines. The effort in the south, though, was secondary, for it was in the north that control of Laos would be won or lost. Air America had to redouble its supply efforts out of Udorn as a result of the successful recruitment. The US now had a second armed force upon which to draw in Laos and the secret war appeared to be going well.

To operate effectively in Laos, the CIA and Special Forces had to try and understand a culture in total contrast to their own. By comprehending Laotian peoples' hopes and fears, it was hoped some could be turned into a motivated fighting force.

LEFT: SPECIAL FORCES SOLDIERS NOT ONLY HAD SUPERB COMBAT ABILITY, BUT ALSO POSSESSED A WIDE RANGE OF SOCIAL, LINGUISTIC AND CULTURAL SKILLS WHICH ENABLED THEM TO FOSTER RELATIONSHIPS WITH ETHNIC MINORITY COMMUNITIES IN SOUTHEAST ASIA.

Laos was one on the great secret battlefields of the Cold War. Not only did the US Special Forces have a presence there, but well over 100,000 NVA troops operated within its borders between 1963 and 1971 alone.

THE GENEVA ACCORDS

As the United States enlarged covert actions in Laos, Kennedy began to push for a negotiated peace. With trouble in Cuba and in South Vietnam, Kennedy believed Laos to be an inappropriate place for a stand against the Soviet Union. By May 1961, 14 nations, including the US and the USSR, began a second Geneva Conference on the future of Laos. On 23 July 1962, the new Geneva Accords were signed. These accords were a compromise agreement aimed at constructing a truly neutral government in Laos. The neutral Phouma would serve as prime minister of Laos and would preside over a coalition government in which Pathet Lao and royalists would share power. In addition all US, Soviet and North Vietnamese forces had to exit Laos. Some 666 US military advisers left the country and abandoned their royalist and Hmong allies. All Soviet advisers left as well. As it turned out, though, the Soviets wielded little practical influence on the Pathet Lao or their Vietnamese allies. The North Vietnamese, who for reasons of logistics had to retain control of their border with Laos, withdrew only a token force of some 40 soldiers. This action alarmed the US, for the CIA estimated that some 6000 North Vietnamese remained behind in Laos in violation of the agreement reached in Geneva. This continued presence worried Kennedy, but he had achieved his main goal of avoiding superpower confrontation in Laos. In addition, by this time the American focus in Southeast Asia had begun to shift to South Vietnam. The war in Laos was not over, but it would become an increasingly secret war fought in the shadow of the larger war in Vietnam.

PATHET LAO 1962–1973

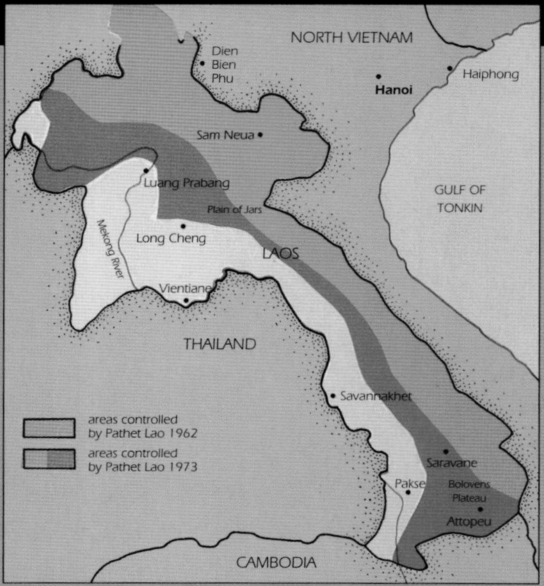

THE RETURN OF THE CIA

The United States soon began to reconstruct its covert presence in Laos. Through a branch of the USAID program in Vientiane military supplies reached forces loyal to US interests. The shipments were controlled through the Military Assistance and Advisory Group Thailand. For military operations within Laos the United States now relied wholly upon the CIA. Its operatives had to retain a level of 'plausible deniability', which meant that if they were caught within the boundaries of Laos the US government would disavow them.

The CIA rekindled its relationship with the Hmong, and even brought several hundred tribesmen, under the command of the Hmong general Vang Pao, to Thailand for training. Once again only the efforts of 'civilian' Air America pilots, who flew their tiny aircraft into small airstrips in remote and dangerous jungle locations, often navigating only with dead reckoning, made the covert war possible.

THE MONTAGNARDS

Several distinct ethnic minorities inhabited the mountains of Southeast Asia. To Americans serving in South Vietnam these people were usually referred to as Montagnards, which is French for 'mountain people'. A tribal people with a comparatively primitive lifestyle, the Montagnards' relationship with the Vietnamese was full of animosity and violence. The Vietnamese regarded them as inferiors and used the pejorative term *moi*, or 'savages', to describe them. Within the ranks of these mountain tribes there were various distinct cultures and religions. The main peoples numbered the Jarai, Rhade, Sedang and Bru. They loathed the Vietnamese in return and would do almost anything to remain independent from their rule.

US WEAPONS DISTRIBUTION.

Into this dynamic relationship stepped US Special Forces and the top-secret Studies and Observation Group (SOG). These US forces hired the Montagnards as mercenaries to fight the North Vietnamese and Vietcong both inside South Vietnam and as part of the American secret war waged in North Vietnam, Laos and Cambodia. The Montagnards were usually happy to serve, and with training and modern arms proved to be loyal friends and determined fighters. Montagnard forces served several functions during the US war in South Vietnam: large groups of them manned Special Forces camps near the borders with Cambodia and Laos in an effort to interdict supplies; and Montagnard troops made up the bulk of personnel in the secret SOG missions into Laos and Cambodia. The Montagnards fought hard for the American cause, but the eventual US withdrawal left them vulnerable to violent ethnic-cleansing operations at the hands of the victorious communists.

LEFT: ACTING AS VIETCONG, POPULAR FORCES SOLDIERS IN VIETNAM UNDERGO A TRAINING EXERCISE AT THE LONG HAI TRAINING CENTER, MARCH 1970. US TRAINING OF VIETNAMESE FORCES RAPIDLY INCREASED AS THE US STARTED TO PULL ITS TROOPS OUT OF THE FIRING LINE.

Studies and Observation Group soldiers faced an appalling future if captured. With the government not acknowledging their presence and many VC/NVA deaths on their hands, they were often subjected to torture.

RIGHT: THE US USED MANY CIVILIAN AIRCRAFT TO CONDUCT ITS MISSIONS AND RECONNAISSANCE OVER TERRITORIES SUCH AS LAOS AND CAMBODIA. THE AIRCRAFT HERE IS A N91572 ICCS VOLPAR BASED AT THE TAN SON NHUT AIRBASE IN SOUTH VIETNAM.

In 1963 and 1964 events transpired in Laos and Thailand which placed the US State Department, and the ambassador in Vientiane, Leonard Unger, in charge of US war efforts in Laos. The power-sharing agreement stipulated by the Geneva Accords quickly broke down and the Pathet Lao, and its North Vietnamese allies, again began to place military pressure on the Phouma government. The main area of conflict was around the Plain of Jars, where the communist forces won victories against the outmatched Laotian military. As a reaction to the deteriorating military situation the US sent USAF units to the Air America base at Udorn to train Thai and Laotian pilots in order to provide combat air support for the Royal Lao Army. In a top-secret move the CIA recruited several American fliers to pilot combat missions in Laos. The Americans flew planes marked with Royal Lao Air Force colours and were designated the 'A Team'. Unger also pressured Phouma into allowing overt USAF and US Navy reconnaissance flights, codenamed 'Yankee Team', over communist-controlled territory. Unger and the US State Department controlled the operations of both the 'A Team' and the reconnaissance flights.

THE WAR GROWS

In November 1964 a new leader, the incoming US ambassador William Sullivan, took over the secret war in Laos. He wielded unprecedented power for a diplomat, even overruling General William Westmoreland in matters concerning Laos. His power derived from the role Kennedy had given to Unger, but Sullivan increased both his power and the US involvement. Sullivan commanded the force of US advisers in Laos, CIA operatives, Air America, USAF and US Navy flights, as well as the irregular Hmong army under Vang Pao.

By 1964 the Hmong army had become a formidable fighting force, advised and supplied by Sullivan's CIA agents. Within the Hmong army there existed the Special Guerilla Unit. Its task was to harass the communists' positions and supply lines, especially during the monsoon season. At that time the torrential rain forced the Pathet Lao and their Vietnamese allies to operate along roads. The Hmong, using the superior mobility provided to them through the Air America effort, launched raids to destroy the communists' logistic system. When the dry season came, the communists would counter-attack and methodically capture Hmong mountain villages. The secret war between the Hmong and the communists followed this pattern until the end of the conflict in Laos. By the late 1960s the clashes between the two sides had grown in size and intensity. Entire companies of Hmong used airmobile tactics, aided by Air America, to helicopter-assault into enemy-held territory. When operations took place special covert US Forward Air Controllers (FACs), or 'Ravens', circled overhead and CIA, USAF and US Navy air strikes pummelled the communists' positions. The war, though still covert, had become in some ways more traditional in nature than the growing conflict in South Vietnam, and every bit as intense. Bomb tonnage can be used as a way to illustrate the extent of the size of the war in Laos and the clandestine US involvement in it – in 1967 and 1968 US forces dropped 500,000 tons (510,000,000kg) of bombs on North Vietnam, but during the same period US forces dropped 350,000 tons (355,000,000kg) of bombs on Laos. The increase in the intensity of the fighting in Laos had a very dark side. A bitter rivalry developed between the Hmong and the communists, and both sides engaged in atrocities. The Pathet Lao and the North Vietnamese came to loathe the Hmong and adopted as their goal the utter destruction of their fearsome ethnic minority adversaries.

Below: US supply aircraft ensured many special operations units remained operable in the field for long periods.

Above: A light aircraft takes off from its dirt-strip runway. Its short landing capability made it ideal for special operations deployments.

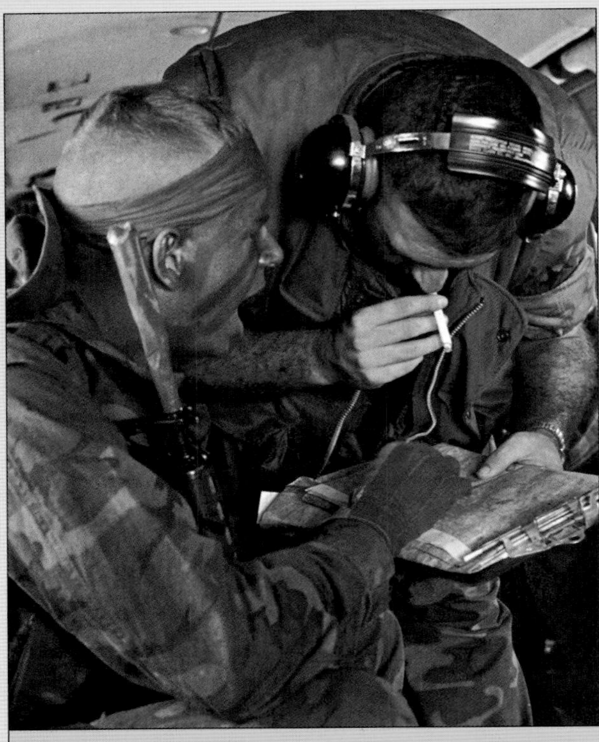

An SOG mission in progress.

SOG

In 1964 the United States formed the top secret Studies and Observation Group (SOG) to coordinate clandestine activity both in and outside South Vietnam. The volunteer unit was subdivided into five sections whose missions included everything from psychological warfare to infiltration into North Vietnam. SOG circumvented the normal chain of command, and its commander reported directly to the Joint Chiefs of Staff. Often the president himself had to approve super-sensitive SOG missions. Their units, usually 12-man teams made up of three Americans and nine indigenous soldiers, had as one of their main missions cross-border surveillance of the Ho Chi Minh Trail. In addition SOG units rescued downed pilots, sabotaged communist materiel, rescued prisoners and carried out assassinations. SOG units were usually inserted into Cambodia or Laos by helicopter, whereupon they attempted to avoid detection while surveying communist supply activities. The units were in the heart of enemy territory, and if they were detected they had to request emergency helicopter evacuation or face annihilation. Once in a position of safety SOG could direct devastating air strikes upon enemy positions in Cambodia and Laos. As the war continued such missions became ever more dangerous as the North Vietnamese began to devote more time and effort to stopping them. In the end some 40,000 communist troops were designated to guard the Ho Chi Minh Trail in the face of the SOG threat. Although SOG usually attempted to avoid battle, when forced to fight it was quite a formidable unit – these secret warriors killed an estimated 150 enemy soldiers for each member of their own lost in battle.

Below: A US supply aircraft gathers speed for take off.

Another aspect of the Hmong war was the reconnaissance in enemy territory. Especially as the conflict in South Vietnam widened, the US found itself in desperate need of intelligence about traffic on the Ho Chi Minh Trail. The Hmong, along with covert Thai irregular forces, formed Road Watch (RW) commando units to undertake these important missions. Helicopter-insertion missions, dubbed the 'Pony Express', carried these RW teams to their ultimate locations, sometimes even into North Vietnam itself. While there the small teams attempted to avoid detection and survey the traffic on the trail system. Intelligence results were then radioed to circling aircraft for evaluation. The NVA was well aware that it was being watched and did its utmost, including the use of bloodhound dogs, to locate and destroy the Hmong teams. These valuable surveillance missions thus resulted in a high mortality rate among the Hmong commandos.

A SECRET WAR BECOMES PUBLIC

In 1969 the US Congress, which was aware of the poorly kept secret of US involvement in Laos, began to hold hearings on the covert war. By March 1970 President Nixon was forced to announce that the US had over 1000 citizens working for and with the Laotian military. Neither the Soviets nor the Chinese, though, made an issue of the US admission, and the war went on as usual, albeit more publicly.

Also in that year Vang Pao's irregular Hmong force made a desperate and ambitious bid for victory on the Plain of Jars. The surprise attack, codenamed Operation About Face, caught the Vietnamese and Pathet Lao off guard and initially scored a major victory. However, the communists regrouped and counter-attacked the Hmong with a sizeable armoured force. Vang Pao was virtually defenceless against such an assault and Laos appeared ready, finally, to fall to communism. In an effort to rescue their tottering ally the Americans unleashed B-52 strikes upon the communists for the first time, and the Plain of Jars suffered immense destruction as a result. The Hmong force had been saved, but the momentum of the conflict had switched irrevocably to the communists.

The Royal Lao Army was a corrupt and weak force that was unable, no matter the amount of American aid, to stand up to the enemy. For this reason the Hmong had shouldered the burden of the secret war in Laos for years. The effects of the fighting were beginning to tell. The Hmong had suffered over 10,000 fatal casualties, and over 100,000 of their people had been forced to flee their ancestral homeland. The steady losses forced

BELOW: A CLANDESTINE US AIRSTRIP. BECAUSE US TROOPS HAD NO OFFICIAL JURISDICTION IN A PLACE SUCH AS LAOS, MILITARY AIRCRAFT WERE NOT USED.

the Hmong to call up 13-year-old fighters by 1970. Although they fought on, Vang Pao and his tribal army had been defeated. They relied on continued American air support for survival. Their strength, though, was gone and it was only a matter of time before their merciless Pathet Lao and Vietnamese enemies hunted them down.

A KIND OF PEACE

US involvement in Laos wound down in the 1970s, following the pattern of the end of the Vietnam War. By 1972 peace talks were being held in Vientiane, even as the Hmong continued to struggle with the communists. Phouma and the Laotian government realized that the US was ending its involvement in Southeast Asia, leaving them to face the communists without meaningful support. Feeling abandoned, on 21 February 1971 the government came to terms on a power-sharing agreement with the Pathet Lao. Laos became a neutral nation, and once again US forces exited the country even though up to 60,000 North Vietnamese did not. But much like the ceasefire in South Vietnam, the peace in Laos was short lived.

LAOS & CAMBODIA INCURSIONS

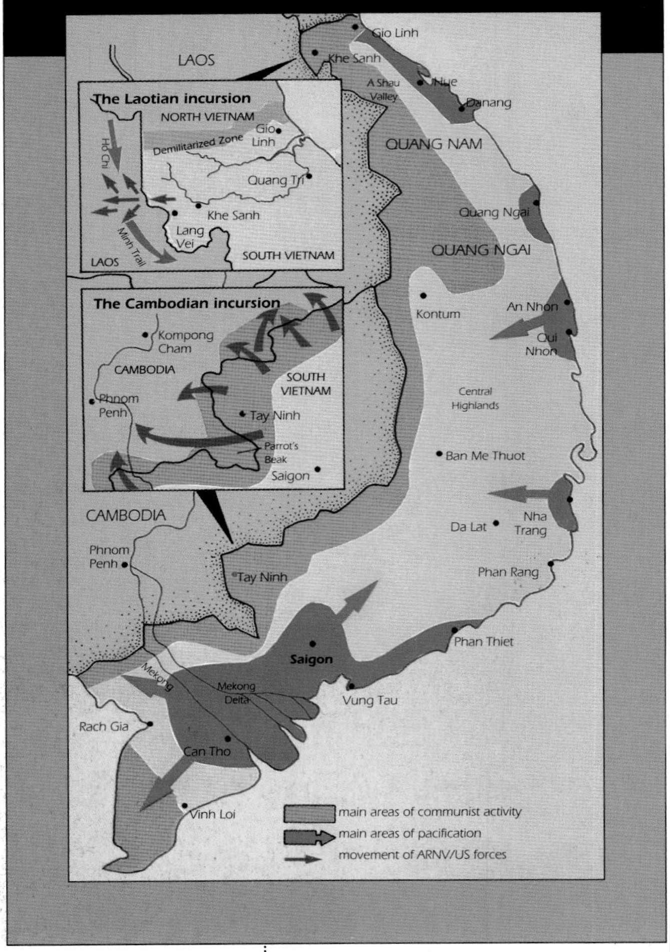

The Pathet Lao and their Vietnamese allies continued to place pressure on the tottering Hmong army and their inept Royal Lao allies. The government and the few remaining US personnel attempted to bring a halt to the fighting, but could not. In many ways the United States had started, and funded, the war in Laos, and without massive American military aid the government forces were at a loss as to what to do. The Pathet Lao scored victory after victory and within a short time most non-communist members of the government had recognized the inevitable and fled to Thailand. As for the Hmong, who had been but simple farmers before the CIA recruited them to fight an American war, the end was at hand. As the communists closed in for the kill, Vang Pao beseeched the United States for aid – and received it. In its last major operation of the secret war the United States used air power to remove several thousand Hmong from their last base near the Plain of Jars. Most would become refugees in Thailand. Those who were unable to flee suffered as victims of the savage communist ethnic cleansing of the nation. In December 1975 the Pathet Lao proclaimed the founding of the Lao People's Democratic Republic. The United States had lost the secret war.

From 1965, the communists' presence in Cambodia gradually increased in strength and confidence. The US found itself with another threat to nearby Vietnam and turned to its Special Forces and American air power.

LEFT: A GROUP OF KHMER ROUGE GUERRILLAS MOVE THROUGH THE COUNTRYSIDE IN WESTERN CAMBODIA.

BELOW: CIVILIAN REFUGEES HEAD FOR THE THAI BORDER THROUGH FLOODED RAINY SEASON FIELDS. CAMBODIA'S POPULATION ULTIMATELY BECAME VICTIMS OF ONE OF THE GREATEST GENOCIDES IN HISTORY.

CAMBODIA

The efforts of the United States in Cambodia took quite a different form than the secret war in Laos had. Cambodia, under Norodom Sihanouk, had achieved its independence from the French in 1953, and was made neutral as a result of the Geneva Accords of 1954. Sihanouk, hoping to keep his nation out of the growing conflagration in Southeast Asia, attempted to remain neutral and balance his nation between the conflicting demands of the communists and those of the United States. Failure doomed his nation to suffer a holocaust.

Initially Sihanouk sought out the aid of the United States during the formation of his military. Seeing Cambodia as a possible bulwark against communism, the US provided Sihanouk with funding of over $85 million, and established a 30-person Military Assistance and Advisory Group in Cambodia to aid in the training of the Cambodian Army. Unlike Laos, Cambodia suffered from no sizeable native communist insurgency. The threat came from the North Vietnamese who coveted the border regions of Cambodia for use in the Ho Chi Minh Trail complex.

SPECIAL FORCES ON PATROL.

DANIEL BOONE

By May 1967 supplies streaming through Cambodia to the communist forces in South Vietnam had become so important to supporting the war that the United States authorized SOG to undertake clandestine surveillance missions – known as 'Daniel Boone' missions – to locate the Ho Chi Minh Trail complex. US forces would operate in a 'sterile' environment, meaning that they wore plain uniforms, carried no identification, and were usually armed with enemy AK-47s. The SOG units were instructed to avoid combat at all costs and if US personnel were captured they would be disavowed. One such 'Daniel Boone' mission took place in 1969. US intelligence believed it had located in Cambodia the ever-elusive COSVN, or the communist's command headquarters in the south. In April 1969 an Arc Light strike pummelled COSVN, but the US needed proof of the strike's effectiveness. As a result SOG prepared a 'Hatchet Force' company to survey the damage and it was inserted by helicopter even as the bombs of the B-52s exploded. The resulting operation was disastrous. The SOG men landed inside an area of communist-prepared defence and fell under withering enemy gunfire almost immediately. Indeed the gunfire was so heavy that the helicopters could not return for an evacuation. In an effort to save their compatriots several SOG troopers charged headlong into the devastating field of fire surrounding COSVN. Only after a bombing support run could the beleaguered SOG evacuate the area. Its losses were heavy and the bravery and sacrifice of the troopers went unnoticed, for their actions were so secret that they could not receive medals. If they were killed they were listed as MIA or were said to have been killed inside South Vietnam.

CRUMBLING US RELATIONS

The marriage of convenience between Cambodia and the United States soon became troubled. As the war in South Vietnam intensified, it carried over into Cambodia. By 1960 North Vietnamese troops were making overt use of northeastern Cambodia to infiltrate South Vietnam. More seriously NVA and VC forces were constructing logistic bases within the borders of Cambodia to use as safe havens in their war. Sihanouk, again unwilling to involve his country directly in the growing war, formally protested, but in the main turned a blind eye to the actions. The Cambodian Army thus monitored communist activity in Cambodia, but did not directly intervene.

During the secret bombing missions over Cambodia, B52 pilots would take off expecting to attack targets in South Vietnam, only to be rerouted mid-flight to a cross-border destination.

The United States regarded Sihanouk's actions as quixotic. He accepted US aid, but seemed to do nothing constructive with it. Although barred from entering Cambodia by the Geneva Accords, South Vietnamese forces and US advisers often followed Vietcong forces across the border in 'hot pursuit'. The Cambodians protested about such actions, and in response to them they opened diplomatic relations with China in 1958. Sihanouk also became convinced that the CIA was behind a secret plot to oust him from power and replace him with a more stalwart anti-communist. He was facing a rightist insurgency in Cambodia led by the Khmer Serei, an uprising which Sihanouk believed had the backing of the United States. The situation worsened in 1965 when US forces in South Vietnam began to recruit irregular forces from a Cambodian minority known as the Khmer Krom for service with the Studies and Observations Group (SOG). This ethnic minority was also

LEFT: A US SPECIAL FORCES COMMANDER INSPECTS THE WEAPONRY OF TROOPS FROM THE VIETNAMESE MOBILE STRIKE FORCE, TRAINED BY US ADVISERS AND SPECIALISTS.

BELOW: A GOVERNMENT SOLDIER GUARDS A SHRINE IN PHNOM PENH, CAMBODIA.

a stalwart part of the insurgency against Sihanouk's rule and the relationship between the US and Sihanouk quickly fell apart. In 1965 Cambodia severed diplomatic relations with the United States and all American military advisers were forced to leave the nation.

COMMUNIST INVOLVEMENT

Cambodia then began to receive military aid from the communist bloc. In addition Sihanouk allowed the North Vietnamese access to the deep-water port of Sihanoukville. From there supplies poured into the burgeoning NVA and Vietcong base areas along the Cambodian border with South Vietnam. Ironically, as Cambodia's relations with the communists warmed, a peasant uprising in 1967 led to the formation of a communist insurgency against Sihanouk led by Saloth Sar (alias Pol Pot) in charge of the Khmer Rouge.

The United States was well aware of the communist build-up and their base camp system in Cambodia. Special Forces teams, with small numbers of local mercenaries, had been crossing the border since 1967. These so-called 'Daniel Boone' missions were designed to discover and monitor these base camps and the activities of the communists. As the Tet Offensive had made clear, these bases were crucial to the

RIGHT: US ARMOUR PREPARES TO GO INTO ACTION DURING AN INVASION OF CAMBODIA IN MAY 1970.

BELOW: US TROOPS FOLLOW IN THE WAKE OF ADVANCING ARVN TROOPS DURING OPERATION LAM SON 719, THE SOUTH VIETNAMESE INVASION OF LAOS IN EARLY 1971.

overall communist strategy in the war. As the United States began its slow withdrawal from the conflict, or Vietnamization, the importance of these Cambodian bases grew. Destruction of the base areas would give the South Vietnamese time to prepare to defend themselves on their own.

SECRET BOMBING MISSIONS

In March 1969 the United States launched a series of bombing missions over the bases in Cambodia, dubbed the 'Menu Series'. The raids at least had the tacit support of the ever-wavering Sihanouk who had now come to fear the extensive communist presence in his country. During the 'Menu Series', US B-52 bombers flew some 3630 raids into Cambodia. These raids violated the Geneva Accords and were thus kept secret from the American public. B-52 pilots were told that they would be bombing locations in South Vietnam and were only rerouted to Cambodia in flight. In addition the Pentagon resorted to a system of 'dual reporting' of their missions in order to falsify the records and keep the activities secret from the US Congress.

The raids were effective, and drove the communists deeper into Cambodia in search of safer havens. This act forced confrontations between the communists and Cambodian forces. A powerful member of the Sihanouk government, General Lon Nol, believed that the prime minister was not acting with enough vigour against this enemy within and in March 1970 he staged a coup and formed a much more pro-US government.

LON NOL AND THE FALL OF CAMBODIA

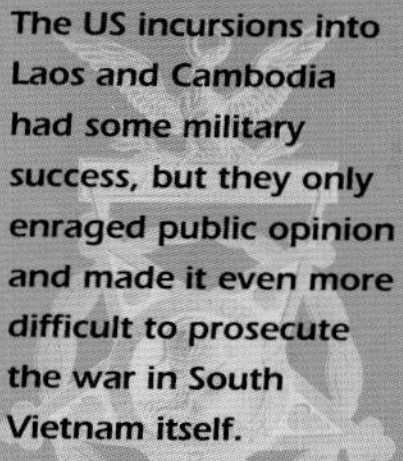
The US incursions into Laos and Cambodia had some military success, but they only enraged public opinion and made it even more difficult to prosecute the war in South Vietnam itself.

The communists feared that Lon Nol would do what Sihanouk never would and allow the US to act in Cambodia. As a result, they began to move their safe havens ever deeper into Cambodia. The process quickened when US and South Vietnamese forces invaded in late April 1970. For the purposes of the Vietnam War the invasion of Cambodia was a success, dislocating the communists' supply lines. However, the invasion had far-reaching consequences for the regime of Lon Nol. The retreating North Vietnamese conquered much of northeastern Cambodia and turned the land over to the Khmer Rouge, a force that now counted the popular Sihanouk among their number. These developments thus reinvigorated and strengthened a communist insurgency that had been moribund.

As the threat to Lon Nol's regime rose, so did renewed US aid for the beleaguered government. Between 1970 and 1975 the US would send some $1.8 billion in aid in an effort to contain the advance of communism. However, the Cambodian Army, like the Royal Lao Army, was to prove no match for the rising strength of the Khmer Rouge or their North Vietnamese allies.

By 1973 and the end of American involvement in South Vietnam, the Khmer Rouge controlled nearly 70 per cent of the Cambodian countryside. Lon Nol's forces had suffered a series of military setbacks and had fallen back upon the capital of Phnom Penh. The Khmer Rouge stood ready to destroy the government's forces and end the war in Cambodia. President Nixon, though, was not yet ready to 'lose' Cambodia and unleashed the B-52s once again. The raids, also known as Arc Light strikes, had continued in a rather on-again, off-again fashion since the 'Menu Series', as and when they were needed. However, the weight of the bombing used to defend Phnom Penh was unprecedented. The raids drove the Khmer Rouge back into the countryside, having caused them considerable losses. They would not return to attack the capital again for nearly two years.

The air strikes, though, also had terrible effects on both Cambodia and the Lon Nol regime itself. In all some 540,000 tons (5,490,000kg) of bombs were dropped on Cambodia, more than three times the amount dropped on Japan in World War II. The bombing destroyed the fragile Cambodian economy and killed over 100,000 people. Lon Nol now had little to defend but refugees, with an army that was disintegrating. As pressure in the United States rose to end all military involvement in Southeast Asia, the Cambodian regime lost its last supporter. When it became clear to the Khmer Rouge that the B-52s would not return, they attacked and once again bore down on the capital. The bombings had played a pivotal role in converting the Khmer Rouge into a brutal killing machine. By April 1975 the Khmer Rouge had emerged victorious and begun to exact a terrible revenge on their enemies.

BELOW: VICTORIOUS KHMER ROUGE TROOPS ENTER PHNOM PENH FOLLOWING THE FINAL DEFEAT OF GOVERNMENT FORCES. THIS VICTORY WAS ONLY THE BEGINNING OF CAMBODIA'S BLOODY TROUBLES.

CHAPTER 11

The Home Front

A US TROOPER STANDS GUARD OVER A BURNING BUILDING IN WASHINGTON, D.C., FOLLOWING RIOTS IN THE WAKE OF THE ASSASSINATION OF DR MARTIN LUTHER KING, JR. THE TIME OF THE VIETNAM WAR WAS ONE OF INTENSE WORLDWIDE CIVIL PROTEST AND POLITICAL UPHEAVAL, AND VIOLENCE STARTED TO SPREAD FAR BEYOND THE BOUNDARIES OF SOUTHEAST ASIA.

Television put the realities of combat in the Vietnam War directly into people's home. They were often shocked by what they saw, and that shock grew into angry protest against US government policy.

The United States entered the Vietnam War as a society generally united in favour of the conflict. Within a few short years, though, the support for the war dwindled and the country seemed to be on the verge of revolution. The Vietnam War cannot be isolated from the 1960s and the racial and social discord that beset the nation during the period interacted with the war and the draft system in a dynamic way. These related forces converged in 1968, a year of assassinations, riots and political discord. It was the year in which the fate of the Vietnam War was decided on the home front.

The Vietnam era was a turbulent one and some historians believe that the United States came perilously close to revolution While such claims are too strong it is certainly safe to say that the cracks that appeared in the American edifice were the most serious since the American Civil War. The 1960s would have been a difficult decade for the United States even without the war: it was the era of civil rights and sex equality; the 'baby boom' generation came of age and demanded its due; the modern American

RIGHT: THE POWER OF THE MEDIA. A US WAR CORRESPONDENT FILES A REPORT TO CAMERA AT A MILITARY BASE, FOR LATER BROADCAST IN THE US.

A CIVIL RIGHTS DEMONSTRATION, 1965.

THE GREAT SOCIETY

The presidency of Lyndon Johnson centred around the implementation of what he called his 'Great Society', which entailed sweeping changes in the structure of society and the economy to make the United States more inclusive. As a result Johnson fundamentally altered the American welfare state, and passed considerable legislation supporting civil rights. The Civil Rights Act and the Voting Rights Act did away with legalized segregation in the Deep South, but did not do away with racial violence or intolerance. Johnson worked hard to make his 'Great Society' a reality. So hard in fact that he had relatively little time to devote to the burgeoning war in Vietnam. The American commander-in-chief was distracted. In addition, Johnson believed that he had to retain the support of the majority of Americans to be able to implement his plan of sweeping societal change. As a result he was unwilling to risk the national consensus by involving the country in a true war in Vietnam. Partly out of concern for political unity in favour of the 'Great Society' project, then, Johnson placed limitations on the nation's involvement in Vietnam that would make the war unwinnable. In the end the gamble failed and the lost war destroyed the national consensus for reform, dooming the Great Society. Johnson would leave the presidency a beaten man, having failed both in Vietnam and on the home front.

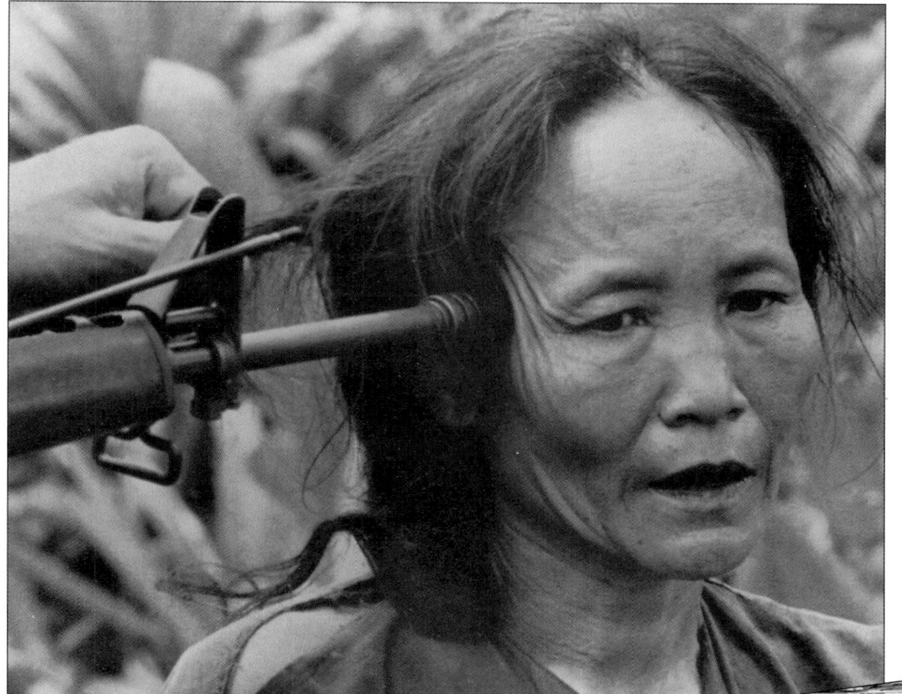

LEFT: IMAGES SUCH AS THIS, INVOLVING CIVILIANS, SERVED ONLY TO INFLAME ANTI-WAR SENTIMENT IN THE UNITED STATES.

BELOW: A 73-YEAR-OLD BUDDHIST MONK BURNS HIMSELF TO DEATH IN A PROTEST AGAINST THE SAIGON GOVERNMENT. IN 1963 THIS PICTURE SHOCKED THE WESTERN WORLD.

welfare state was born; the counter-culture experimented with drugs and new modes of thought; and the new, more decadent form of rock-n-roll music became the language of the day. These factors alone would have forced a difficult social transformation upon America. When the difficulty of Vietnam was added to the mix it became almost too much for the American body politic to bear. The fortunes of the decade and the war are intertwined so completely that to understand the outcome of the war, one must understand the nature of the decade and life on the home front during it.

In the 1950s America had been a confident superpower. With the trusted President Eisenhower in command the United States seemed to be immune from foreign challenges and free from internal strife. Although the Soviet Union had 'the bomb', the US retained a significant edge in world power. At home nobody questioned authority and the American family resembled the perfect one portrayed on television's *Leave it to Beaver*. The new decade of the 1960s dawned with the election to office of charismatic young John F. Kennedy who urged the people to 'Think not what your country can do for you, but what you can do for your country'. All seemed to bode well for the new decade.

Right: A defiant reversal of hippie philosophy is scrawled on the helmet of this US soldier in Vietnam. The psychological gulf between Vietnam veterans and US civilians could be profound.

Below: Dr Martin Luther King, Jr., leads a crowd of around 10,000 people during a 50-mile (80km) protest march in Alabama on 25 March 1965.

THE TURBULENT 1960S

Roiling beneath the surface calm, however, were currents that would threaten the country's unity of purpose during the coming decade. Most importantly, the landmark US Supreme Court decision in Brown vs Board of Education ruled out segregated schools, shining a glaring light on American race relations and fuelling the Civil Rights Movement. Advocates of civil rights would find their leader in the person of Rev. Martin Luther King, Jr. The nation, and the world, watched in wonder as Dr King led peaceful marches protesting against the inequities of the segregated South. White southerners did not want change, however – peaceful or otherwise. King was arrested several times, his marchers were beaten, leaders were assassinated and the racist Ku Klux Klan terrorized the night. Advocates of civil rights persevered, and perfected the tactics of civil disobedience, such as sit-ins, that would later be adopted by anti-war elements. Kennedy, who was beginning the American involvement in Vietnam, had to intervene in what was a worsening situation. But before he could make a substantive difference he was assassinated, leaving the war and the problems of the home front to his successor, Lyndon B. Johnson.

LEFT: AS US INVOLVEMENT IN VIETNAM GREW, PROTESTS AT HOME ESCALATED. HERE MARCHERS PASS DOWN PENNSYLVANIA AVENUE IN FRONT OF THE WHITE HOUSE, ADVERTISING THEIR MESSAGE ON BANNERS AND THROUGH CHANTS.

Although the political power of protesters was in many senses limited, the anti-war mood caught on with many in the wider electorate and left government leaders looking politically indecisive.

THE BEGINNING OF PROTEST

As American involvement in the Vietnam War began in 1965, Johnson's social and foreign policy enjoyed widespread support. Most Americans believed in the Cold War theory of containment and agreed that defence of South Vietnam was critical to the security of their own nation. However, the manner in which the United States became involved in the conflict aroused suspicion among many and added to the problems. Several inconsistencies, from campaign promises that American 'boys' would not be sent to Vietnam to fight a war to the seeming falsehoods surrounding the Gulf of Tonkin incident and the dictatorial nature of the regime in South Vietnam, caused doubt concerning the US role in Southeast Asia. Many Americans were critical of Johnson and called on him to launch more devastating attacks upon North Vietnam and end the war quickly. Most noticeable, though, were protesters who believed that the country should exit the conflict. Anti-war sentiment was concentrated in the universities, where protest groups were formed, the most important of which was the Students for a Democratic Society.

Anti-war elements were an amorphous group. Due to their disorganization protesters never wielded any true political power, though they were adept at causing trouble and grabbing headlines. Most protesters were students or members of the counter-culture who vaguely believed that American involvement in Vietnam was wrong and participated in protests as part of the 'in thing' to do. There were, however, some minor groups of people who were true radicals and sought to bring down the existing system. The most infamous group was the Weathermen, anarchists who bombed Reserve Officer Training Corps' (ROTC) buildings. Most popular protest, then, had as its goal the ending of a conflict that was wasting American lives – not a fundamental restructuring of power within the United States. Thus, as painful as the protests became, they never portended revolution.

DEFECTIONS AND DECISIONS

BELOW: THE EMINENT BABY AND CHILD CARE SPECIALIST DR. BENJAMIN SPOCK FRONTS AN ANTI-WAR PRESS CONFERENCE, ONE OF MANY HIGH-PROFILE PROTESTERS.

Much to Johnson's growing concern, events on the home front only fuelled the fire of protest. In February 1966 Senator William Fulbright, having rethought his role in passing the 'Gulf of Tonkin Resolution', held public hearings questioning American involvement in Vietnam. The hearings were seen on television by millions and helped to legitimize anti-war views. In spring 1967 the Civil Rights Movement became intertwined with the anti-war movement when Dr Martin Luther King, Jr., went public with his anti-war sentiments. He contended that the United States had become so caught up in fighting communism that it had lost its way and become involved in oppression. In addition Dr King stated that the billions spent on killing in Vietnam could be better spent in an effort to end poverty and want in the USA. Other influential people, including Muhammed Ali and Jane Fonda, added their voices to the growing chorus of protest. Although the defection of national leaders from the wartime cause anguished Johnson, it was his own actions that caused the greatest amount of turmoil in the country.

When the involvement in Vietnam began, the American economy was robust and Johnson was fully aware that a strong economy makes for happy citizens and a political consensus. For this reason Johnson was wary of dislocating the economy in wartime. The spectre of recession and hardship thus played an important role in his decision to not call out the National Guard and Reserve to provide troops for Vietnam. But the president's efforts to avoid discord failed, for he and his military advisers chose to rely on the draft system to supply the manpower that was needed and nothing would do more to polarize the home front than the inequities of the draft.

RIGHT: DRAFT CARDS ARE DEPOSITED IN A BOX PASSED AROUND AT A DEMONSTRATION IN FRONT OF A FEDERAL BUILDING IN SAN FRANCISCO.

THE DRAFT

The draft system in the United States during the Vietnam War caused a public outcry. Perhaps the most controversial aspect of the draft was the number of deferments available to those with either the money or the intelligence. First and foremost college students were deferred from service during their years in school. Enrolment at universities and colleges rocketed as the massive 'baby boom' generation took full advantage of the loophole. Universities, already bastions of liberalism, became filled with students of draft age who desperately wanted to avoid service in the war. For this reason universities from Berkley to Harvard became centres of anti-war feeling. Other forms of deferment existed for those not attending college: it was well known that the National Guard would not be sent to Vietnam, so the waiting list for this 'safe' form of national service grew to staggering lengths; a note from a sympathetic doctor to a draft board stating that the draftee was infirm was enough to obtain one; homosexuals and married men with children did not have to serve; finally those employed in exempted professions received deferment – in short, men with connections and cash could avoid service if they chose to do so.

The result of the inequities of the draft was an army that relied on conscripts taken from the lower strata of society. Many men certainly made themselves available for the draft or enlisted out of a sense of honour and duty to country. However, most of the men who served were too poor or uneducated to avoid service. As a result, citizens from the rural hinterlands, inner-city poor and minorities were over-represented in the war. It would take time for the effects of the draft to be felt in the armed forces, but the potent mix of race and class pressure – when blended with a losing effort and societal indifference – caused the effectiveness of the American military to drop after 1968.

TARGETING THE DRAFT.

To its credit the military altered the draft system in 1970 and began to rely on a lottery system based on birthdates that put an end to many deferments. The damage, however, had already been done and can be seen reflected in the following numbers.: during the war some three million men and women saw service in Vietnam, but a staggering 16 million found some way to avoid it. Such was the true American verdict on the Vietnam War

DRAFT PROTESTS

In the United States most anti-war protest had its roots in the draft. By 1967 anti-draft and anti-war demonstrations had become commonplace. Rightly or wrongly many young people felt as if their generation was being persecuted by the older one. They felt as if they had no say in the making of national decisions but had to pay the price for them. Ironically, most of the young protesters who spoke out against the war or the draft did so in relative safety, already having procured a deferment of some type. Most protests in this early stage of the war were peaceful and were as much social happenings as anything else. All across the nation men burned their draft cards, staged sit-ins and picketed ROTC buildings on university campuses. In October 1967 the biggest protest to date took place in Washington, D.C., attracting over 100,000 people. Portending the future, a more radical segment of the crowd attempted to invade The Pentagon, sparking a battle with the

The draft took ordinary US citizens and forced them into directly participating in the war in Vietnam, though more often than not it was the uneducated or the poor who found themselves transported thousands of miles to the front line.

The Vietnam War gave rise to some of the ugliest episodes in US political history, during which some departments of the government abused civil liberties through the use of surveillance and misinformation.

RIGHT: PROTESTERS GATHERING AT THE LINCOLN MEMORIAL DURING THE AUTUMN OF 1967.

police. The violence erupted as the authorities resorted to force to remove the activists. The numbers of people attending such demonstrations only tells the smallest part of the story. Their presence, however, forced the government to respond by turning up the pressure, which in turn caused more protest.

THE TET OFFENSIVE

Johnson was outraged at the growing level of internal protest. He decided that it was time to strike back. In a maneouvre reminiscent of Senator McCarthy during the earlier 'witch-hunts' of the 1950s, Johnson sought to discredit the leaders of the anti-war movement as being 'communist'. In addition, elements of the CIA and FBI were involved in secretly, and illegally, infiltrating the anti-war movement. As these actions came to light the credibility gap plaguing the government widened even further. Johnson also sought to counter-attack through a public relations campaign about the war. As a result several military and political figures, including General Westmoreland himself, promised the nation in late 1967 that victory was in sight.

BELOW: DR TIMOTHY LEARY (CENTRE) HOLDS AN ANTI-WAR CONFERENCE. NOTE THE JOHNSON AS HITLER REPRESENTATION IN THE BACKGROUND.

The North Vietnamese and Vietcong foiled Johnson's campaign by launching the massive Tet Offensive on 30 January 1968. Everywhere American troops were victorious, but the public refused to see Tet as a victory. The attack indicated to many that Johnson had been misleading them about the state of the war. It seemed that the war would in fact intensify and last longer than anyone had expected. Proof of this viewpoint was given for many by General Westmoreland's request for 206,000 additional troops. Members of the public asked themselves, why would he need more troops if the enemy had just suffered a debilitating defeat? The result was a firestorm of protest, and for the first time polls indicated that the anti-war elements were gaining significant ground among the hitherto pro-war middle class. Riots and protests now engulfed universities across the nation. The results of the Tet Offensive and the increasing domestic discontent forced a tired and defeated president to announce to the nation on 31 March that he would not seek another term. The protesters thought that they had won, for the architect of the war was leaving. However, the political struggle over the war was actually just beginning.

ASSASSINATIONS AND VIOLENCE

As the election process began a wave of incredible violence shook the nation. The Civil Rights Movement had entered a new, more difficult stage. Laws had been changed, but now Dr King set about the more difficult task of changing minds. He was unable to complete the task for an assassin's bullet struck him down on 4 April in Memphis, Tennessee. That night riots tore through the impoverished inner cities of America – a stunning 130 cities were wracked by violence. The government called out a total of 75,000 troops to keep order and even mounted machine-gun emplacements on government buildings in Washington, D.C. Fires blazed through the night, laying waste to several ghettos. Thousands were injured and government troops killed at least 46 people in the wake of the death of a beloved national leader. It is certainly ironic, though, that the passing of so gentle a man was marked by such violence.

The Republican Party stood united behind their 'law and order' candidate, Richard Nixon, in 1968. The experienced 'Cold Warrior' hoped to have a chance to avenge his defeat of 1960. The Democratic Party was divided and lurched towards disaster. Two anti-war candidates, Robert Kennedy and Eugene McCarthy, duelled in the primaries with Vice President Hubert Humphrey, widely seen as the 'business as usual' candidate. The charismatic Kennedy seemed well on his way to victory and uniting the party against the war when another assassin's bullet split the night. On 5 June Sirhan Sirhan shot Kennedy when he was busy celebrating a victory in California. Once again the nation mourned. Assassinations, protests and riots appeared to be tearing the United States apart. Robert Kennedy's death threw the election into a shambles and set the stage for a showdown between pro- and anti-war factions during the Democratic Party convention to be held in Chicago.

BELOW: THE OTHER SIDE OF PROTEST. PEOPLE PROTESTING AGAINST THE ANTI-WAR FACTION DISPLAY A US FLAG IN A NEW YORK STREET.

MUHAMMED ALI OUTSIDE A HOUSTON COURTHOUSE.

MUHAMMED ALI

Throughout the history of America, celebrities and athletes had been called into the army through the draft, both in times of war and peacetime. Glen Miller, Joe Dimaggio and even Elvis Presley had sacrificed years of their careers or even their lives when their nation called them to duty. Vietnam was different and is represented by the case of Muhammed Ali. The mercurial heavyweight champion, formerly Cassius Clay, had become a member of the Nation of Islam. Known as the 'Black Muslims', the sect propounded black pride and separatism. Led by Elijah Muhammed, the Black Muslims denounced the war in stark racial terms. When called to serve in the army in 1967 Muhammed Ali refused induction and asked for conscientious objector status on religious grounds. The draft board refused his request, asserting that the Nation of Islam, unlike the Quakers, was not against all war. Ali was left with a difficult choice – jail or service in what was deemed to be a 'white man's war' against another oppressed race. Choosing to side with his religious convictions, Ali refused to serve and was stripped of his heavyweight title and sentenced to five years in prison. To many in America Ali's actions seemed to border on treason; others saw him as a brave martyr for the cause of peace and racial equality. Ali remained free on bond while his conviction was appealed, and his case eventually reached the US Supreme Court where his conviction was overturned. Although he was somewhat vindicated, Ali had sacrificed five years of what many believe to be the best-ever heavyweight boxing career to an act of opposition to the Vietnam War. He would regain the heavyweight title, but many Americans would never forgive him for his wartime actions. Others would forever revere him for his brave stand and sacrifice. The story of Muhammed Ali and his legacy is truly representative of the various fractures within American society caused by Vietnam.

Anti-war feelings filtered through to all sectors of society and people. Even the previously hawkish Robert McNamara told President Johnson in 1967 that the war was becoming unacceptable.

THE DEMOCRATIC NATIONAL CONVENTION

Humphrey held the lead as the convention neared. Protest groups, though, decided to make a last stand and called a massive rally in Chicago in an effort to influence the party's stance. Thousands of protesters, some truly radical and some just enjoying the show, descended on Chicago. By the time of the convention some 12,000 activists had gathered, mainly in the Grant Park area. The mayor of Chicago was Richard Daley, one of the last scions of 'boss politics' in America. Chicago was his city and he was determined to see that the demonstrators did not besmirch its image. As a result he gathered a force of over 20,000 police and National Guard to keep order. On 24 August the convention began. At first confrontations were few as the two sides waited for news from the convention floor. On 28 August, though, Humphrey emerged victorious and adopted a pro-war policy. Chicago then exploded into violence.

LEFT: CONFRONTATION. PROTESTERS TAUNT US MILITARY POLICE OUTSIDE THE PENTAGON IN OCTOBER 1967. SUCH SITUATIONS WERE EXPLOSIVE AND COULD LEAD TO LARGE-SCALE VIOLENCE.

BELOW: THE FOLK SINGER JOAN BAEZ TALKS WITH THREE US PRISONERS OF WAR DURING A VISIT TO HANOI. BAEZ WAS ONE OF SEVERAL ANTI-WAR US PERSONALITIES TO TRAVEL TO NORTH VIETNAM.

An attempt was made by the crowd to rush the building. The masses of police retaliated and attacked using clubs and tear gas. Television crews were on hand to record the violence and what they showed was stunning, often being referred to as a 'police riot'. Inside the building delegates watched the televisions in horror, accusing Daley of using 'Gestapo tactics' against the protesters. For a short period violence even erupted within the convention itself. By the end of the night over 1000 people had been injured and the Democratic Party had been ripped apart.

The 'Battle of Chicago' was perhaps the most important anti-war protest event of the entire era. It split the Democratic Party, leaving it easy prey for Nixon in the presidential election. Even more importantly, though, it typified a divided nation. The middle ground was gone and the country had become polarized. Viewers all over the nation judged the events in Chicago. Many regarded the police as representatives of an almost fascist state that had perpetrated wrongs in Vietnam; others saw the protesters as long-haired traitors who were doing a great injustice to America's righteous war effort. One thing nobody did was ignore the events in Chicago; everyone took sides. The nation seemed to be disintegrating and only a solution to the war itself would put things right.

ABOVE: NOT VIETNAM BUT WASHINGTON, D.C. THREE SOLDIERS KEEP WATCH FOLLOWING RIOTS IN RESPONSE TO THE DEATH OF MARTIN LUTHER KING, JR. HIS ASSASSINATION WAS NOT DIRECTLY LINKED TO VIETNAM, BUT WAS FELT BY THE PUBLIC TO BE PART OF THE GENERAL ASSAULT ON PEACE.

NIXON'S VICTORY

A battered Democratic Party limped into the election against Richard Nixon. Although Vietnam was but one of many issues in this complicated campaign, the war and politics interacted in a very disturbing way. Once they saw the alternative the peace wing of the Democratic Party belatedly endorsed Humphrey. It still seemed that he had little real chance of victory, though. As a result both sides in the election would play politics with the war and the lives of American and Vietnamese citizens. Johnson desperately wanted the Democrats to retain power and on 31 October in an eleventh-hour bid to influence the election he announced a halt to all bombing of North Vietnam and indicated that substantive progress had been made towards a peace settlement. The revelation gave Humphrey's candidacy the required boost and he surged in popularity. Nixon had to respond. He did so by promising that he had a secret plan to end the conflict, but could not reveal its nature. Nixon's evasive tactics worked and he won victory in the memorable election of 1968 by the narrowest of margins.

As it turned out Nixon had no real plan to end the Vietnam War. He, like Johnson before him, would lie and even carry out extra-legal activities against American citizens in

It is a gross misrepresentation that mainstream US society was anti-Vietnam War. Huge sections of the nation supported the anti-communist efforts throughout the war.

LEFT: CHICAGO POLICEMEN MOVE IN TO BREAK UP AN ANTI-WAR DEMONSTRATION OUTSIDE THE CONRAD HILTON HOTEL, THE DEMOCRATIC CONVENTION HEADQUARTERS; 1000 PEOPLE WERE INJURED.

BELOW: RICHARD NIXON AND SPIRO AGNEW DURING THE 1968 PRESIDENTIAL CAMPAIGN.

the name of the ongoing conflict in Vietnam. Nixon's main idea concerning the war was a gradual process in which the South Vietnamese took over the war and American troops withdrew – a process called Vietnamization. For most in the anti-war movement the withdrawal was too slow, and protests continued. In summer 1969 matters became worse when the *New York Times* exposed the secret bombing of Cambodia and began to publish the Pentagon Papers, containing secret Defense Department documents on Vietnam. To many members of the public it seemed that Nixon was secretly widening the war even while he promised he was ending it. Once again protests swept across the nation. Making matters more frustrating for the president, trusted national security advisers were implicated in leaking sensitive information to the media. Nixon was livid and believed himself to be beset by 'communist enemies' both from within and without his administration. He set out to discredit his detractors by forming a special group called the 'plumbers'. Their task, through wiretapping and various other illegal activities, was to find the evidence necessary to destroy Nixon's foes. The incubus of the Vietnam War thus caused Nixon to begin a pattern of illegal activity so serious that it would eventually destroy his presidency.

A BRIEF RESPITE

Ironically, Nixon was quite successful in converting Vietnam into a non-issue in American life. He stated firmly that America was in the process of exiting the conflict, and backed his words with actions. In June 1969, 25,000 American soldiers left Vietnam in the first true evidence of Vietnamization. The troop withdrawals

Right: A pro-Vietnam War group confronts anti-war marchers.

Below: Tear gas scatters students protesting at the state university in Kent, Ohio, where four people were shot dead by National Guardsmen.

would continue, sometimes cynically timed near election days for maximum effect. Protests continued though, and in October 1969 one million people gathered across the country for a day of peace. By withdrawing troops, Nixon had to a certain degree pre-empted the protests. In addition Americans were simply tired of the upheavals of the 1960s and yearned for a return to normality. These people, who Nixon called his 'silent majority', were satisfied with Vietnamization and tired of protest. The president also made use of fear to warrant the slow pace of the American exit from the war. He made a speech in November 1969 that recalled the chilling scenes of slaughter in Hue during the Tet Offensive. He asked his listeners to have patience, for an over-quick American withdrawal would only lead to the slaughter of millions of innocent civilians. One final factor in diminishing protest was the implementation of the draft lottery system. Once the numbers had been chosen each year the lucky 'losers' of the lottery no longer had to fear the draft call, and in the main they drifted out of the body of protesters.

WOODSTOCK AND ALTAMONT

Rock-n-roll music was the voice of American youth in the 1960s and was often also the voice of anti-war protest. Artists from Marvin Gaye to Crosby, Stills, Nash and Young spoke out against Vietnam in their lyrics. Perhaps the lines of one song summed up the anguish many felt, when Country Joe McDonald sang in his 'I Feel Like I'm Fixin' to Die Rag':

'And its 1-2-3 what are we fightin' for?
Don't ask me I don't give a damn,
Next stop is Vietnam.
And its 5-6-7 open up the pearly gates,
Ain't no time to wonder why,
Whoopee we're all gonna' die.

Never in the history of warfare had youth spoken out so vehemently for peace. Although never in the majority, anti-war youth and members of the counter-culture had a tremendous impact on the American home front during the conflict in Vietnam. At Woodstock the counter-culture and their music would make a statement. Concert organizers rented Max Yasgur's farm near Bethel, New York, and hired the great bands of the day, from Jimi Hendrix to Creedence Clearwater Revival to perform. In far greater numbers than expected, hippies and rock-n-roll fans from all over the nation flocked to Woodstock causing the greatest ever traffic jam in New York history. By the beginning of the event on 15 August 1969, over 400,000 fans had arrived. The overcrowding could have been disastrous, but the young people worked together and made it into a wonderful 'happening'. 'Mind-expanding' drugs, 'free love' and rock music were everywhere. The 1960s' generation felt it had come of age and had found a better way.

Organizers in California were anxious to recreate Woodstock and hired many of the same bands to perform at a free concert at the Altamont Speedway only four months later. It was intended to be another example of the counter-culture at its best. This time 300,000 fans appeared, but the results were very different. The Hell's Angels motorcycle club had been given $500 of beer to guard the stage during the concerts. Periodically, as bands performed, struggles broke out near the stage. The violence culminated when several Hell's Angels beat and stabbed a black man to death as a stunned Mick Jagger looked on while singing 'Street Fighting Man'. In the violent episode the counter-culture lost its innocence. To many the 1960s and the promise that had been demonstrated at Woodstock, ended at Altamont. The older generation began to lose patience with the counter-culture and the younger generation began to question whether or not they could actually change the world at all.

THE FLOWER GENERATION, PARTCULARLY VOCAL IN ITS OPPOSITION TO THE WAR IN VIETNAM.

CAMBODIA

Although Americans longed for a return to normality and were beginning to become rather indifferent towards the war, the troubles were not yet over. In May 1970 US and ARVN forces invaded Cambodia. Nixon limited the scope of the incursion in part to deflect criticism at home, but his efforts failed. There were violent protests on university

campuses where students viewed the incursion as yet another attempt by Nixon to widen the war rather than end it. At Kent State University in Ohio a confrontation erupted which resulted in four students being shot dead by National Guardsmen. The killings prompted more campus disruption across the nation and most universities were paralyzed by protest and had to close. Bombers struck at ROTC buildings at over 20 universities. Finally a violent protest at Jackson State University in Mississippi ended with police killing two students. In reaction to the chaos pro-war activists took to the streets of New York and over 100,000 blue-collar workers, or 'hard hats', marched in favour of Nixon's war policies and denounced the radical violence erupting on campuses.

The chaos and death during the protests of 1970 signalled a sorely divided country but one which yearned for peace. Nixon, for his part, had learned his lesson. The pace of Vietnamization quickened and there would be no more incidents like the Cambodia incursion. There would be controversies over attacks into Laos and the Christmas bombings of 1972, but these occurred after the vast majority of American troops had left Vietnam and provoked little in the way of protest. By this time Americans were sick of war and tired of clashes on the home front. By the time of the 1972 election the war was a non-issue and Nixon was poised to defeat his Democratic challenger, George McGovern, by a landslide. However, old habits died hard for Nixon. To ensure his victory he sent the 'plumbers' into the Democratic headquarters in the Watergate Hotel. Although he did achieve re-election, his presidency would end in disgrace.

ABOVE: THE AFTERMATH OF A DEMONSTRATION BY WAR VETERANS IN WASHINGTON, D.C., DURING WHICH MANY DISCARDED THEIR WAR MEDALS IN VERY PERSONAL ACTS OF PROTEST.

RIGHT: TERRIFIED CHILDREN, ONE NAKED AND BURNT AFTER TEARING OFF HER MELTING CLOTHES, RUN FROM THEIR VILLAGE AFTER A US NAPALM ATTACK.

AFTERMATH

Events on the home front and the battlefront were inexorably linked during Vietnam. The manner in which the United States entered into and prosecuted the war had caused a firestorm of opposition. The protest, in turn, had affected the prosecution of the war and had unseated a president. Many will remember the 1960s as an era of violence, assassinations and near-revolution. Others will remember the decade as one of almost limitless promise ruined by a senseless war.

The turmoil at home also had an effect on those whom America sent to fight the war. By 1968 many American soldiers had realized that much of their nation had turned against them. After the advent of Vietnamization many soldiers realized they were being asked to fight and possibly die in a war the United States had no real intention of winning, adding further to the immense tragedy of their situation. Morale plummeted in the US armed forces as the war drew to its conclusion. As the veterans of the conflict made their way home they had to re-enter America's fragmented society. The returning soldiers were not greeted with open arms; some were spat upon, but most were just met with indifference as Americans rushed to put the horror of the period behind them. There were no parades and no national welcome home. The memory of the war and the men who fought it was to be collectively ignored. The legacy of the war had already begun.

BELOW: RICHARD NIXON DELIVERS HIS RESIGNATION SPEECH IN 1974. HIS FALL FROM GRACE WAS NOT THE FAULT OF VIETNAM ALONE, BUT HIS HANDLING OF THE CONFLICT HAD SEPARATED HIM FROM THE SUPPORT OF MANY IN THE ELECTORATE.

Chapter 12

The South Fights Alone

A mixed Thai and US crew man an armoured personnel carrier around an air base in Thailand in 1972. The US was no longer the dominant player in the Vietnam War by the early 1970s, and South Vietnam found the confidence to strike out on its own.

RIGHT: US MARINES MOURN THEIR DEAD. US PUBLIC OPINION COULD NOT TOLERATE THE LEVELS OF CASUALTIES FOR THE RELATIVELY LIMITED GAINS MADE IN THE WAR.

BELOW: AN EXHAUSTED US SOLDIER SLUMPS IN THE VIETNAMESE MUD. ALTHOUGH WITHDRAWAL BEGAN IN EARNEST IN 1970, US TROOPS WOULD STILL BE ON THE GROUND UNTIL 1973.

By 1971 South Vietnam was facing a vulnerable future. For nearly a decade, the US had been either building or maintaining an awesome protective force within its boundaries. US and allied guardianship, however, was now entering its final chapter. The early 1970s brought increasingly rapid troop withdrawal as the US emphasized that South Vietnam should now repossess its own military and social destiny.

Responsibility for this fell on the shoulders of the Army of the Republic of Vietnam (ARVN). In 1971 three specific US policies or measures started to take their effect on the ARVN: Vietnamization, withdrawal and US-North Vietnam peace talks. Vietnamization, and its corollary of withdrawal, was the most significant. Vietnamization was President Nixon's attempt to return responsibility for the Vietnam War to the South Vietnamese, withdrawing American troops while investing in the expansion of South Vietnamese forces. It was not a new policy: it was conceived during the Johnson administration in 1967, and as a general principle even further back by Kennedy in 1963. Yet it was only from Nixon's presidency in 1968 that it started to bite.

In 1969 there were just over 540,000 US servicemen in South Vietnam, but by December 1971 that number had fallen to 156,000, and dropped by a further 20,000 over the next two months. Most remaining US personnel were now operating in support, logistical and advisory roles rather than combat duties, though these were vital for Nixon's political credibility, as he was walking a fine line between appearing to abandon South Vietnam to its fate and continuing to pursue an unpopular war. Australia and New Zealand were also pursuing withdrawal, and on 18 August the respective governments finally announced their aim of a complete pull-out from Vietnam. Of the 47,000 Australians who served there, the last would be withdrawn by December 1972.

It was therefore a key year in the withdrawal process. Nixon was facing an impending presidential election, so the numbers were increased to around 14,300 US troops a month to satisfy the mounting public desire for a conclusion to the conflict and to try to quench the massive anti-war protests that were sweeping the country. Air power, however, was retained in both carrier- and land-based forms, though to maintain the appearance of withdrawal, many aviation units were now concentrated in Thailand rather than South Vietnam itself. US air power would continue to play a forceful role in Vietnam for the next two years.

Furthermore, US ground troops were still in combat in 1971, albeit more under the guise of pacification duties. Nixon's Accelerated Pacification Campaign placed an emphasis upon village security as a way of isolating communist insurgents, and it was reasonably successful. However, pacification included the immensely controversial Phoenix Program, a joint Vietnamese-US intelligence-gathering operation which aimed to expose VC personnel and place them under the jurisdiction of South Vietnamese law. The Phoenix Program straddled military and civilian action, and torture and killing became widespread techniques of investigation: 26,369 VC suspects were killed and over 33,000 imprisoned between 1968 and 1972.

Despite air power and aggressive US pacification programmes, the fact remained that South Vietnam was increasingly going to have to fight its own war. But did it have the army to do so?

As US withdrawals increased, more emphasis was placed on pacification actions such as the Phoenix Program. These actions were actually very successful, and threatened the Vietcong with total extinction.

THE ARVN

A major mobilization programme in the early 1970s, especially under Nguyen Van Thieu who was elected president in 1971, significantly pushed up ARVN troop numbers. By the end of 1971 South Vietnam had just over a million soldiers at its disposal

BELOW: GOING HOME. MOST VIETNAM VETERANS WERE GLAD TO RETURN TO THE UNITED STATES, BUT SOME FOUND THAT HOSTILE ATTITUDES TO THE WAR MADE THEM SOCIALLY UNWELCOME BACK HOME.

Despite years of investment by the US, the ARVN still couldnt match the motivation or discipline of their Northern opponents. Instead they tried to rely on the superior weaponry the US had left behind.

RIGHT A US ROAD PATROL OPENS UP WITH A JEEP-MOUNTED 0.50IN CALIBRE MACHINE-GUN WHILE CLEARING A HELICOPTER LANDING ZONE.

BELOW: THAI SOLDIERS GIVE OUT GRAIN CAPTURED FROM THE VIETCONG TO VIETNAMESE CIVILIANS AROUND SAIGON.

(almost equally divided between regulars and territorials), an increase of over 200,000 since 1968. These troops were now handling almost all the major combat operations in Vietnam (and were losing about 21,000 men a year in doing so). Basic US equipment was in good supply – all soldiers had M16 assault rifles, the navy had received hundreds of ships and more ARVN helicopter units were created.

Yet mobilization brought with it many problems. The ARVN did have some excellent men, such as the marine, airborne and ranger units and the 1st Infantry Division, yet expansion brought a dilution of military experience within units and officers, the latter often recruited on the basis of high social class and who had little empathy with common soldiers. Alienation and corruption resulted, and though the number of desertions actually fell in 1971 the problem remained significant. In addition, the US attempts to train up ARVN soldiers in sophisticated weapons technology suffered from a simple lack of time and the difficulty of transferring English-language information to thousands of Vietnamese-speakers. The problems of corruption, preferentialism, inadequate training and desertion dogged the ARVN for the rest of the war. But despite this, in 1971 the South Vietnamese government felt itself ready to take on more military responsibility – this found expression in Operation Lam Son 719, a pre-emptive strike against the enemy.

INTO LAOS

1971 may have seen a decline in fighting within South Vietnam, but NVA military activity across the border in Laos was a wholly different story. NVA infiltration and supply had dramatically increased there as a result of the events in Cambodia during 1970 when Prince Sihanouk was ousted and replaced by an anti-communist government, severely affecting the NVA's ability to use the Cambodian section of the Ho Chi Minh Trail.

By late 1970 the build-up of NVA forces in the Laotian panhandle just west of the DMZ was becoming worryingly large, suggestive of an impending offensive. NVA troops in the area numbered around 18,000, all armed with tanks and heavy artillery and supported by the incredibly effective efforts of Transportation Group 9, the 150,000 strong unit responsible for the maintenance of the Ho Chi Minh Trail. Yet such a build-also presented an opportunity to hit the enemy hard and this was the aim of Operation Lam Son 719.

The name derived from the place (Lam Son) of a successful Vietnamese uprising against the Chinese in 1427, the year of the operation (1971) and the main invasion route down Route 9. The plan fell into four phases: Phase One – clear Route 9 from Quang Tri

ABOVE: TRAINING THE ARVN. A US SOLDIER INSTRUCTS HOW TO USE A COMPASS TO BRING IN A HELICOPTER LANDING.

BOEING B-52 STRATOFORTRESS

Operational as part of the Strategic Air Command (SAC), from 1954, the Boeing B-52 Stratofortress could deploy a massive 69,996lb (31,750kg) payload of conventional bombs in a single pass. This awesome destructive force was the result of the 'Big Belly' modification programme in 1965 during which 85 B-52s had their payloads increased by more than 50 per cent, with the rest of the B-52Ds receiving the upgrade by September 1967. A significant increase in bombing effectiveness came with the development of the Combat Skyspot in 1966, a ground-directed bombing system which enabled ground troops to direct the B-52s accurately to their target and initiate bomb release. Working in multiple 'cells' of three aircraft, the Skyspot-directed B-52s could carpet a target area three miles square (7.8 sq km) with high-explosives, a capability which took a huge toll on communist troops and targets in Vietnam, Cambodia and Laos. The main variants used in the Vietnam War were the B-52D, -F and -G. The first years in Vietnam were spent in Arc Light operations, but later they pounded North Vietnam itself with the Linebacker raids of 1972. In all these roles their destructive impact had a significant influence on the course of the war.

A B-52 DROPPING HIGH-EXPLOSIVES OVER NORTH VIETNAM.

province up to the border with Laos, reopening the Khe Sanh supply base and massing forces ready to enter Laos;

Phase Two – 16,000 troops cross into Laos and attack along Route 9, terminating with the capture of the town of Tchepone, a major NVA consolidation point along the Ho Chi Minh Trail; Phase Three – clear the Tchepone area of further resistance and defend against counter-attacks; and Phase Four – withdraw back to South Vietnam having achieved all the objectives.

Below: Standing alone. ARVN troops attend a pre-battle briefing.

The operation would not just be an ARVN affair; the US was heavily involved too and their part of the operation was called Dewey Canyon II. It was under the jurisdiction of Lieutenant General James W. Sutherland, the commander of XXIV Corps in the 1 Corps area. The US priorities lay in Phase One of the operation, particularly in the setting up of artillery FSBs and helicopter support to enhance ARVN mobility. In addition to using 600 helicopters and 10,000 troops, the US would also be bombing with 2000 fixed-wing aircraft, including Boeing B-52 Stratofortresses. Because of the Cooper-Church Amendment of 29 December 1970, which prohibited funding for US operations outside South Vietnam, no US helicopters or troops were actually supposed to enter Laos, though US bombers were free to cross the border and US artillery within South Vietnam could maintain cross-border fire. However, by the end of the operation US transport and attack helicopters had flown some 90,000 sorties into Laos.

Operation Lam Son 719 involved the biggest helicopter assault of the entire war when, on 6 March during Phase Two, two ARVN battalions staged an attack in 120 UH-1H Iroquois helicopters.

Lam Son 719/Dewey Canyon II began on 30 January. Khe Sanh was quickly occupied through a helicopter landing of the 1st Brigade of the US 5th Infantry Division and by 1 February artillery units were arriving and forming a fire-support base. Another FSB was then established on 3 February in the Phuoc Loc area, followed by a huge build-up of armour, artillery and helicopters on the Laotian border.

On 8 February, after 11 early morning B-52 raids on NVA positions in Laos, 12,000 ARVN troops under the command of Lieutenant General Hoang Xuan Lam crossed over into Laos led by the 1st Armoured Brigade and the Airborne Division. US 105mm and 175mm howitzers blasted NVA positions in the path of the advance. As progress was made down Route 9, the 1st infantry Division and the Airborne Division were heli-landed at significant points either side of the main advance and helped establish further FSBs.

The initial advance was successful, but bad weather set in on 9 February and started to hamper US air operations and helicopter deployment. Furthermore, momentum was lost only a week into the operation owing to indecisiveness on the part of the ARVN officers

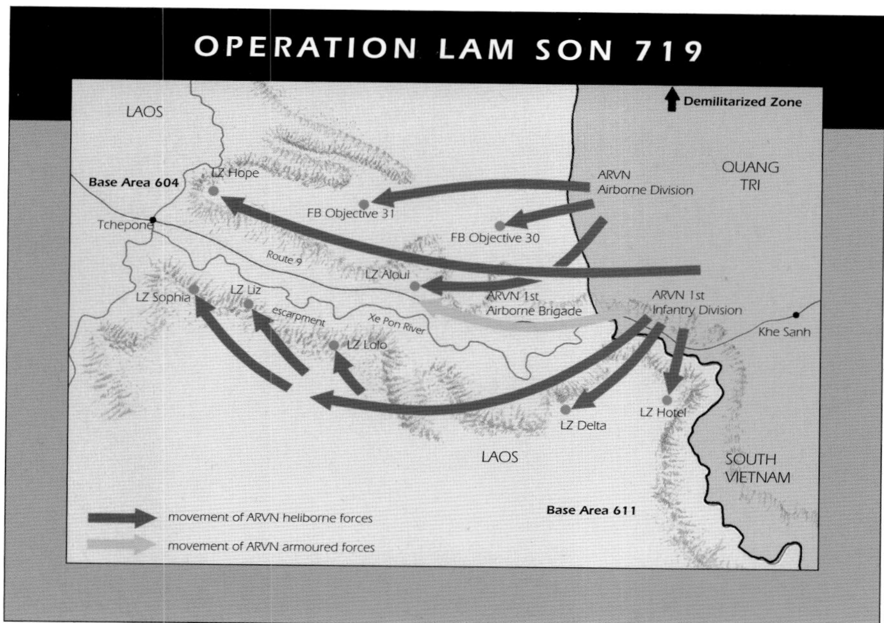

and the Saigon government. From this point onwards resistance from three NVA divisions, supported by T-54/55 and PT-76 tanks plus heavy mortars and 103mm and 122mm artillery, became more pronounced – particularly as they realized that the Route 9 assault was the main invasion and not a diversionary tactic. From 17 February regimental-size elements of the NVA 308th and 320th divisions started to smash away at the ARVN's northern FSBs, while NVA anti-aircraft batteries prohibited resupply or evacuation. The ARVN Ranger Battalions in particular started to lose hundreds of men; Ranger South suffered 330 dead and was forced to withdraw.

On 25 February, the soldiers of the 3rd Brigade, Airborne Division, had to abandon FSB 31 to the north of A Luoi after two days of communist artillery strikes followed by an assault from 2000 NVA soldiers and around 20 PT-76 tanks.

Alarmed by the impending strategic collapse, Lam changed his tactics to revolve more around airborne assaults directed at Tchepone itself. On 6 March, 120 Bell UH-IH Iroquois helicopters flew two ARVN battalions from Khe Sanh to Tchepone, the biggest and longest helicopter assault of the Vietnam War.

BELOW: AN ARTILLERY OFFICER ORDERS FIRE-SUPPORT FOR AN ARVN OPERATION AGAINST NVA TROOP CONCENTRATIONS.

DESTROYING A RAILROAD BRIDGE.

LINEBACKER I AND II

Linebacker I was Nixon's powerful response to the NVA's Easter Invasion of 1972. Between 8 May and 23 October US B-52 bombers dropped 155,000 tons (158,000,000kg) of bombs in some 41,000 sorties. The initial target was Haiphong harbour, the entrance of which was mined by Grumman A-6 Intruders and Vought A-7 Corsairs dropping 2000lb (900kg) sea mines, and other North Vietnamese ports such as Dong Hoi received similar treatment. Bridges and railway yards followed next, the devastation increased by the more frequent use of 'smart bomb' technology. The range of targets was extended across North Vietnam and the 25,000 tons (25,400,000kg) of supplies coming into the country's ports each month was almost entirely stopped, while imports from overland destinations – such as communist China – were reduced by 140,000 tons (142,000,000kg) a month.

Linebacker I coerced North Vietnam back to the Paris peace talks, but when these fell through Linebacker II was put into action on 18 December. The targets were almost all major infrastructural sites around Hanoi and Haiphong. A shift system was established whereby B-52s attacked at night (to limit MiG and SAM intervention), while General Dynamics F-111s and A-6 strike aircraft bombed during the day. Anti-aircraft fire during Linebacker II was extraordinary – over 1000 SAMs were fired (practically North Vietnam's entire stock) and 15 B-52s (out of 729 sorties flown) and 11 other US aircraft were shot down by the close of the operation on 30 December. In 11 days, US planes had dropped 49,000 tons (49,800,000kg) of bombs and the scale of devastation meant that North Vietnam was unable to execute its final invasion of South Vietnam until 1975.

RIGHT: TWO VIETCONG GUERRILLAS ARE FLUSHED FROM THEIR HIDING PLACE BY AN ARVN PATROL. THE ARVN AND THE VIETCONG TREATED EACH OTHER WITH EQUAL CRUELTY, AND IT WOULD BE FAR FROM UNUSUAL IF THESE SUSPECTS FAILED TO REACH A DETENTION CENTRE.

This force, added to the earlier B-52 bombings around the town, enabled the ARVN to capture the final objective of Lam Son 719's Phase Two and proclaim operational success.

Despite the capture of Tchepone, Lam recognized that his forces were vulnerable to gathering NVA counter-attacks, and by 10 March he had ordered the retreat back to South Vietnam. This became a horrifying ordeal for the weary ARVN soldiers. Over 35,000 NVA troops attacked the retreating columns with everything from machine-guns and mortars to tanks and rockets. The evacuation efforts of the US 101st Airborne Division kept casualties to a minimum, yet the ARVN invasion force had lost 1529 men killed and 5483 wounded by the time the remainder reached home (some US analysts put the casualty figures above 9000). NVA losses were substantially higher with 19,000 killed and more than 170,000 tons (173,000,000kg) of ammunition, 1250 tons of rice and thousands of weapons, ranging from AK-47s to tanks, destroyed or taken. Furthermore, the flow of NVA supplies down the Ho Chi Minh Trail was severely disrupted and would take many months to resume normal levels.

Yet there was no doubt that an initially promising operation had turned into a bloody rout, and ARVN morale plummeted to an all-time low. Lam Son 719 had been strategically weak, isolating individual units on exposed flanks in the attempt to secure FSBs. Ironically, both Thieu and Nixon proclaimed the operation to be indicative of South Vietnam's new level of confidence and self-dependence. Thus Nixon felt fully justified in accelerating the withdrawal of US troops, and he would push the numbers down to 47,000 in 1972.

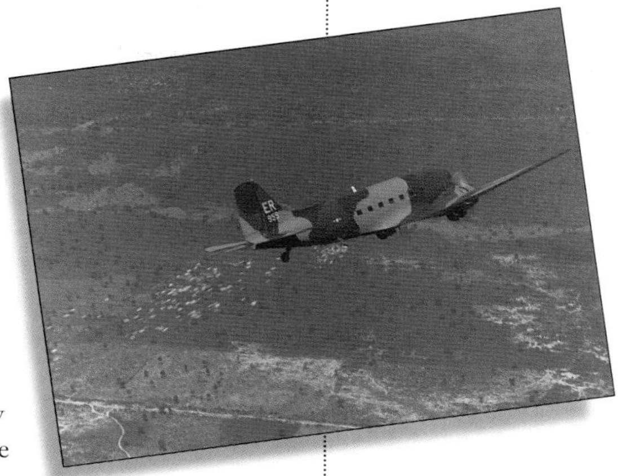

ABOVE: A C-47 SKYTRAIN DEPOSITS PROPAGANDA LEAFLETS ON AN ENEMY AREA AROUND NHA TRANG, ONE OF THE MANY US PACIFICATION TACTICS.

LEFT: UH-1 HELICOPTERS ARE GUIDED INTO A SPECIAL FORCES CAMP.

The South Vietnamese leadership desperately needed Lam Son 719 to be a success. Politically they claimed that it was, though military it was a bloody ordeal that showed some fundamental weaknesses.

Right: Pleiku, 1972. Jeep-mounted recoilless rifles, such as are seen here, proved to be invaluable weapons in the ARVN arsenal when defeating the enemy armour used in the NVA invasion of 1972.

THE SPRING 1972 INVASION

US air strikes continued over Laos for some months after Lam Son 719, in an effort to stop the rebuilding of damaged sections of the trail and also in support of Royal Lao Army forces in the north of their country who were waging their own war against the NVA and the communist Pathet Lao guerrillas. But negotiations with the North Vietnamese were also in train, as Nixon revealed on 25 January 1952. Nixon informed the world that since 1969 Dr Henry Kissinger, the National Security Advisor, had been in negotiations with Hanoi. Nixon also announced that if an agreement to withdraw all US and NVA troops from South Vietnam could be reached, then supervised South Vietnamese elections could be held to determine its future. With these cards left on the table, Nixon awaited the North Vietnamese response. His full answer would come on 30 March 1972.

THE EASTER OFFENSIVE

The reasons why North Vietnam launched the Nguyen Hue campaign, otherwise

The North hoped that the Easter invasion would conclude their domination of South Vietnam. Yet, despite all its imperfections, the ARVN was ready to take it on with surprising resistance.

LEFT: A VIETCONG PRISONER IS FORCED ACROSS A STREAM IN THE MEKONG DELTA, ACTING AS A LIVING MINE DETECTOR. THE PRISONER LATER DIED FROM INJURIES INFLICTED BY ARVN TROOPS.

BELOW: A TESTAMENT TO ARVN FIREPOWER. SOVIET-MADE T-54 TANKS DESTROYED BY ROCKETS AND AIRCRAFT LIE NEAR CAM LO, SOME 35 MILES (56KM) SOUTH OF THE DEMILITARIZED ZONE.

known as the Easter Offensive, in March 1972 are varied, but essentially revolve around three primary objectives. First, Giap hoped to destroy the ARVN once and for all; this would, in turn, gain the second objective – namely, discrediting the Vietnamization programme (which was actually having a profound effect on VC operations) and President Thieu (and, potentially, Nixon); and the third objective was quite simply that of territorial gain – to acquire as much of Vietnam as possible before any subsequent negotiations.The build-up to invasion had been sensed some months before when US air reconnaissance warned of a

ABOVE: GATHERED AROUND A KNOCKED-OUT NORTHERN TANK, ARVN TROOPS RAISE THEIR ARMS IN VICTORY AFTER THE DEFEAT OF NVA FORCES AT AN LOC IN JUNE 1972.

RIGHT: DESPERATE, WOUNDED ARVN SOLDIERS CLING TO THE SKIDS OF A DEPARTING HELICOPTER IN AN ATTEMPT TO FLEE THE BATTLE ZONE, BUT THEY WERE KICKED OFF AS THEY TRIED TO CLIMB ON BOARD.

huge increase in NVA logistical activity just north of the DMZ. Fighting also escalated in Quang Ngai province, especially in the two weeks prior to the main invasion.

Yet all this was nothing to compare to the Easter invasion itself, when 12 NVA divisions with a total of 150,000 men, all supported by new tanks, artillery and SAM weapons which had been acquired from the Soviet Union and China during 1971, smashed into South Vietnam, operating on three fronts.

The first assault was a four-division thrust directly across the DMZ into Quang Tri province, while other units drove from the A Shau Valley in the west to attack Hue – both attacks aiming to capture South Vietnam's two northernmost provinces. The second – and simultaneous – element of the invasion was the attempt to take Kontum in the Central Highlands and Qui Nhon in the coastal province of Binh Dinh, thereby splitting South Vietnam in two. Finally, three NVA divisions would strike towards Saigon in the south, the main objective being the occupation of An Loc, the capital of Binh Long province, just over 60 miles (96km) north of Saigon. If all these attacks succeeded, then South Vietnam would effectively be in the hands of the NVA.

The initial thrust into Quang Tri province was irresistible. The NVA sent thousands of artillery shells into 3rd ARVN Division positions on the DMZ before attacking with a full range of modern weaponry including tanks and shoulder-launched SAM-7 missiles to neutralize South Vietnamese air power. Northern FSBs and the town of Dong Ha fell in quick succession, and ARVN troops found themselves taking up defensive positions in Quang Tri City. There they held on against attacks from two NVA divisions and two regiments of tanks, their defence supported by quality marine and ranger reinforcements and by huge US air strikes. Persistent NVA artillery power, however, was too overwhelming and on 1 May ARVN troops started the withdrawal from Quang Tri City. It ended in a desperate and panicked flight across the Thach Han River, where the ARVN defensive line was established.

Hue now became the focus of the NVA's northern invasion forces. Yet by mid-May, Hue was defended by the elite 1st Infantry Division, and marine, airborne and ranger soldiers, now under the more effective 1 Corps leadership of General Ngo Quang

Once the Easter invasion was launched, the NVA were exposed to the tremendous force of US air power. B-52s in particular decimated the NVA ranks with accurate and awesome bombing runs that enabled the ARVN to gain a military foothold.

LEFT: A BADLY WOUNDED SOUTH VIETNAMESE SOLDIER IS HELPED BY HIS COMRADE.

BELOW: ELITE ARVN PARATROOPERS CLING TO THE SIDE OF A TRUCK AS THEY ARE RUSHED TOWARDS AN LOC AS PART OF AN ARMOURED RELIEF COLUMN.

The Easter invasion saw Giap make key strategic mistakes. The Vietcong and NVA were masters of guerrilla war, but in conventional campaigns against ARVN troops and US airpower they often over-reached themselves.

M72 66MM HEAT LIGHT ANTI-ARMOUR (LAW) ROCKET

The defeat of the Easter Invasion in 1972 can in good measure be attributed to the new weapons technology available to ARVN troops. One invaluable weapon was the M72 HEAT Light Anti-Armour Weapon (LAW) rocket, which gave the individual ARVN soldier the capability to destroy many of the NVA's T-54/55 and PT-76 tanks. The M72 was a single-shot disposable anti-tank rocket launcher. Made from two interlocking fibreglass tubes (one carrying the missile, the other carrying the trigger and sight) which were drawn out and locked for firing, it weighed only 5lb (2.3kg) yet its HEAT (High-Explosive, Anti-Tank) shell could punch through 12in (30cm) of armour at 990ft (300m). Early use of the M72 (1968) was hampered by poor anti-tank training among its users, but by 1972 it was competently applied and took a heavy toll on NVA tanks operating around urban areas.

QUANG TRI BLAZES AS ARVN TROOPS, ONE WITH A LAW, CELEBRATE THE NVA'S EXPULSION.

Truong. NVA attacks on Hue were constantly blunted and ARVN forces even started to make successful counter-attacks, despite being outnumbered by six divisions to three. The tide was turning in the north, and by 28 June ARVN attempts to retake Quang Tri City began, supported all the while by US B-52s and the shells of South Vietnamese naval and land-based artillery.

Meanwhile, the NVA was energetically pursuing the invasion in other sectors. The NVA's drive towards Kontum and Qui Nhon was rapid, quickly destroying ARVN FSBs, capturing the town of Tan Canh on the approaches to Kontum and destroying the divisional headquarters of the 22nd ARVN Division at Dak To, while communist forces on the coast secured much of the territory there.

Attacks on Kontum itself began in mid-May and would take the defenders to within hours of losing the city. Yet it was not to be. As well as the incredible resistance of defenders, US air power devastated the ranks of NVA infantry and armour. US B-52s and attack helicopters equipped with US TOW-missiles (Tube-launched Optically-tracked Wire

Left: South Vietnamese troops gather around the bodies of two NVA soldiers killed near Dong Ha during the Easter invasion.

Guided) worked in a close-support role with ground troops (equipped with LAW anti-tank rockets) to create a lethal environment for NVA armour. NVA losses grew so profound that by the end of May it was retreating from Kontum.

A similar picture of NVA advance and retreat was evident in the most southerly part of the invasion. In the first week of the invasion the NVA made two thrusts: one towards Tay Ninh City, which was actually a feint for the main attack towards Binh Long's provincial capital of An Loc. Following the fall of An Loc's main airstrip on 7 April, the city's 6000 remaining inhabitants and 3000 military defenders came under siege. Once again, the NVA made heavy armoured assaults which once more fell victim to infantry anti-armour weapons and air strikes. Yet their persistence enabled them to take the northern half of the city in a fierce street-by-street battle. From 10 to 14 May, seven NVA regiments launched their final

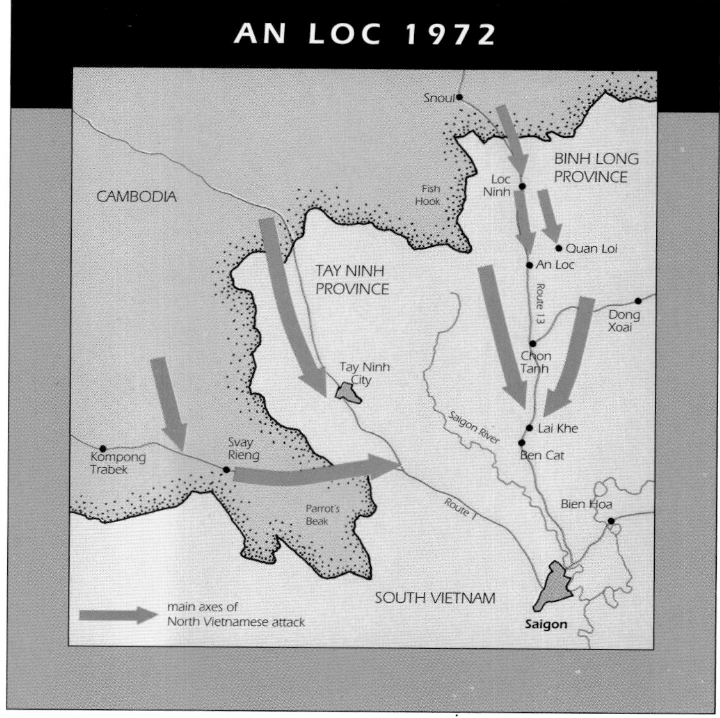

The crushing of the Easter invasion smashed the NVA military, yet in some senses it was a victory. The North had acquired key areas of the South and the peace accords left a way open to invade again in the future without the US presence.

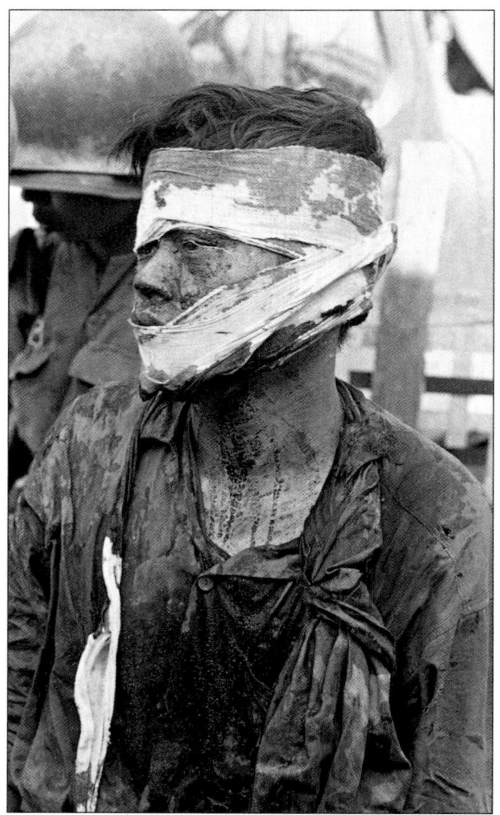

RIGHT: HIS SHIRT SOAKED IN BLOOD FROM HEAD AND CHEST WOUNDS, A VIETNAMESE SOLDIER WAITS FOR TREATMENT.

BELOW, RIGHT: DECEMBER 1972. A RELAXED MOMENT DURING A CLEARING OPERATION SOME 27 MILES (45KM) FROM SAIGON. MILITARY ACTIONS CONTINUED RIGHT UP TO THE FINAL SIGNINGS OF THE PARIS PEACE ACCORDS.

all-out assaults to take An Loc. Yet once again B-52 raids delivered such awesome destructive power that all the attacks were shattered. The situation became unsustainable for the NVA. By 17 May all of Kontum was in ARVN hands and the NVA in general retreat or defence, not just at Kontum but throughout the country.

The Easter Invasion cost the NVA the lives of 120,000 soldiers, a figure which could not be countenanced even by North Vietnam. Several elements contributed to its defeat: troops were wasted in open frontal assaults; NVA efforts were strategically scattered across the invasion's many fronts; and, perhaps most significantly, they did not reckon on the effect of US bombing raids.

The signature aircraft of the Easter Offensive was the B-52. Three B-52s in tandem with the Combat Skyspot system of ground radar could totally destroy anything within an area of ground three miles square (7.8 sq km), wiping out entire NVA battalions in a single pass. B-52s played an especially integral role in the Linebacker raids of 1972. Linebacker I was launched by Nixon on 8 May in response to the Easter Invasion. This six-month campaign resumed the bombing of North Vietnam, starting with the mining of Haiphong harbour on 8 May before systematically destroying almost the entire infrastructural base around Hanoi. As well as thunderous bombing raids by B-52s, F-4 Phantoms and other US strike aircraft now deployed a wide range of laser-guided and electro-optically guided weapons to devastating effect on targets such as bridges and oil storage

Above: A group of ARVN soldiers regroup after heavy fighting around Duc Co near the border with Cambodia.

facilities. Linebacker I slashed the North's supply input by over 155,000 tons (157,500,000kg) a month and effectively drove them to the negotiationg table.

THE PARIS PEACE ACCORDS

In July 1972 the US and North Vietnam discussed possible terms for peace, the key figures being Kissinger and North Vietnam's negotiator Le Duc Tho. Compromises were reached on both sides. The United States stopped pushing the issue of North Vietnamese withdrawal from the South, while Le Duc Tho accepted that Thieu could remain in power, though only in the coalition with the Provisional Revolutionary Government of South Vietnam (PRG). (The PRG was the old National Front for the Liberation of Vietnam and, by the Paris Peace Accords, was the dominant communist structure in the South, operating with the North's backing.) On 8 October, Kissinger accepted a proposal which called for a ceasefire, prisoner exchange and the withdrawal of US troops within 60 days of the agreement. Yet, crucially, the agreement was an entirely US and North Vietnamese

Vital to the NVA was that they managed to secure the removal of US air forces from Vietnam. As long as those remained, the possibilities for further invasions were doomed to failure.

RIGHT: A US AIR FORCE AC-130 GUNSHIP FLIES HIGH OVER SOUTH VIETNAM, ITS AWESOME CANNON WEAPONRY CLEARLY VISIBLE ALONG THE FUSELAGE.

BELOW: A NORTH VIETNAMESE RAILYARD DESTROYED BY B-52 RAIDS.

affair which allowed the North Vietnamese to keep any southern territorial gains. Thieu refused to sign. Nixon attempted to force Thieu's hand with Operation Enhance Plus – the contribution of large amounts of military hardware (including 300 aircraft and 2000 trucks) to the South Vietnamese forces.

The talks got nowhere, and by December the North had withdrawn itself from the negotiations. In an extraordinary move, Nixon gave North Vietnam 72 hours to return. When this elapsed without response, he launched Linebacker II on 18 December. Mostly carried out by B-52s, Linebacker II destroyed storage facilities, railways, bridges and a vast array of other targets in the North. US losses were high, however, with 15 B-52s shot down out of 26 US aircraft lost. F-4 and F-105 strike aircraft had to work hard to take out SAM sites throughout the North.

Linebacker II provoked an international outcry, but by 28 December Hanoi had come back to the talks. On 8 January 1973, the Paris Peace Accords were signed by the US, South Vietnam, North Vietnam, and the Vietcong's PRG. The details of the agreement were little different from those of October 1972. It returned to an acceptance of the oneness of Vietnam – as in the 1954 Geneva Accords – and provided 60 days for prisoner exchanges and the final and irrevocable withdrawal of all US and allied troops from Vietnam, and all foreign troops from Laos and Cambodia. Troop withdrawals would be overseen by the Four Party Joint Military Commission (FPJMC). Finally, differences between North and South would be humbled by a new Council of National Reconciliation and Concord.

The Paris Peace Accords held and America's war in Vietnam was over. Some 58,000 US servicemen had died and over 153,000 had been wounded in Southeast Asia since the early 1960s, and many analysts felt that what was being portrayed as a negotiated settlement was actually a desperate attempt to be rid of the Vietnam millstone. Certainly, the government of South Vietnam remain terribly vulnerable to North Vietnamese expansionism, especially now that almost all the western border zones were under communist control. Kissinger and Le Duc Tho would go on to receive the Nobel Peace Prize for their efforts, though the next two years would show that peace was still a long way away as far as South Vietnam was concerned.

BELOW: A TROOPER OF THE 101ST AIRBORNE DIVISION RECEIVES THE VIETNAMESE CROSS OF GALLANTRY FROM A SOUTH VIETNAMESE GENERAL OF THE 1ST ARVN DIVISION DURING A STAND-DOWN CEREMONY IN JANUARY 1972.

308

Chapter 13

The South Falls

A UH-1 helicopter is pushed over the side of the USS *Blue Ridge* to make space for other helicopters coming in as a result of the evacuation from Saigon. The US project of containing communism had failed as the North launched its final, dramatic invasion of the South.

President Thieu's belief in 1973 that US air power would come to his assistance if necessary was a sadly mistaken one. South Vietnam was now truly on its own, and the North knew it had liberty to act.

The end of the American phase of the Vietnam War had instant repercussions across Southeast Asia. The loss of US resolve boosted communist forces throughout the region and placed renewed and intense pressure on the governments in Laos and Cambodia – their countries already severely weakened by the warfare which had spilled across their border with their larger neighbour – to reach their own agreements with insurgents. But in South Vietnam itself, now alone, the military capabilities were there to delay defeat considerably longer, and perhaps even to avoid it completely.

In Laos, which had been busy fighting its own civil war for years, the government recognized the meaning of American withdrawal and signed a peace agreement and a power-sharing arrangement in 1971 with the forces of the communist Pathet Lao. The agreement quickly fell apart and the insurgents renewed their campaign for total control. Without covert American support the Royal Lao Army was unable to withstand the pressure and Laos fell to communism. The Pathet Lao and their North Vietnamese allies then proceeded to hunt down and kill those who had supported the pro-American regime.

In Cambodia matters were even worse. General Lon Nol and his pro-American forces waged a continuing, desperate struggle against the communist Khmer Rouge and the invading NVA forces. By early 1973 the communists in Cambodia had victory within their grasp and were massing for an attack on the capital of Phnom Penh. In an effort to save the situation President Nixon approved an airlift for the city and the bombing of the Khmer Rouge by American Boeing B-52s. The giant bombers took a fearsome toll on the Cambodian communists, claiming 20,000 lives, and drove the weakened Khmer Rouge away from the capital. In addition the action all but destroyed the fragile Cambodian economy and created nearly two million refugees. Indeed the victory was transitory, for a

PRESIDENT THIEU

Born in 1923, Nguyen Van Thieu would become president of South Vietnam as well as a lasting symbol of the problems that plagued the government there. Thieu had served briefly in the Vietminh, but later joined the Vietnamese army serving the French. He graduated from the Dalat Military Academy and received training in the United States. By 1963 Thieu had become a powerful general, a strong supporter of the United States and of vigorous action against the communists. He took part in the coup against Diem and as a result was promoted. American backing secured him a cabinet post in 1965 and he made continued use of American support to rise to power as president in 1967. Once in power Thieu, even though he relied on American aid, proved to be intractable. His regime relied on dictatorial tactics to remain in place, and did little to win the support of the South Vietnamese people that would have been vital in a victorious war. Graft and corruption ran rampant in his government, dividing the nation and weakening the armed forces. Thieu stood against US withdrawal from the war or any negotiation with the North Vietnamese. As the war drew to a close he railed against American abandonment of his people, but did little to help them himself. As communist forces approached Saigon in 1975, Thieu resigned power and fled the nation. Although disgraced and defeated, Thieu went into exile in possession of millions of dollars. The money had been sent as aid to the South Vietnamese people, but had wound up in Thieu's foreign bank accounts. His own corruption had helped to destroy South Vietnam

THIEU TAKES THE OATH OF OFFICE.

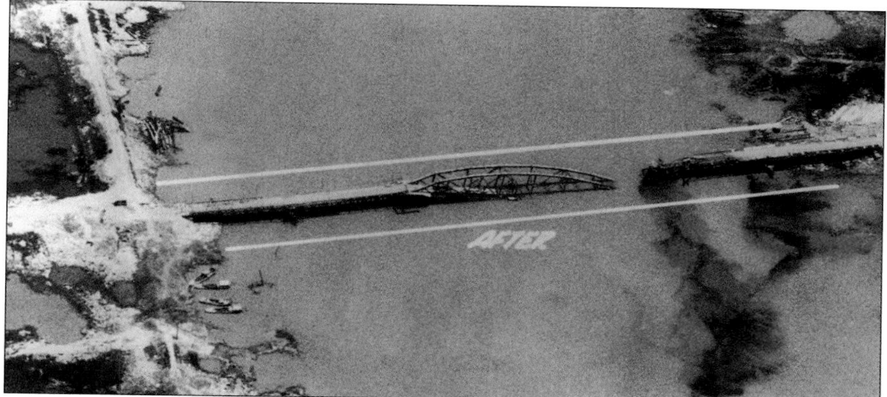

LEFT: THE INFRASTRUCTURE OF NORTH VIETNAM HAD BEEN SEVERELY DAMAGED BY YEARS OF US BOMBING, AS IS EXEMPLIFIED BY THIS SEVERED RAIL BRIDGE.

BELOW: THE REBUILT RAIL BRIDGE AT LONG BIENH IS REOPENED WITH A CEREMONY IN MARCH 1973 .

disgruntled US Congress halted the bombing effort by cutting off all the funding for it. The communists once again gathered their strength and by early 1974 they had launched a renewed offensive against the embattled capital.

By April the Khmer Rouge was once again poised to seize power in Cambodia. Although the US tried to arrange a peace accord, and the president tried to arrange over $200 million in emergency aid, there was no stopping the inevitable collapse of the Lon Nol regime, and by 17 April the capital was in the hands of the communists. The results of the conquest were horrific. The Khmer Rouge espoused a brutal, agrarian form of Marxism. Their goal was to convert the country into a rural, peasant's paradise. Towards that end the Khmer Rouge forcibly transferred the urban citizenry to the countryside to 're-educate' them and convert them into hard-working peasants. The reality behind the doctrine was exceedingly brutal. Bourgeois intellectuals were murdered out of hand, deemed to be agents of 'capitalist oppression'. Just wearing glasses or speaking correctly was enough to be killed for. The result was a Cambodian holocaust in which millions lost their lives in the 'killing fields'.

A NEW WAR IN THE SOUTH

In South Vietnam the peace agreement did not stop the war; it only altered it. In 1973 the South Vietnamese found themselves in a very strong position. The ARVN had more than one million men under arms and was in possession of the very latest American weaponry. The strength of the VNAF gave the South Vietnamese a tremendous firepower

RIGHT: A SOUTH VIETNAMESE SOLDIER ARMED WITH AN M79 BLOOPER GRENADE LAUNCHER PAUSES, CAUTIOUSLY ASSESSING THE DANGER AHEAD.

BELOW: ONE OF THE FIRST SOLDIERS TO LEAVE VIETNAM AFTER THE 1973 CEASEFIRE RAISES HIS LUGGAGE IN EXHILARATION AFTER LANDING AT TRAVIS AIR FORCE BASE IN CALIFORNIA.

advantage over its enemies, just as the Americans had enjoyed. Finally South Vietnam was awash in financial aid provided by the United States. The NVA, by contrast, had yet to recover from the serious beating it had received the previous year. There were only around 150,000 men and women in the communist forces in South Vietnam and they were only in control of 25 per cent of the countryside, both recent lows. In addition the logistic network of the NVA had been shattered. President Thieu of South Vietnam realized his advantage and chose to use it before the North Vietnamese had managed to regroup.

Thieu, however, overestimated his strength. While ARVN numbers and weaponry were impressive, its leadership remained poor and its morale at times non-existent. Politically, neither Thieu nor his predecessors had done what was necessary to win the loyalty of their own people. The regime was thoroughly corrupt and despotic. The situation was worsened further when South Vietnam's economy, overdependent on US aid, collapsed in early 1974 and millions became further impoverished. When the military situation worsened and Thieu had to call upon the loyalty of his own population, he found that there were actually very few people who supported him and his government. If all else failed Thieu believed that he could call upon American military support to save the situation. He could not imagine that the United States, after having invested so much, would allow his nation to fall. In that too he was wrong. The US Congress, controlled now by 'Doves', passed the War Powers Act over Nixon's presidential veto in November 1973. If the US Congress had given up too much power in the 'Gulf of Tonkin Resolution', it now seized some of the president's power. The War Powers Act required that the president notify the US Congress within 48 hours of a decision to deploy troops overseas. Unless there was congressional approvement for the deployment, the troops had to be removed in 60 days. Also Nixon, who certainly desired to defend South Vietnam, found himself struggling for his political survival in the wake of the Watergate scandal. In August 1974 the embattled president resigned rather than face impeachment. His successor was Gerald Ford, who had previously been appointed vice president to replace the disgraced Spiro Agnew. Ford was unelected and his mandate for firm action was weak. Thus the peace-making faction ruled Washington, D.C., and neither American men nor bombers would ever return to Vietnam. Thieu would have no military aid.

After the costly Easter offensive, North Vietnam set to work rebuilding its forces to invasion strength. By the end of 1974 it had increased its number of troops by some 50 per cent, up to 300,000.

BELOW: VIETCONG PRISONERS ARE GATHERED AT LOC NINH AIR BASE PRIOR TO THEIR RELEASE.

THE WEAKNESS OF THE SOUTH

Once removed from the war, the US felt less obliged to maintain large financial contributions to South Vietnam. With such crucial support in decline, the instability of South Vietnam's economy – and its military – became acutely apparent.

While South Vietnamese forces gained ground in the new war, the North Vietnamese were content to fall back. It was the communists' intention to reconstruct their logistical system to enable it to support a massive conventional ground assault. Therefore, while Thieu thought himself to be winning, the NVA was merely biding its time. The South Vietnamese period of prosperity and victory was quite brief, partly due to the breathtaking corruption rampant in Thieu's regime. Of the billions of dollars South Vietnam received in US aid, much of it found its way to the pockets of Thieu and his cronies. Promotions were bought and sold, units actually had to pay extra to receive their supplies and pilots demanded a high additional payment to fly their aircraft into combat. ARVN officials actually sold US military supplies to their communist foes in their never-ending search for profit. Public anger over the corruption grew as the situation in South Vietnam worsened.

It had never been a major US priority to build a functional economy in South Vietnam, and instead the country developed into a parasite, feeding off the United States. When left to fend for itself the fragile economy had ground to a total halt by 1974, its inherent problems exacerbated by the absence of money once spent by the now departed US troops. Inflation skyrocketed to nearly 200 per cent, destroying the lives and hopes of many and increasing disaffection with the government. Protests erupted in Saigon against Thieu and his corrupt regime. Millions were unemployed and homeless. As the North watched with intense interest, South Vietnam began to collapse under the weight of its own problems.

The army and the air force still retained their all-important edge in firepower though, and they stood ready to crush any NVA attempt at invasion. However, the economic problems plaguing South Vietnam also rendered its armed forces all but useless. The South

BELOW: A SLICE OF EVERYDAY LIFE IN DOWNTOWN HANOI, 1973. CIVILIAN AND MILITARY PERSONNEL WERE ALWAYS MORE INTERTWINED IN THE NORTH, AS THIS PHOTOGRAPH SUGGESTS.

Vietnamese military was powerful but it was also very expensive. Relying on technology, motorized transport and mobile operations, it required a budget of $3 billion a year in order to function. Corruption, of course, also played a role in the cost of operating the ARVN. The South Vietnamese economy, even in the best of times, could produce but a tiny fraction of the amount of money required to supply the armed forces, much less the needs of the nation. The economic collapse meant that South Vietnam became ever more reliant on US military aid.

The economic boom in the United States had ended by the early 1970s, worsened by the onset of the OPEC oil embargo. Recession stalked America, and the US Congress was not in a charitable mood regarding monetary aid to South Vietnam. In 1973 the United States sent $2.3 billion in military aid to South Vietnam. The total was slashed to $1.1 billion in 1974. Thieu railed against the cutbacks, but the US Congress paid him no heed. As a result the effectiveness of the ARVN and the VNAF fell dramatically. The South Vietnamese could not afford fuel, spare parts or even maintenance on the majority of the vast stockpile of American weaponry. Tanks, jet aircraft, artillery and trucks all sat idle because the South Vietnamese could not afford to use them. When the NVA did attack it found that the ARVN and VNAF had lost their critical edge in firepower. In fact most of the ARVN divisions would be immobile, paralyzed by a lack of fuel. As a result the NVA could pick them off one by one. In the end, then, Nixon's policy of Vietnamization had been bankrupt, as Thieu had realized when he protested against the peace agreement. Vietnamization had been a plan for American departure from the war, with little real heed paid to the needs of South Vietnam. Without massive US aid South Vietnam was not able to defend itself as a viable nation.

Below: February 1973. Troops cheer with the announcement of the ceasefire.

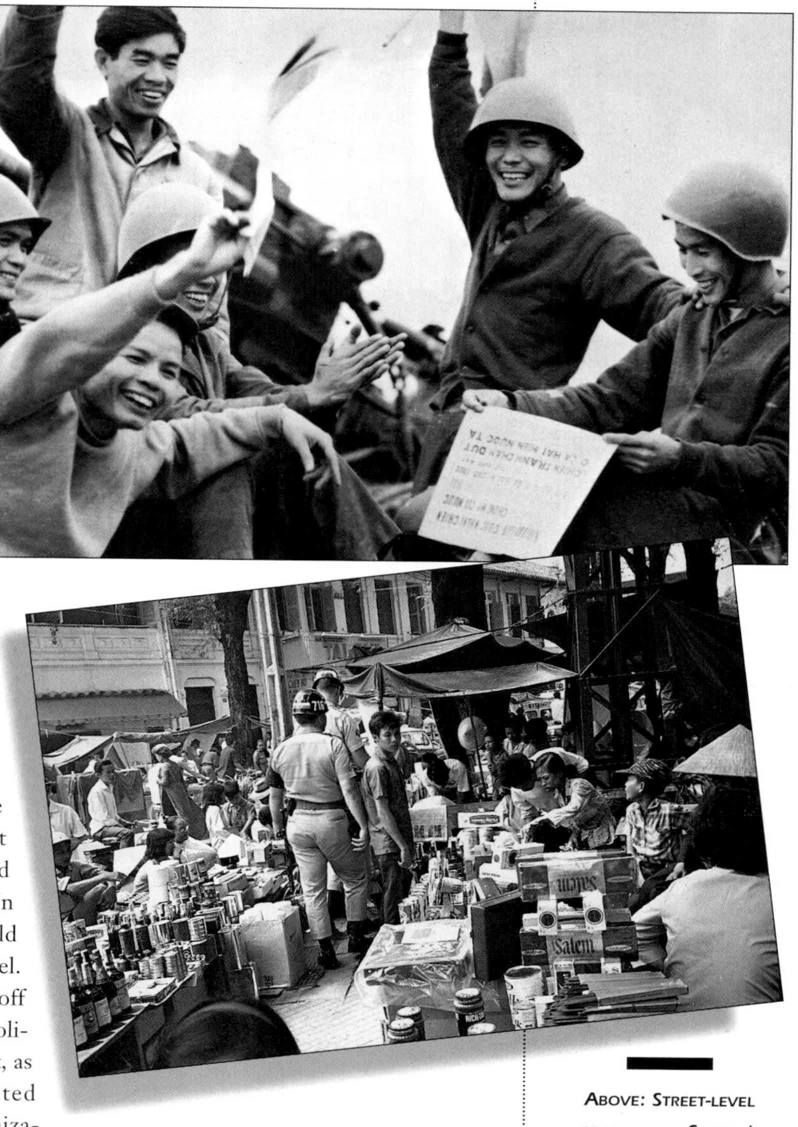

Above: Street-level corruption: Saigon's black market, where almost anything could be bought and sold.

THE NORTH ATTACKS

Since their defeat at the hands of American bombers in 1972 the North Vietnamese had contented themselves with rebuilding their logistical lines and troop strength. These efforts also involved additional training and practice in the conduct of conventional ground offensives. In addition the North put an emphasis on the acquisition of the very latest Soviet weaponry. Mistakes of the past would not be repeated. The communists looked on with a growing interest as the Watergate scandal engulfed the United States and the South Vietnamese government and economy slowly imploded. The time seemed to be ripe for an attack designed to reunify the nation. Several within the communist power structure pushed for an immediate offensive, but others feared that such action might cause the B-52s to return. In the end Le Duan, a politburo member, developed a compromise. As a result General Van Tien Dung, who had replaced Giap as chief of staff, ordered North Vietnamese forces to attack Phuoc Long province in South Vietnam. The two divisions involved in the operation were under the command of General Tran Van Tra.

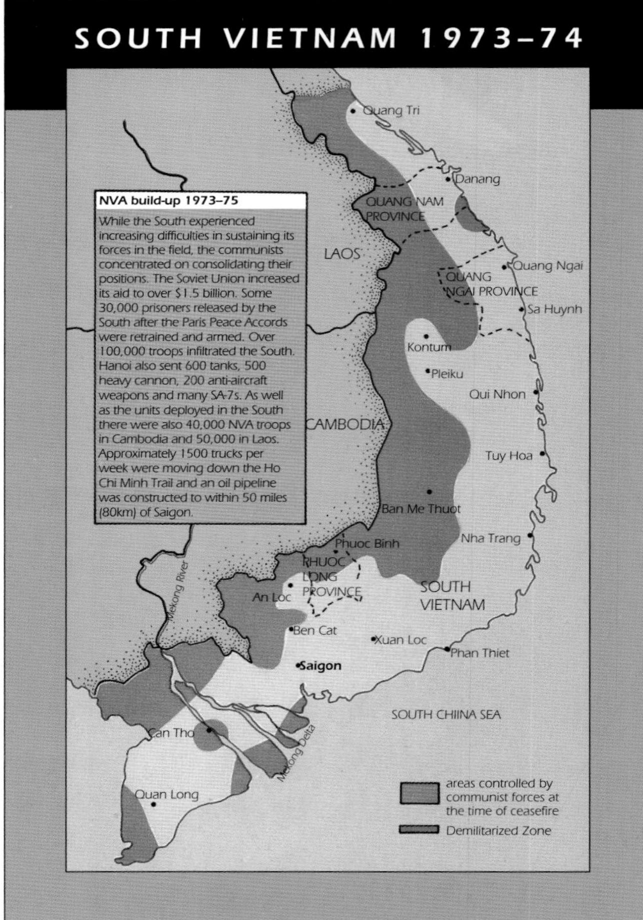

The North Vietnamese ordered this limited attack on an unimportant South Vietnamese province for several reasons. First the North wanted to see how well the formidably large and technologically superior ARVN would fight in a pitched, conventional battle. The North would also use the offensive as a test of its own abilities to conduct a conventional offensive. Finally the communists wanted to see how Gerald Ford, the new American president, would react. Nixon had promised continued support for the government of South Vietnam, and few in the North believed that the US, after investing so much blood and wealth, would stand by and watch the South fall.

The attack rolled forward in mid-December 1974. Initially, ARVN troops in the area fought hard, but they were unable to stem the tide. The ARVN lacked, in this and the coming battles, the firepower advantage that they and US forces had enjoyed for the entire war hitherto. The VNAF and the ARVN artillery simply lacked the power to pound the NVA offensive into dust, while NVA firepower had increased dramatically. As a result the NVA overran the entire province in three weeks, winning its first true conventional victory of the war. Even though the North had violated

LEFT: DURING THE NORTH VIETNAMESE ATTACK INTO THE CENTRAL HIGHLANDS, ARVN GUNNERS NEAR KONTUM REPLY WITH 105MM SHELLS.

BELOW: AN NVA SOLDIER OF AN ANTI-AIRCRAFT COMPANY MAINTAINS HIS POST AROUND A BRIDGE OVER THE MA RIVER. IT WAS CLAIMED TO HAVE DOWNED 100 US AIRCRAFT, BUT BY THIS STAGE OF THE WAR IT NO LONGER NEEDED TO GO INTO ACTION.

the peace agreements and President Thieu clamoured for support, the United States did nothing. It had become clear to the communists that they were now at liberty to launch an offensive designed to end the war, free from the fear of American reprisals. One communist leader even quipped that the Americans would not return to Vietnam, 'even if we offered them candy'.

ASSAULT IN THE CENTRAL HIGHLANDS

General Dung himself commanded the next phase of the offensive. His plan was exactly what Westmoreland had expected for the entire war: a thrust through the Central Highlands designed to sever South Vietnam in half. Some five NVA divisions, including tanks, artillery and engineers, rolled forward on 1 March. The ARVN commander in the area, General Phu, had an equal number of men under his command and hoped to blunt the communist assault at Pleiku. However, Dung did not proceed as his adversary hoped, but manoeuvred south to the poorly defended but critical road junction at Ban Me Thuot. The 1000 defenders there fought very bravely but succumbed to

Above: The exodus. US advisers and ARVN troops run for helicopter evacuation from Quang Tri in January 1972.

the onslaught within one week. Phu's position at Pleiku had now been flanked and his forces were in danger of being surrounded. The NVA effort to bisect South Vietnam had almost succeeded.

As the NVA advanced, President Thieu made his most misguided decision of the war. He ordered his troops in the north to withdraw to a line from Tuy Hoa on the coast to the border with Cambodia. In essence he chose to surrender the northern half of his country to the enemy and at the same time as attempting to form a defensive line to the south. His decision called for the ARVN to undertake the most difficult operation in warfare, a fighting retreat. Its leadership and morale, however, were not up to the challenge. Thieu's orders called for General Phu to retreat from the Central Highlands. He obeyed by boarding the nearest aircraft, abandoning his men and an increasing number of refugees to fend for themselves. The roads from the region quickly became jammed with a 200,000 strong rabble of soldiers and civilians all fleeing toward the distant safety of Tuy Hoa. The NVA unleashed a 'hailstorm' of firepower on the unsuspecting mass of humanity, thereby transforming the retreat into a road of death. Over 100,000 perished or were captured during the desperate flight. The strategic retreat had become a deadly rout.

Left: The papers say it all. Stood in front of The White House, two tourists read about the resignation of President Richard Nixon. Thieu's situation looked even bleaker as a result.

Below: The troubles continue. A bloodied South Vietnamese man is led away after being injured during fighting in Saigon.

DISASTER IN THE NORTH

During the disaster in the Central Highlands five additional NVA divisions attacked the northern provinces of South Vietnam. Once again, after initial strong defence, ARVN troops quickly retreated. These men and women were in the most perilous position of all. Once Thieu had ordered the evacuation of the Central Highlands, soldiers and civilians in the northern provinces realized that they were trapped. Their only hope of avoiding a fate of death or re-education seemed to lie in flight to the coast where it was hoped that the South Vietnamese government or the Americans would evacuate them by sea. Millions streamed toward the coastal cities of Hue and Danang in a final bid for freedom. Some ARVN soldiers threw down their weapons and fled along with the civilians, trying to blend unnoticed into the refugee population. The South Vietnamese government attempted an airlift of civilians from Danang. However, the effort was made too late and the airplanes that did leave were often commandeered by soldiers, sometimes gunning down the civilians they were supposed to protect in their own brutal effort to flee the coming carnage.

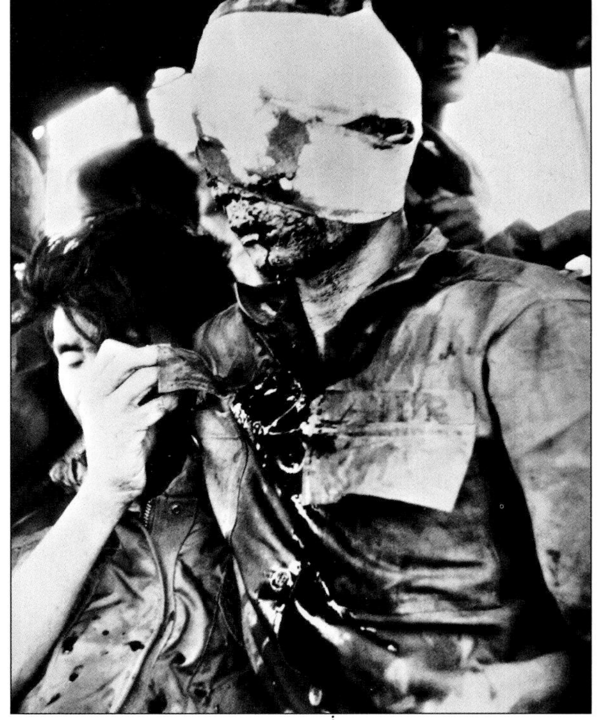

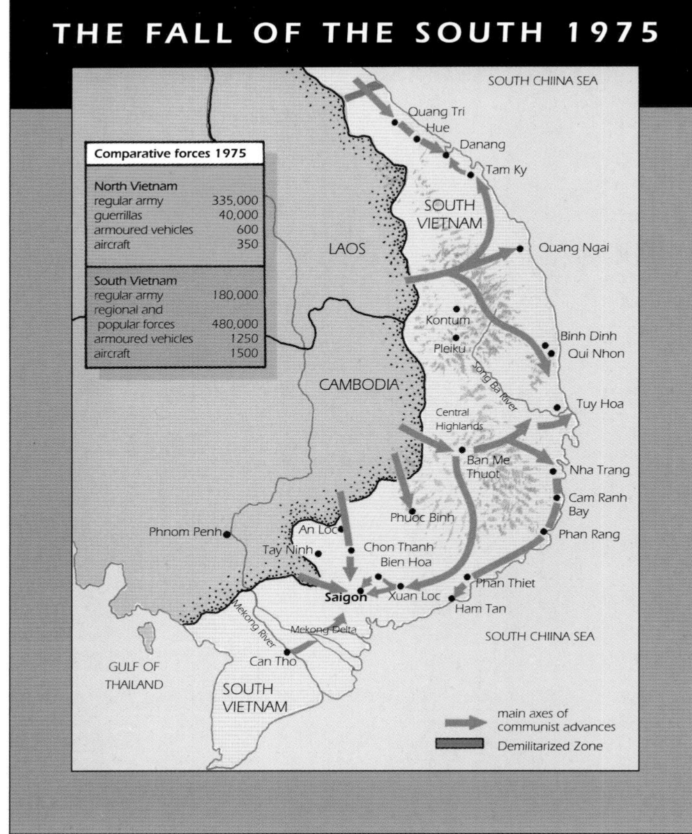

On 26 March the city of Hue fell without a fight, and NVA forces closed in around the last northern bastion of Danang. The communists briefly held back their attack on Danang in an effort to allow any Americans caught up in the defeat to make their way out of the stricken city. Dung wanted there to be no American casualties to serve as a possible lever for a US entry into the fray. On 30 March communist forces captured Danang without a fight. Of the two million who had sought refuge there only a mere 50,000 had escaped southwards before the fall of the city. During April the NVA advance continued down the South Vietnamese coast. The ARVN was in such full flight that the NVA sometimes had difficulty keeping pace. The collapse continued.

Neither North Vietnamese nor US officials had expected the quick victories of March 1975. For their part the communists had expected the ARVN to fight hard and maintain the war for a year with continued American support. United States' intelligence had not even expected a NVA attack in 1975, much less the complete ARVN collapse that resulted. Both nations now struggled to deal with the completely unexpected.

RIGHT: AS DISASTER LOOMED PANIC SEIZED THE CROWDS IN SAIGON. HERE AN AGITATED MOB SURROUNDS THE PRESIDENTIAL PALACE.

Left: Some of the 5000 US citizens evacuated from Saigon by helicopter arrive at the amphibious command ship the USS *Blue Ridge* during frantic airlift operations in late April 1975.

DECISION IN THE UNITED STATES

Communist officials informed General Dung on 23 March to concentrate all of his forces in an effort to capture Saigon. The NVA had to press its advantage, allowing the ARVN no time to recover. Dung was instructed to capture Saigon before the onset of the monsoon season in May. If the rains came before Saigon fell the NVA offensive would stall and thereby give Thieu and his still powerful forces time to regroup and organize a defence of the densely populated southern third of the nation. Any delay would also give Thieu an additional opportunity to plead for renewed American involvement in the conflict. In the United States President Ford and Secretary of State Kissinger searched for ways to support their tottering ally. Both realized that the use of American force was out of the question given the political reality of the times. Ford did try to do the next best thing, and on 10 April went on television to make an emotional request for $722 million in emergency military aid for the South Vietnamese. The American people and the US Congress, however, were tired of the conflict. The American interest in the war was over and the people of the United States were now worried about issues such as the moribund American economy. There would be no further funding for Thieu and his regime. In a speech on 23 April Ford made it official and informed the nation that the war in Vietnam was being lost and that American involvement in it was finished.

Below: Vietnamese refugees are held on a US merchant ship in the South China Sea off the coast of Vietnam.

ATTACK ON SAIGON

As all hope of any last-minute American involvement ended, Dung's forces converged on the doomed city of Saigon. The last obstacle in their way was the ARVN 18th Division, which held the critical road junction at Xuan Loc some 35 miles (56km) north-east of Saigon. Here, in mid-April, 40,000 NVA soldiers, artillery and tanks attacked the lone ARVN division. An epic battle ensued in which the 18th Division held off the advance of the NVA for an entire week. Although it was heroic, the sacrifice of the 18th Division could do little but momentarily halt the victorious advance of the communist forces. By 21 April the battle at Xuan Loc had ended and the NVA had breached the defences of Saigon. Nothing could stop them now.

BELOW UH-1D HELICOPTERS LIE DESTROYED ON AN AIRFIELD AS NVA TROOPS TAKE OVER.

On the same day that Xuan Loc fell, and as his nation crumbled all around him, President Thieu resigned. In a departing speech he lashed out at the United States for abandoning South Vietnam. A few days later he too abandoned South Vietnam and fled the country.

Thieu passed power to his vice president, Tran Van Huong, who resigned in turn leaving power to General Minh. The new leader, who had also ruled South Vietnam for a short period after the ousting of Diem, sought to negotiate a settlement with the North Vietnamese while he still had some leverage. But the North, with total victory in sight, refused his request.

ABOVE NVA SOLDIERS RUSH ACROSS THE TARMAC OF THE TAN SON NHUT AIRBASE IN SAIGON. THE FALL OF THE CITY IS CLOSE.

Only at this last minute did the United States begin an effort to evacuate its personnel and the thousands of South Vietnamese who had been integral to the American war effort. Rescue operations had been planned for quite some time, but had not been implemented for fear that the evacuation would cause panic in Saigon. Also US planners, including Ambassador Martin, believed that Saigon would be able to hold out for some time. they were wrong. The first plan for evacuation called for the use of military transport planes at Tan Son Nhut airbase. Some 50,000 people were evacuated in this manner. On 29 April, though, the communists began an attack on the airbase which forced the Americans to rely on helicopter evacuations from within Saigon itself.

Even as rockets slammed into Saigon the United States launched Operation Frequent Wind, its last operation of the Vietnam War. Buses were to pick up Vietnamese and

FLIGHT TO FREEDOM FROM DANANG

As North Vietnamese soldiers closed in on Danang, nearly two million South Vietnamese civilians and ARVN forces scrambled to escape the doomed city. The slaughter in Hue during the Tet Offensive indicated to the panic-stricken mob that only torture and death awaited those who failed to make their way south. The efforts of the South Vietnamese government to save its countrymen and women were woefully inadequate. There seemed to be no escape. However, partly for its news value, the president of World Airways had a Boeing 727 fly into Danang and rescue as many women and children as possible while camera crews covered the moving story. As the plane began to load its human cargo a mob of ARVN soldiers, realizing that it would be the last plane to leave Danang, rushed aboard the aircraft. Women and children, including the children of the soldiers themselves, were trampled in the melee. The heavily armed soldiers packed themselves on board and commandeered the aircraft. As the frightened pilot prepared to take off several ARVN who had been unable to board the plane attacked it using their rifles and grenades. If they were not leaving, then no one would. The overloaded plane received minor damage and struggled into the air. The pilot was stunned to find that he could not retract his landing gear once aloft. The problem was not mechanical in nature – several desperate ARVN troops had sought refuge in the wheel wells in a final bid for freedom. Some were crushed by the attempt to raise the wheels and some plummeted to their deaths but others held on for dear life for the entire 90-minute flight to Saigon and survived. when the plane touched down safely in Saigon it was discovered that only five women and children had ever made it aboard.

THE FIGHT TO GET ON BOARD.

LEFT: SOUTH VIETNAM'S SURRENDER IS ANNOUNCED, AND SOLDIERS THROW AWAY THEIR UNIFORMS IN FRONT OF THE PALACE. ANY IDENTIFICATION WITH MILITARY OR POLICE AUTHORITIES COULD PROVE DANGEROUS.

As the last US helicopters left Saigon, the city fell into a strange silence. No one knew what to expect when the new masters arrived. At midday on 30 April, NVA T-52 tanks rolled through the gates of the Presidential Palace.

RIGHT: A NORTH VIETNAMESE TANK ROLLS INTO THE GROUNDS OF THE PRESIDENTIAL PALACE IN SAIGON, CRUSHING THE GATES BENEATH ITS TRACKS.

BELOW: THE FLIGHT TO FREEDOM. A HELICOPTER SITS ATOP A BUILDING WHILE US CITIZENS LINE UP TO BE AIRLIFTED TO US NAVY SHIPS OFF SHORE.

foreign nationals eligible for evacuation and take them to helicopter landing points across the city. The transport was soon overwhelmed by mobs of civilians desperate to flee the city, most of whom carried the correct documentation. Hysterical South Vietnamese surrounded the American Embassy pleading for their very lives. US Marines inside the embassy had to use their rifle butts to beat back people who tried to scale the wall. In the morning of 30 April the last helicopter took off, leaving behind within the embassy grounds some 500 South Vietnamese nationals who were eligible for rescue. The airlift had removed 7000 people from Saigon, while a naval operation rescued an additional 70,000 people. However, the evacuation had come too late for many. Tens of thousands of South Vietnamese who had been followers of the American-backed regime were left to face the wrath of the impending communist takeover. Many would be killed or 're-educated'. Still others would eventually make their way out as refugees. In all, it was a sad conclusion to America's involvement in a tragic war.

THE WAR ENDS

Communist forces now stood ready to carry out the last act of the capture of Saigon, in what they called the 'Ho Chi Minh Campaign'. The defences of the city had evaporated, and in most places the streets were deserted as the NVA burst into Saigon. NVA armour rolled down the

ABOVE: FOLLOWING THE SURRENDER OF PRESIDENT MINH, MEMBERS OF THE PRG STAND ON THE BALCONY OF THE FORMER PRESIDENTIAL PALACE AND TAKE IN THEIR VICTORY.

streets unopposed, with exultant infantry often clinging to the sides of the tanks. At noon on 30 April a group of tanks approached the Presidential Palace, the centre of power in South Vietnam. The tanks burst through the gates. Waiting inside the palace was General Minh and his staff. The ranking NVA officer present was Colonel Bui Tin, actually present to cover the proceedings as a reporter for the NVA newspaper. He was somewhat surprised to find himself accepting the surrender of the South Vietnamese government. As he walked into the upstairs office Minh announced, 'I have been waiting since early this morning to transfer power to you.' Tin replied, 'There is no question of your transferring power. Your power has crumbled. You cannot give up what you do not have.'

The North Vietnamese were victorious and had reunified their nation. During the epic struggle the Vietnamese had faced the Japanese, the French, the Americans and the South Vietnamese. The war had lasted over thirty years and cost millions of lives. The effects of the war had spread throughout Southeast Asia and had killed millions in other nations as well. Even as the Vietnamese set about their reunification and revolution it became apparent from Cambodia to the United States that the effects of the Vietnam War would live on for many decades to come.

POW★MIA
YOU ARE NOT FORGOTTEN

CHAPTER 14

The Legacy of Vietnam

THE POW/MIA BANNER IS HOISTED DURING PENTAGON CEREMONIES IN 1993. THE VIETNAM WAR WAS ONE OF THE MOST PSYCHOLOGICALLY, POLITICALLY AND MILITARILY TRAUMATIC EVENTS OF THE TWENTIETH CENTURY. IT IS NOT EASILY FORGOTTEN.

Although the war in Vietnam effectively ended in 1975, the people of Vietnam, Laos, Cambodia and Thailand had more years of violence, displacement and human tragedy stretching ahead of them.

The Vietnam War left in its wake a legacy of death and discord. In Southeast Asia the victors exacted their revenge, slaughtering millions and then fighting among themselves. The continuing struggle caused economic chaos and forced untold numbers to flee the area as refugees. In the United States the people, used to winning, had to come to terms with losing. As a result Vietnam, and the men who fought there, were in some ways forgotten, while in other ways America could not forget its defeat, and its legacy lived on to crush the nation's innocence.

In the decades that have passed since the beginning of the American involvement in Vietnam it has become clear that the conflict marked a watershed in American history. Even today the subject sparks fierce debate and Vietnam still matters in a meaningful way in both domestic politics and foreign policy. President George Bush had to assure the nation that his war in Iraq would not be 'another Vietnam'. President Bill Clinton had to justify his anti-war stance to secure his political fortunes. Ex-Vice President Dan Quayle faced serious questioning over managing to join the National Guard rather than serve in Vietnam. The war changed America in a fundamental way – before the conflict Americans saw their nation as something of a shining example to the rest of the world, but Vietnam forced them to take a long, hard look at the reality. It was the end of American innocence. It was also the beginning of a new time of troubles for the Vietnamese people themselves.

The most obvious legacy of Vietnam is contained in simple numbers. Although estimates vary, some 1.5 million Vietnamese citizens perished and over three million were wounded during the fighting from 1945 to 1975. Over 300,000 Vietnamese are still listed as missing. Deaths in the adjoining nations of Laos and Cambodia, due to the war and the following revolutionary butchery, totalled over two million. Since the conflict ended over 1.5 million refugees have fled Vietnam for other nations. During their own war in Indochina some 30,000 French soldiers died (plus even more of their allies) and 140,000 were wounded, while the United States suffered 58,000 fatal casualties along with approximately 300,000 wounded.

Above: French soldiers on patrol in the First Indochina War. Some 30,000 of them lost their lives in the war.

Right: The plight of Vietnamese refugees, the 'boat people', in 1975 moved the world and compounded the US defeat.

The above figures do not take into account those who suffered serious mental trauma during and after the war, or the countless millions who grieved for the loss of a loved one. Against the backdrop of human loss and suffering, the monetary cost of the war seems almost trivial. The United States alone spent over $160 billion on the war effort. Once that of all the combatant nations is factored in, the Vietnam War cost a staggering half a trillion dollars.

THE PRICE OF INDEPENDENCE

With the fall of Saigon in April 1975, the North Vietnamese had achieved Ho Chi Minh's cherished goals of Vietnamese independence and reunification. The war, though, had left lasting scars beyond the human ones. The landscape was ravaged, as was the economy. Some 25 million acres of cropland and 12 million acres of forest had been destroyed or rendered useless – as well as potentially deadly – by US efforts at defoliation. The economy was in a shambles and the national infrastructure devastated. The numbers of destitutes emphasize the scale of the tragedy that was post-war Vietnam: in 1975 there were some 200,000 prostitutes, 879,000 orphans, 181,000 disabled persons and over one million widows. As the superpowers moved on to new confrontations elsewhere, the stream of aid money began to dry up, leaving the economy weaker still. Millions of displaced people, the human flotsam and jetsam of war, crowded into urban areas and huge slums resulted. Vietnam had to rebuild itself.

BELOW: AIR CAVALRY HELICOPTERS LANDING DURING OPERATION EAGLE CLAW IN 1966. THE UH-1 HAS BECOME A POTENT SYMBOL OF THE WAR, MYTHOLOGIZED IN FILMS SUCH AS *APOCALYPSE NOW*.

With the war ended, the time for internal reckoning was also at hand. Although not as all-encompassing as the slaughter in Hue in 1968 had indicated might occur, the victorious North Vietnamese began to purge southern society of its unwanted elements. Officials of the South Vietnamese government and the ARVN who had not already fled the country paid with their lives. In the decade after the war over 60,000 such 'undesirables' were executed. In addition hundreds of thousands of South Vietnamese had to undergo so-called 're-education' in camps.

Perhaps the best indicator of internal strife is the fact that some 1.5 million Vietnamese fled the new regime. Many of these desparate people sought refuge in Cambodia, only to find themselves in an even worse situation. The most popular method of flight, however, was to put to sea – earning them the name 'boat people'. Many of the boats and passengers were lost at sea, while others were boarded by pirates who sold their captives into slavery. Plenty of course made good their escape to another country in the region, only to be held

The genocide in Cambodia parallels the mass killings enacted by Hitler and Stalin. The slightest connection with a colonial or intellectual past would be cause for execution – whole communities were killed on the most groundless suspicions.

REMEMBERING THE MISSING.

MISSING IN ACTION

After the close of the war in Vietnam the United States listed some 2387 American servicemen as 'missing in action'. The majority of the MIAs were American pilots shot down during the war whose bodies were never recovered. The peace agreement stipulated that the MIA issue was to be solved by a joint US-Vietnamese military team, but cooperation soon broke down. The MIA issue remains controversial to this day. Many within the United States believe that Americans remain prisoners of the Vietnamese, held in remote jungle locations. These claims are backed by several supposed sightings of MIAs, and many American groups work diligently to find these men and release them. Relatives of the missing often claim that their government is hiding information about their loved ones. In the 1980s Ronald Reagan gave many hope when he declared that he would do everything in his power to solve the MIA issue. Even under his presidency, though, no hard evidence was ever discovered that demonstrated that the Vietnamese still held Americans. In the early 1990s the subject erupted again when Senator John Kerry, a veteran, held hearings on it. As a result of the publicity, and their need for normalized economic relations with the United States, the Vietnamese began to cooperate with American efforts to account for missing soldiers. As a result of this information, and the continuing work of US MIA teams in Vietnam, all but one of the MIAs have been declared legally dead. The one remains as symbolic of the continuing American resolve to fully account for the missing. All evidence now points to the conclusion that no Americans remained behind in Vietnam against their will after the release of the American POWs.

in squalid camps where they had to await their fate. Eventually about one million 'boat people' made their way to France or the United States where most had to begin life anew, penniless and unable to read or speak the language, while also serving as rather unwelcome reminders of a nation's wartime tragedy.

Even as Vietnam began its period of recrimination and rebuilding, the regional war in Southeast Asia continued in a different guise. In Laos the victorious Pathet Lao took their revenge on the Hmong people who had sided with the United States. In a campaign of genocide, the Hmong were either driven from Laos or systematically wiped out. In Cambodia the Khmer Rouge achieved their victory in 1975, and in an effort to form their 'agrarian Marxist utopia' the communists emptied most cities of their population and forced the people, irrespective of age or health, into agricultural concentration camps in the countryside. Under their brutal leader Pol Pot, the Khmer Rouge began to slaughter those who were deemed too intellectual or bourgeois for the new society. A brutal orgy of killing went on unchecked until the advent of a new war in 1979. Estimates of the scale of the slaughter vary, but some 1.8 million people, or 30 per cent of the entire population, are thought to have lost their lives in the 'killing fields'.

BELOW: WAR GOES ON. THE THAI-CAMBODIA BORDER: OFFICER CADETS OF THE KHMER PEOPLE'S LIBERATION FRONT.

Fighting lingered on along the Cambodia-Vietnam border after 1975. The situation then exploded on 25 December that year, when Vietnam invaded Cambodia. The Khmer Rouge put up little resistance and Phnom Penh fell on 7 January. The victorious Vietnamese then placed a puppet government in power. However, China viewed Vietnam's actions as a threat and after several tense years it invaded Vietnam in February 1979. For sixteen days the Chinese laid waste to the northern sections of Vietnam, leaving after they had taught the Vietnamese a sufficient 'lesson'. Meanwhile, the Khmer Rouge had reverted to insurgency, this time aimed at the Vietnamese-dominated government. The ongoing insurgency would plague the region for nearly 20 years.

All this continued conflict and social upheaval hindered Vietnamese efforts at rebuilding their shattered nation. Purges and ill-advised attempts at Stalinist economic reform, assured continuing poverty and economic weakness. Cut off from all American trade, and eventually Chinese as well, Vietnam became ever more reliant upon aid from the Soviet Union. Adding to the difficulty was the fact that Vietnam insisted upon retaining a huge army, which drained some 20 per cent of the nation's annual GNP. Almost all foreign aid, though, came to a halt with the collapse of the Soviet Union. Vietnam was left among the poorest nations in the world, so during the 1980s a concerted effort was made to attract foreign trade and investment. The national economy slowly began to grow. Finally, in 1994 the United States lifted its trade embargo. The Vietnamese victory in war had been impressive, but social turmoil and economic failure have made that victory seem quite hollow to many.

The limits of military technology were clearly demonstrated in Vietnam. Great destruction was visited upon the enemy, but the cultural and political war was underestimated and mishandled.

THE LEGACY OF DEFEAT

The Vietnam War left the United States worn and defeated. Certainly the war was not a military defeat in its truest sense; in fact it has often been stated that US forces won every battle in the war. Such reasoning, however, did not soften the impact of defeat and quite possibly made the loss even harder to bear. The apparently invulnerable United States had to face the fact that the war had been a colossal blunder. Those who supported the war believed the blunder to be in the political dominance over the military, tying the hands of the war machine; those who were against the war saw the blunder as a more fundamental failing of American policy and values. All could agree, though, that the United States had finally lost a war. For the first time American blood shed in war seemed to have been spilled in vain.

It is very difficult today to understand the feeling of American exceptionalism that had existed before 1965. The country had been founded on the principle that it would right the mistakes made by the Old World. America, the land of liberty and justice, would

BELOW: A US ARMY PARACHUTE DISPLAY TEAM PROUDLY FLIES THE POW/MIA BANNER.

RIGHT: THE COST OF THOUSANDS OF US DEAD CAUSED THE PUBLIC TO QUESTION THE ENTIRE MEANING OF WHAT WAS BEING DONE IN VIETNAM.

stand as a shining example of what a nation should be. America was the shining 'City on the Hill' and this grand idea remained fundamentally intact until beset by the storms of the 1960s and Vietnam. The conduct of the war forced many to alter their view of their nation; the United States, it seemed, did not have all of the answers. Many simply lost faith in the infallibility of their country. Innocence was gone and in some ways the United States, saddened and somewhat wiser, had come of age.

The great consensus that had been built in America after World War II was shattered, leaving the country in political turmoil. The war deeply eroded the unquestioning respect of the people for their government and political leaders, as well as causing a loss of trust in the armed forces. To some degree then, American foreign policy after the war found itself disabled. The so-called 'Vietnam syndrome' made the United States question its ability and power in the wake of defeat. The symptoms were so serious that in 1983 Ronald Reagan, in a thinly veiled attempt to make America feel 'good' again, launched an invasion of

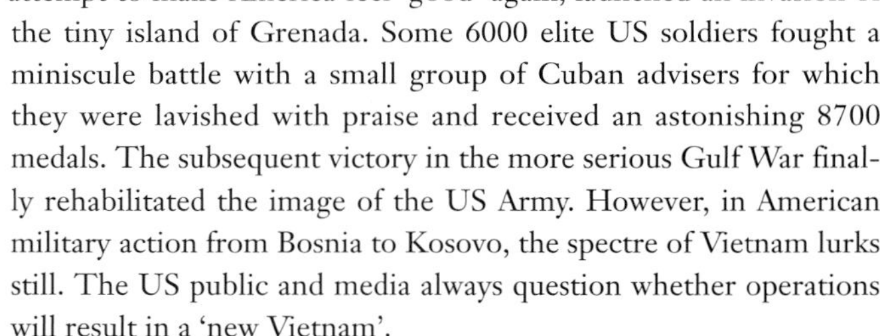

the tiny island of Grenada. Some 6000 elite US soldiers fought a miniscule battle with a small group of Cuban advisers for which they were lavished with praise and received an astonishing 8700 medals. The subsequent victory in the more serious Gulf War finally rehabilitated the image of the US Army. However, in American military action from Bosnia to Kosovo, the spectre of Vietnam lurks still. The US public and media always question whether operations will result in a 'new Vietnam'.

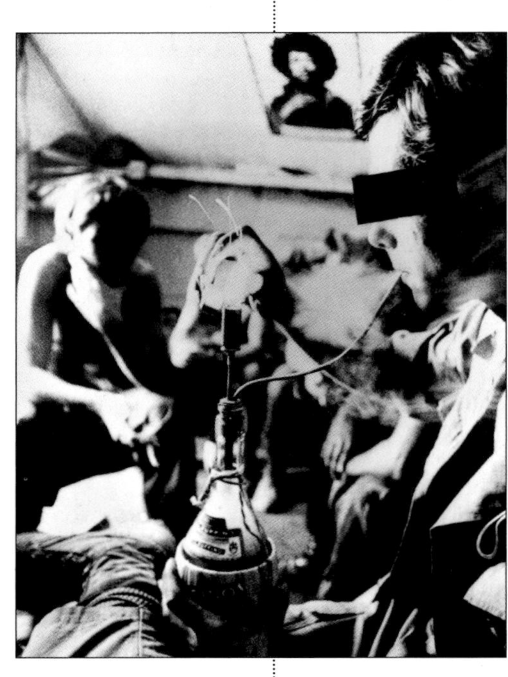

BELOW: DRUG ABUSE WAS ONE OF MANY PRACTICES OF THE GIS IN VIETNAM THAT SHOCKED AMERICAN CITIZENS BACK HOME.

The war was also an economic disaster for the United States. Spending totalled over $160 billion. When coupled with the expenditure required for President Johnson's social programmes, the economy was sent into a spiral of inflation. The pattern of economic decline lasted for a decade, forcing Americans to live through some of the worst periods of economic hardship since the Great Depression. Johnson was a Franklin D. Roosevelt 'New Dealer' at heart and he sought to deliver the great good done by the New Deal to a wider number of people through the welfare state. The Vietnam War, and its expense, was instrumental in leaving the job only half done and only half thought out. The welfare state, as created during that period, remains one of the most politically turbulent topics in American political life.

SEARCHING AMONG AND SILENTLY REFLECTING OVER THE NAMES.

THE VIETNAM WAR MEMORIAL

Perhaps the best known symbol of America's continuing effort to come to terms with the legacy of Vietnam is the Vietnam Veteran's War Memorial in Washington, D.C. Designed by Maya Ling Lin, the memorial was dedicated in 1982. The stark, black granite rises slowly out of the earth and then disappears back into it. On its polished stone panels are carved the names of the 58,201 American men and women who died in Vietnam. Thousands visit it each day, journeying there to come to terms with an American tragedy. Some just visit out of curiosity, but others come out of a deep sense of need. Comrades reach out to touch the names of friends whom they held during their last moments of life. Mothers and fathers remember the children they sent off to war, but never saw return. It is a moving and wonderful place where a nation comes to terms with itself. It is the one single place where the legacy of the Vietnam War is most clearly evident. Each name represents a person who desperately wanted to live, but died on a distant battlefield. Such is the legacy of war.

Although controversial and cathartic, Vietnam tragically became the forgotten war. Few Americans had ever truly understood the war or the social turmoil caused by it. All could remember the pain of the conflict, though, and wanted to put it behind them as soon as possible. Lost in the shuffle were the Vietnam veterans who had suffered directly and watched friends die. Tragically they returned home to a nation that turned its back on them as reminders of a war best forgotten.

The average age of the combat soldier in Vietnam was 19, a time in life when most people are discovering their own sense of self. The soldiers had to spend this most important period of their psychological development witnessing constant multiple tragedies. Unlike previous wars in which soldiers trained and then fought together, the draft system during Vietnam placed most American soldiers into battle as single replacements. Thus they entered the conflict as strangers, without the traditional support group of beloved comrades that make the horrors of war easier to take. Friendships came to some, but were often tragically short and painful. After a year of combat, watching and causing death, the soldier suddenly rotated out, boarded a plane and was home at the family dinner table, often within 24 hours. Even in the best of times such a situation would allow the veteran little time to readjust and work through the tortured memories of war.

In addition to this trauma, veterans often returned to ignorance and apathy at best and hostility at worst on the part of much of the public. The veteran did not

BELOW: THE SEEMINGLY ENDLESS LIST OF NAMES ON THE VIETNAM VETERANS WAR MEMORIAL HAS AN IMPACT ON MOST VISITORS.

Right: A personal memento left at the Vietnam Veterans War Memorial brings some names to life.

Below: A 'Welcome Home' parade in 1985 in Chicago. On their original return, many veterans faced a hostile reception.

win his war, and did not return to find parades and a national 'welcome home'. Many Americans had turned against the war, and others had even turned against the soldiers. One man recalls his homecoming: 'On returning from Vietnam, minus my right arm, I was accosted twice . . . by individuals who inquired, "Where did you lose your arm? Vietnam?" I replied, "Yes." The response was, "Good. Serves you right." '

For many Vietnam-era veterans this was all the more difficult to take for they could remember taking part in the national 'welcome home' for their own World War II-veteran fathers. There would be no memorial or parade for decades, as America hastened to forget the tragedy that was Vietnam. The veterans were painfully aware of this process. They knew that they were unwanted losers in a society full of winners. Many were unable to deal with the pain of this rejection, and sank back into themselves.

LEFT: THE REMAINS OF AN UNKNOWN SERVICEMAN IS CARRIED ACROSS THE MEMORIAL BRIDGE TO ARLINGTON NATIONAL CEMETERY ON 28 MAY 1984. THOUSANDS OF PEOPLE LINED THE ROUTE TO PAY THEIR RESPECTS. THE DISTANCE OF TIME THAT HAS PASSED SINCE THE VIETNAM WAR HAS LED TO A COLLECTIVE GUILT ABOUT THE POOR WAY VETERANS WERE TREATED ON THEIR ORIGINAL RETURN.

Due in part to the circumstances of Vietnam and its conclusion many veterans carry the trauma of war with them to this day. It still haunts them in the form of nightmares and even flashbacks. Many never speak of their pain, but it is there. These veterans, who had bravely done their duty but had returned to rejection, suffered alone for years. The psychiatric community did not recognize their pain and suffering in an organized way until 1980, and the US government did not begin to aid these veterans until nearly 15 years after the fall of Saigon. These veterans have Post-traumatic Stress Disorder and recent psychological studies estimate that a staggering 850,000 veterans, or some 25 per cent of the total, suffer from it.

Films such as *Apocalypse Now* and *Platoon* showed how the killing of civilians in Vietnam was part of a general insanity bred by fear, fatigue and prolonged exposure to terrible violence.

Another controversial legacy of the Vietnam War swirls around the use of the chemical defoliant Agent Orange used during Operation Ranch Hand. After the war veterans who had been exposed to it reported high rates of cancer and other health problems. The government refused to admit responsibility, but by the 1980s the health risks posed by the chemical had become clear and veterans brought a lawsuit. The suit was settled out of court in 1985, but an apology was not forthcoming.

Military control of the media during times of war has been much tighter in recent conflicts. Vietnam taught that a single powerful image of death or injury can sway the opinions of an entire nation.

RIGHT: US MARINES POSE FOR A PHOTOGRAPH OUTSIDE THE US EMBASSY IN KUWAIT FOLLOWING THE LIBERATION OF THE CITY FROM IRAQI FORCES.

During the 1980s and 1990s America finally started to come to terms with its lost war. It was slowly becoming history and for the first time movies, from *The Deerhunter* to *Apocalypse Now*, were released that explored the conflict from almost every angle, including the American errors made during the war. The film *Platoon* is instructive regarding one American conclusion about the nature of Vietnam; the war was in some ways a great American morality play, in which good and evil struggled for dominance over the collective American soul. Although less critically acclaimed, movies like *Rambo*, based around a maltreated veteran, also dealt with serious repercussions. America had lost the war, but in the 1980s Americans wanted to feel good about their country once again. During that decade several larger than life heroes, including movie stars Sylvester Stallone and Chuck Norris, returned to Vietnam on the silver screen and finally 'won' the war by rescuing prisoners and outwitting the Vietnamese.

For years history courses at most universities almost always ended in 1945 and ignored Vietnam, leaving it America's dark secret. Today, though, the interest level in the study of Vietnam has soared. Students, often the children of veterans, rush to discover the mysteries of the forgotten war. Veterans are stunned and gladdened that American youth, 'Generation X', finally wants to know about their involvement and sacrifice. America has begun to realize its folly in denying its soldiers their due. The process of healing the wounds caused by the war has begun. One only has to hear the anguished, eloquent words of veterans who witnessed the horror of war, only to be forgotten, to realize that much healing remains to be done:

'Even today, I feel like so much of me died in Vietnam, that at times I wished all of me had died over there. For those who came back, the price of living is never easy or cheap. Laughter and happiness is rare. The nightmares, the flashbacks, the pains, waking up soaked in sweat are the norm. The sounds and smells of combat, the smell of sweat and dust, of the damp earth and vegetation, of the hot sun and exhaustion, of ambushes and firefights to full-blown battles, and of blood and death, enter my daily life. The moans of the wounded, some cursing, others calling for their mother, someone screaming for the corpsman or moans of "Oh God, Oh God" Like so many other Vietnam vets, I feel so much rage in me that it exhausts me and isolation is my only sanctuary.'

Vietnam will continue to exert a pull over world politics and military action for years to come. In recent conflicts, such as those in the former Yugoslavia, UN and NATO leaders watch for the danger signs of 'gradual escalation'.

THE GULF WAR

In a very real way the American effort in the Middle East's Gulf War was a direct legacy of Vietnam. The United States had made some fundamental military and political errors in its prosecution of the war in Vietnam, and by the late 1980s it had re-evaluated the American way of war. The leaders of the US involvement in the Gulf War, Norman Schwartzkopf and Colin Powell, had both served in Vietnam and were fully aware of the dangers posed by fighting a limited war. They pressed upon President George Bush the importance of overwhelming force and achievable goals. There would be no graduated escalation or involvement of military force in solving political problems in the region. It was not without a sense of irony that Schwartzkopf and his staff, again made up largely of Vietnam veterans, dubbed the planned air campaign against Iraq 'Instant Thunder'. Air power, using weapons and tactics that had been perfected in Vietnam, was unleashed with few restrictions. It was the massive bombardment that so many had called for during Vietnam. By the time of Operation Desert Storm, the Coalition forces in the Gulf numbered near 500,000 – almost exactly the wartime high for US forces during the Vietnam War. As the tanks and helicopters rumbled forward once again America watched the progress of a war on the evening news. This time, however, the coverage was different. The military restricted media access, resulting in a tight control over public perception of the conflict. As Coalition forces rolled over the outmatched Iraqis, for many the Vietnam War finally ended. The US military had been vindicated, and defeat was but a distant memory. Even President Bush stated, 'By God, we've kicked the Vietnam syndrome once and for all.' When Schwartzkopf returned to the US he and his forces were greeted by a ticker tape reception in New York City. It was the welcome home he had never received upon his return from Vietnam. The general made certain he did not forget his old comrades and included a large group of Vietnam veterans in the parade. It was victory and celebration, but for many it had come over 30 years late.

PRESIDENT CLINTON HONOURS COLIN POWELL.

CHRONOLOGY

1945

9–11 March Japanese establish an independent Vietnam under the leadership of Emperor Bao Dai.

15 August Surrender of Japan. World War II ends.

2 September Vietminh led by Ho Chi Minh takes power and declares a Democratic Republic of Vietnam in Hanoi.

13 September British forces start to disarm the Japanese and return power to the French.

1946

March France recognizes the Democratic Republic of Vietnam as an independent state within the Indochinese Union. The recognition has little value.

23 November Haiphong is shelled by French warships.

December The Vietminh launch attacks on French garrisons. The First Indochina War begins.

1949

8 March Vietnam becomes an associated state within the French Union and Bao Dai subsequently becomes its nominal leader.

1 October The People's Republic of China is established.

1950

January China and Soviet Union recognize the legitimacy of Ho Chi Minh's Democratic Republic of Vietnam.

26 July President Truman grants $15 million of aid for the French war effort in Indochina.

1953

October Laos gains independence from France, though it remains in the Indochinese Union.

9 November Cambodia declares its independence from France.

1954

25 January International peace talks are timetabled for the conflicts in Korea and Indochina.

13 March The battle of Dien Bien Phu begins.

7 May French forces surrender at Dien Bien Phu.

16 June Ngo Dinh Diem becomes South Vietnam's prime minister.

20–21 July Signing of the Geneva Accords. First Indochina War ends with Vietnam divided at the 17th Parallel.

8 September South-East Asia Treaty Organization (SEATO) established.

11 October Vietminh take over leadership of North Vietnam.

24 October President Eisenhower promises an increased package of direct US aid to support Ngo Dinh Diem's regime.

1955

May US begins to supply military aid and military training to South Vietnamese forces.

16 July With US backing, Diem renounces the Geneva Accords and refuses to take part in reunificatory elections.

23 October Diem becomes South Vietnam's head of state after a referendum removes Bao Dai from office. Diem declares the Republic of Vietnam.

1956

28 April Training of South Vietnamese forces becomes the responsibility of the American Military Assistance Advisory Group (MAAG).

1957

January Review of Geneva Accords by International Control Commission concludes that the criteria of the Accords has not been met. The Soviet Union proposes that North and South Vietnam are recognized as separate nations.

29 May In Laos, the communist Pathet Lao attempts to seize control of government.

October Communists increase the scale of guerrilla warfare with major deployments in the Mekong Delta region.

1959

May North Vietnam begins the infiltration of supplies down the Ho Chi Minh Trail into South Vietnam.

8 July Two US advisors are killed by insurgents at Bien Hoa.

September North Vietnam begins the supply of weaponry to communist insurgents in Laos.

1960

April Universal conscription introduced in North Vietnam.

8 November John F. Kennedy secures the US Presidency.

11 November Diem retains power after an abortive coup attempt by South Vietnamese army groups.

December The National Liberation Front for South Vietnam is formed by Hanoi; it is called the Vietcong by the government of South Vietnam.

1961

January Laos establishes a pro-Western government under Prince Boun Oum while North Vietnam and the Soviet Union back Laotian communist factions.

11–13 May Vice-President Lyndon B. Johnson visits South Vietnam and proposes an increase of US aid to Diem.

September Vietcong attacks increase, including the temporary capture of the provincial capital of Phuoc Vinh.

8 October Following a conference in Geneva, opposing forces in Laos agree to the establishment of a coalition government under Souvanna Phouma.

October–November Maxwell Taylor and Walt Rostow conduct an evaluation tour of South Vietnam. With partial acceptance of their report, Kennedy increases aid to South Vietnam.

1962

3 February Initiation of the Strategic Hamlets program.

8 February MAAG becomes the US Military Assistance Command, Vietnam (MACV) led by General Paul Harkins.

May Vietcong units achieve battalion strength in central Vietnam.

June US military presence in South Vietnam reaches 12,000.

August Australian military advisors arrive in Vietnam.

1963

2 January South Vietnamese troops suffer a heavy defeat at Ap Bac.

May–August Anti-Diem riots by Buddhist communities spread across South Vietnam and include the shocking self-immolation of seven monks.

12 November Diem is overthrown and murdered in a military coup. General Duong Van Minh takes over.

22 November John F. Kennedy is assassinated in Dallas, Texas.

1964

30 January Duong Van Minh is deposed by General Nguyen Khanh.

2 June Honolulu conference resolves to increase levels of US aid to South Vietnam.

20 June General William C. Westmoreland takes over command of US MACV.

2–4 August Attacks, or reported attacks, by North Vietnamese patrol boats take place against the USS *Maddox* and USS *C. Turner Joy* in the Gulf of Tonkin.

5 August US aircraft from the Seventh Carrier Fleet bomb North Vietnamese naval and military targets in retaliation for the Gulf of Tonkin incidents.

7 August Tonkin Gulf resolution is passed by the US Congress, which gives President Johnson a free hand to act against communist forces in Vietnam.

24 December A Vietcong bomb in Saigon kills two Americans and wounds 52 others.

1965

February Johnson authorizes Operation Flaming Dart, a series of air assaults against North Vietnam in retaliation for attacks against US installations and bases.

10 February US soldiers die in a Vietcong bombing at Qui Nhon.

13 February Operation Rolling Thunder, a sustained air campaign against North Vietnam, is authorized; begins on 2 March.

8 March Two US Marine battalions land at Danang as the first dedicated US combat troops rather than advisors.

June After a period of political turmoil, Nguyen Cao Ky becomes prime minister of South Vietnam's government.

27 June Large-scale US operations against Vietcong units are launched northeast of Saigon.

October–November Vietcong forces in the Ia Drang Valley are defeated by US units in the first major 'Search and Destroy' campaign of the war.

25 December Operation Rolling Thunder halted in an attempt to bring North Vietnam to the negotiating table.

31 December US troops strength in Vietnam exceeds 180,000.

1966

24 January Secretary of Defense McNamara requests raising US troop levels to 400,000 by the end of 1966.

31 January Operation Rolling Thunder resumes its bombing of North Vietnam.

7–8 February Premier Ky and President Johnson meet in Hawaii and discuss, among other issues, South Vietnamese pacification actions.

April Operation Game Warden begins in which the US Navy attempts to interdict communist supply lines through the Mekong Delta region.

May–June South Vietnamese troops take over Hue and Danang to stop Buddhist rioting.

30 July US surveillance monitors NVA troops passing across the DMZ into South Vietnam.

13–16 December US bombing of a North Vietnamese truck depot brings international condemnation, and General Westmoreland publicly denies targeting non-military sites.

1967

8 January Operation Cedar Falls begins in the Iron Triangle area near Saigon.

22 February US troops launch Operation Junction City, one of the biggest 'Search and Destroy' operations of the war.

28 February The Mobile Riverine Force (MRF) is established in the Mekong Delta.
8 March US Congress sanctions the expenditure of $4.5 billion on the Vietnam conflict.
8 May The NVA launch attacks against the US Marine base at Con Thien, south of the DMZ.
3 September General Nguyen Van Thieu is elected to the presidency of South Vietnam.
4 October The siege at Con Thien is lifted by US operations.
October–December Khe Sanh airbase is reinforced and faces increasing NVA attention.

1968

22 January The 77-day siege at Khe Sanh begins.
31 January Tet Offensive begins.
26 February The city of Hue is recaptured from the NVA.
31 March Following Tet, President Johnson limits bombing operation against North Vietnam and announces that he will not run for re-election.
14 April Khe Sanh is relieved.
3 May President Johnson announces peace talks agreement betweeen US and North Vietnam.
13 May US and North Vietnamese officials meet in Paris for preliminary peace discussions.
11 June Westmoreland is replaced by General Creighton W. Abrams as commander of the MACV.
23 June Khe Sanh base is abandoned by US troops.
5 November Richard Nixon is elected US President and commits the US to a steady retraction from the Vietnam War.

1969

25 January Peace talks open in Paris and include representatives from Saigon and the Vietcong.
18 March Secret US bombing of Cambodia begins.
8 June President Nixon meets with President Thieu and announces a withdrawal of 25,000 US personnel. This is achieved by the end of August.
3 September Ho Chi Minh dies.
16 September President Nixon announces further US troop withdrawals of 25,000.
October–November Huge anti-war demonstrations take place in Washington, DC.
16 November The details of the My Lai massacre (on 16 March 1968), become public.
December While Nixon continues to pledge more troop reductions, Thailand also commits itself to a complete withdrawal of its forces from South Vietnam.

1970

20 February Kissinger opens secret talks with North Vietnamese negotiator Le Duc Tho in Paris.
18 March Prince Norodom Sihanouk of Cambodia is overthrown by General Lon Nol.
29 April President Nixon announces that US forces have participated in actions against communist forces in Cambodia.
10 May Over 80,000 people attend an anti-war protest in Washington, DC, following the Cambodian offensive.
29 June US forces in Cambodia are withdrawn back across the border.
7 October Nixon proposes a stand-still ceasefire but the terms are rejected by North Vietnam.
31 December The Gulf of Tonkin resolution is repealed by the US Congress. US troop strength in Vietnam has now fallen to 335,000, down from 474,000 from the year previously.

1971

8 February Operation Lam Son 719, the South Vietnamese incursion into Laos, begins.
25 March Lam Son 719 concludes four weeks earlier than planned.
13 June *The New York Times* begins its publication of the Pentagon Papers.
August–September Australia, New Zealand and South Korea announce their intention to withdraw all of their troops.
October Nguyen Van Thieu is re-elected as South Vietnam's president.
12 November Nixon commits himself to further US troop reductions of 45,000.
26–30 November Major US airstrikes are directed at North Vietnam in response to the NVA gathering its forces against South Vietnam.

1972

6 January US officials state that US troop levels will be reduced to 69,000 by the end of April.
25 January President Nixon presents a new peace plan following Kissinger's negotiations with North Vietnam.
5 February North Vietnam rejects the US peace plan.
30 March North Vietnam launches a major invasion of the South.
6 April US air campaign is resumed.
8 May Nixon announces the mining of Haiphong harbour.
12 June ARVN forces finally break through the siege at An Loc.
12 August The last US combat troops leave South Vietnam.
16 September Quang Tri city, lost to the NVA on 1 May, is recaptured by the ARVN.
18 December After several abortive peace proposals, Nixon launches a bombing campaign (Operation Linebacker II) against North Vietnam above the 20th parallel.
30 December Following a truce agreement, Nixon stops the Linebacker bombing.

1973

8 January Talks resume between Kissinger and Le Duc Tho.
15 January US military operations against North Vietnam cease.
27 January A peace agreement is formally signed by Kissinger and Le Duc Tho.
21 February A ceasefire agreement between Souvanna Fume and the communists is reached in Laos.
29 March The last US troops finally leave South Vietnam.
15 August The US bombing of Cambodia is stopped following a Congressional resolution in July.
14 September Communist Pathet Lao officials and members of the Laotian government form a provisional administration.

1974

4 January President Thieu declares that the Vietnam War has started again, later pointing to over 57,000 deaths since the ceasefire.
15–28 January Phnom Penh is shelled by Cambodia's rebels.
March The communist Khmer Rouge make significant gains in the civil war in Cambodia.
16 April Talks collapse between President Thieu and the PRG (Provisional Revolutionary Government of Vietnam). Action between ARVN and communist troops intensifies throughout the year.
May Communist forces launch a major offensive in South Vietnam.
9 August President Nixon resigns following the Watergate scandal.
October North Vietnamese leaders decide on a conclusive offensive against Saigon during 1975.

1975

January The NVA continues its military build-up. Attacks against ARVN positions increase.
1 January Khmer Rouge launch a major attack on Phnom Penh.
4 March NVA offensive begins in the Central Highlands.
10–15 April NVA captures An Loc, 40 miles (64km) from Saigon.
17 April Phnom Penh falls.
21 April President Thieu resigns; replaced by Tran Van Huong.
28 April Duong Van Minh replaces President Tran Van Huong.
30 April Saigon falls.
24 August Pathet Lao takes Laos.
December Communist Khmer Rouge forces seize power in Cambodia and the state is renamed Kampuchea.

1977

January President Carter pardons most of the war draft evaders. Talks begin to discuss US recognition of Vietnam.

1978

June Since 1975 Pol Pot's victims believed to number two million.
October US-Vietnam normalization talks break down.
25 December Vietnam invades Kampuchea. Pol Pot is toppled.

1979

January US leads international embargo against Vietnam for its invasion of Kampuchea.
February China invades Vietnam. Its forces withdraw a month later. Small scale border war continues.

1982

February Vietnam agrees to talks on the issue of American MIAs.
11 November The memorial to the veterans of the Vietnam War is unveiled in Washington, DC, inscribed with the names of more than 58,000 US war dead.

1984

Chemical companies agree to compensate 15,000 war veterans damaged by Agent Orange.

1988

Vietnam starts withdrawing troops from Kampuchea.
September US-Vietnam joint field investigations on MIAs begin.

1989

September Vietnam's withdrawal from Kampuchea completed.

1991

The US ban on organized travel to Vietnam is lifted. Relations begin to normalize.

1992

April US eases trade restrictions on US dealings with Vietnam.
December President Bush permits US companies to open offices in Vietnam.

1993

2 July President Clinton ends US opposition to Vietnam's financial arrangements with the IMF and clears the way to a resumption of international capital for Vietnam.
13 September Economic sanctions eased further by US.

1994

27 January US Senate urges President Clinton to lift the economic embargo on Vietnam to further MIA investigations.
3 February US trade embargo ends.

1995

30 April Vietnam celebrates 20th anniversary of the end of the war.
31 May Vietnam provides papers about US servicemen killed or captured during the war.

1997

May Ambassadors take up positions in respective capital cities.

STATISTICS

US Force levels in Vietnam

1960	900	1967	486,000
1961	3000	1968	536,000
1962	11,000	1969	475,000
1963	16,000	1970	335,000
1964	23,000	1971	157,000
1965	184,000	1972	24,000
1966	385,000		

(source: US Dept of Defense (rounded up /down to nearest '000)

In 1967's total of 486,000 men there were 90 combat infantry battalions with 700 men each, 150 of those being support staff. Combat infantry strength was therefore less than 50,000 men overall, or just over 10 per cent of the total. Artillery and engineers accounted for 12 per cent, aviation 2 per cent and 75 per cent were HQ and logistics personnel.

US Congressional Medal of Honor citations were awarded to some 241 men for actions in Vietnam, 1964–1972.

US combat casualties in Vietnam

1960–63	759	1968	14,592
1964	137	1969	9414
1965	1369	1970	4221
1966	5008	1971	1380
1967	9378	1972	300

Total US casualties in Vietnam

Killed: 58,169 Wounded: 304,000
Note that of the 58,000-plus killed, more than 10,000 were non-combat deaths.

Cause of death and injury (per cent of total)

	Death	Injury
Small arms:	51	16
Shell fragments:	36	65
Booby traps, mines:	11	15
Stakes:	0	2
Other:	2	2

Death ratio for those reaching hospital was 2.6 per cent (nearly half that of World War II).

USAF losses, 1962–1973

Aircraft	2257
Killed	2118
Wounded	3460
Missing/captured	586
Approx. cost	$3,130,000,000

US Navy aviator enemy kills 1965–1973

1965	4	1970	1
1966	8	1971	0
1967	16	1972	24
1968	6	1973	1
1969	0		

(source US Naval Historical Center)

Americans unaccounted for

US Army	640
US Navy	412
USMC	256
USAF	674
US Coastguard	1
Civilians	39

BIBLIOGRAPHY

Baker, M. *NAM: The Vietnam War in the Words of the Soldiers Who Fought There*. Berkley Books: New York, 1983.

Barrett, D. *Uncertain Warriors: Lyndon Johnson and his Vietnam Advisors*. University Press of Kansas: Lawrence, Kansas, 1993.

Brende, J and Parson, E. *Vietnam Veterans: The Road to Recovery*. Plenum Press: New York, 1985.

Berman, L. *Planning a Tragedy: the Americanization of the War in Vietnam*. Norton: New York, 1982.

Cable, L.E. *Conflict of Myths: The Development of American Counterinsurgency Doctrine and the Vietnam War*. New York University Press: New York, 1988.

Carhart, Tom. *Great Battles of the Vietnam War*. Hamlyn: London, 1984.

Castle, T. *At War in the Shadow of Vietnam: U.S. Military Aid to the Royal Lao Government, 1955–1975*. Columbia University Press: New York, 1993.

Chinnery, Philip. *Air War Vietnam*. Bison Books: London, 1987.

Croizat, Victor. *The Brown Water Navy: the River and Coastal War in Indochina and Vietnam 1948–1972*. Blandford: Poole, 1984.

Currey, C.B. *The Disintegration and Decay of the United States Army during the Vietnam era*. Norton: New York, 1981.

Cutler, T. *Brown Water, Black Berets: Coastal and Riverine Warfare in Vietnam*. Naval Institute Press: Annapolis, 1988.

Dacy, Douglas C. *Foreign Aid, War and Economic Development: South Vietnam 1955–75*. Cambridge University Press: Cambridge, 1986.

Dalloz, J. *The War in Indo-China. 1945–54*. Barnes and Noble: Savage, Maryland, 1990.

Davidson, Lt. Gen. Philip B. *Secrets of the Vietnam War*. Presidio Press: Novato, California, 1990.

Dorr, Robert F. *Air War Hanoi*. Blandford: London, 1988.

Elliot, W.P. (ed.) *The Third Indochina Conflict*. Westview Press: Boulder, Colorado, 1981.

Farber, D. *The Age of Great Dreams: America in the 1960s*. Hill and Wang: New York, 1994.

Fitzgerald, F. *Fire in the Lake: The Vietnamese and the Americans in Vietnam*. Random House: New York, 1972.

Francillon, Rene. *Vietnam Air Wars*. Hamlyn: London, 1987.

Gardner, Lloyd C. *Approaching Vietnam: from World War II through Dienbienphu, 1941–1954*. Norton: New York and London, 1988.

Hammer, E.J. *The Struggle for Indochina*. Stanford University Press: Stanford, California, 1954.

Isserman, M. and Kazin, M. *America Divided: The Civil War of the 1960s*. Oxford University Press: New York, 2000.

Karnow, S. *Vietnam: A History*. Viking: New York, 1983.

Lee, Steven Hugh. *Outposts of Empire: Korea, Vietnam and the Origins of the Cold War in Asia, 1949–1954*. Liverpool University Press: Liverpool, 1995.

Mangold, T and Penycate, J. *The Tunnels of Cu Chi*. Berkley Books: New York, 1986.

Marolda, Edward J. *By Sea, Air and Land: An Illustrated History of the US Navy in the War in Southeast Asia*. Naval Historical Center: Washington, D.C., 1994.

Marolda, Edward J. *Carrier Operations*. Bantam: Toronto, London, 1997.

Melson, Charles D. *Vietnam Marines, 1965–73*. Osprey: London, 1992.

Moss, G. *Vietnam, An American Ordeal*. Prentice Hall: Upper Saddle River, New Jersey, 1990.

Nalty, Bernard C. *An Illustrated Guide to the Air War over Vietnam: Aircraft of the Southeast Asia Conflict*. Salamander Books: London, 1981.

Nichols, John B. *On Yankee Station : the Naval Air War over Vietnam*. Airlife: Shrewsbury, 1987.

Nolan, K. *Into Laos: The Story of Dewey Canyon II/Lam Son 719*. Presidio: Novato, California, 1986.

Oberdorfer, D. *TET*. Doubleday: New York, 1971.

Olson, J. and Roberts, R. *Where the Domino Fell*. Brandywine Press: St. James, New York, 1999.

Page, Tim and John Pimlott (eds.) *Nam: The Vietnam Experience 1965–75*. Barnes and Noble: London, 1995.

Pike, D. *A History of Vietnamese Communism 1923–78*. Hoover Institute Press: Stanford, California, 1978.

Plaster, J. *SOG: The Secret Wars of America's Commandos in Vietnam*. Simon and Schuster: New York, 1997.

Ross, R. (ed.) *Cambodia: A Country Study*. U.S Government Printing Office: Washington, D.C., 1990.

Schulzinger, R. *A Time For War*. Oxford University Press: New York, 1997.

Shay, J. *Achilles in Vietnam: Combat Trauma and the Undoing of Character*. Touchstone: New York, 1994.

Shawcross, W. *Sideshow: Kissinger, Nixon and the Destruction of Cambodia*. Simon and Schuster: New York, 1979.

Simpson, H.R. *Dien Bien Phu: the Epic Battle America Forgot*. Brasseys: Washington, DC, 1994.

Spector, R. *After Tet: The Bloodiest Year in Vietnam*. The Free Press: New York, 1993.

Stanton, S. *Green Berets at War*. Presidio: Novato, California, 1985.

Summers, H. *On Strategy: A Critical Analysis of the Vietnam War*. Dell: New York, 1982.

Thompson, James. *Rolling Thunder*. University of North Carolina Press: Chapel Hill, 1980.

Tucker, Spencer M. *Vietnam*. UCL: London, 1999.

Turley, G.H. *The Easter Offensive: Vietnam 1972*. Presidio Press: Novato, California, 1985.

Valentine, D. *The Phoenix Program*. Morrow: New York, 1990.

VanDeMark, Brian. *Into the Quagmire : Lyndon Johnson and the Escalation of the Vietnam War*. Oxford University Press: New York; Oxford, 1991.

Warner, W. *Backfire: The CIA's Secret War in Laos and Its Link to the War in Vietnam*. Simon and Schuster: New York, 1995.

Young, M. *The Vietnam Wars*. Harper Collins: New York, 1991.

INDEX

Note
Page numbers in *italics* refer to picture captions; those in **bold** refer to subjects which are treated in depth in boxes. Indochinese personal names are given by the family name which comes first, eg: Vo Nguyen Giap will be found under the letter 'V', Vo being the family name.

PICTURE CREDITS

POPPERFOTO: 180 (b), 182-183, 184 (b), 186 (b), 189, 190 (t), 191, 192, 193 (t), 194, 195 (b),196, 197, 198 (t), 199, 222, 229 (t), 231 (t), 235 (t), 236, 237, 244 (b),

TRH PICTURES: 6-7, 8, 9 (t), 10, 11, 12, 13, 14, 15, 16, 17, 18, 19 (t), 20, 21, 22-23, 25, 26, 27, 28 (US Army), 29, 30, 31, 32, 33 (t) (US Navy), 33 (b), 34 (US Dept. of Defense), 36 (t) (US Army), 36 (b), 37 (t) (US Dept. of Defense), 37 (b) (US Army), 38-39 (USAF), 40, 41, 42, 43, 44, 45, 46, 47, 48 (t), 48 (b) (USAF), 49, 50, 51 (t) (US Navy), 51 (b), 52, 53, 54-55 (US Army), 56 (US Army), 57 (US Dept. of Defense), 58, 59 (US Army), 60 (t) (US Dept. of Defense), 60 (b), 61 (t), 61 (b) (US Dept. of Defense), 62 (t) (US Army), 63, 64 (US Army), 65 (t) (US Army), 65 (b), 66 (US Army), 67, 69 (US Army), 70 (US Army), 71 (t) (US Army), 71 (b), 72-73, 74 (US Army), 75, 76 (US Army), 77 (t), 77 (b) (US Navy), 78, 79 (US Navy), 80 (US Navy), 81 (US Navy), 82 (t), 82 (b) (US Dept. of Defense), 83 (t), 83 (b) (US Dept. of Defense), 84, 85 (t) (US Army), 85 (b) (US Navy), 86, 87, 88-89 (US Army), 90 (US Dept. of Defense), 91, 92 (US Army), 94, 95, 96 (t), 96 (b) (US Dept. of Defense), 97, 98, 99, 100, 101 (t) (US Army), 101 (b), 102, 103 (t), 103 (b) (US Army), 104-105 (US Navy), 106, 108 (US Navy), 109, 110 (US Navy), 111 (US Dept. of Defense), 112 (t), 112 (b) (US Navy), 113 (t) (US Navy), 113 (b), 114, 115 (t) (US Dept. of Defense), 115 (b) (US Navy), 116 (US Dept. of Defense), 117 (t), 117 (bl & br) (US Navy), 118 (t) (US Navy), 118 (b) (US Dept. of Defense), 119 (US Navy), 120 (t & m), 120 (b) (US Navy), 121 (US Dept. of Defense), 122-123, 124 (US Army), 125, 126, 127 (US Army), 128, 129, 130, 131, 132, 133 (US Army), 134, 135, 136 (US Marine Corps), 137 (t) (US Marine Corps), 137 (b), 138, 139, 140, 141 (US Marine Corps), 142, 143, 144-145, 146 (US National Archives), 147, 148 (US Marine Corps), 149 (t) (US Marine Corps), 149 (b) (US Dept. of Defense), 150, 151 (US Marine Corps), 152, 153, 154, 155 (US Army), 156 (US Marine Corps), 157, 158 (US Dept. of Defense), 159, 160 (US Marine Corps), 161 (t) (US Army), 161 (b), 162 (US Army), 163 (US Army), 164-165, 167, 168 (t) (USAF), 168 (b), 169, 171 (t), 171 (b) (US Army), 172 (US Army), 173, 174, 175, 177 (T A Davis), 178, 179, 180 (t) (US Dept. of Defense), 181, 184 (t), 185, 186 (t), 187, 188, 190 (b), 193 (b), 195 (t), 198 (b), 200-201 (USAF), 202, 203, 204 (t) (US Army), 204 (b) (Dept. of Defense), 205, 206, 207, 208, 209, 210, 211, 212, 213, 214, 215, 216, 217, 218 (USAF), 219 (US Army), 220-221 (US Navy), 223, 224 (t) (US Army), 224, 225 (US Army), 226 (USAF), 227, 229 (b), 230, 231 (b), 232, 233 (US Navy), 234, 235 (b), 238-239 (US Dept. of Defense), 240 (t), 240 (b) (US Navy), 241, 242 (t), 242 (b) (T A Davis), 243 (US Dept. of Defense), 244 (t) (US Dept. of Defense), 245 (t) (M. Roberts), 245 (b) (USAF), 246, 247, 248 (US Navy), 249 (US Dept. of Defense).

ILLUSTRATIONS:
All medal and insignia artworks:
Mainline Design

ORBIS PUBLISHING: 9 (b), 19 (b), 24, 35, 47, 56, 62, 68, 91 (b), 93, 100 (t), 106 (t), 107, 111, 114 (b), 127, 132 (t), 148 (t), 166, 170, 176, 207, 210, 215 (b), 228, 232 (t).